TITHE SURVEYS

for Historians

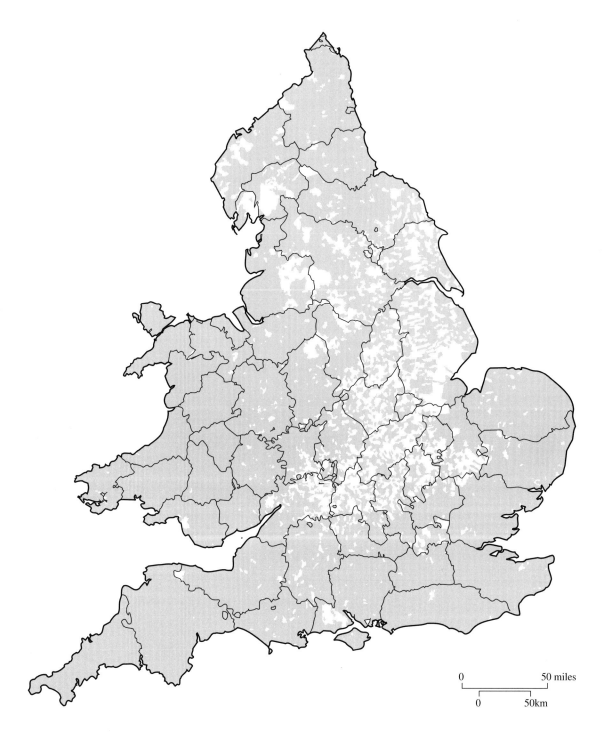

0   50 miles

0   50km

The coverage of England and Wales by tithe surveys. Compiled by Rodney Fry from the 55 county-scale maps in R.J.P. Kain and R.R. Oliver, *The tithe maps of England and Wales: a cartographic analysis and county-by-county catalogue* (Cambridge, Cambridge University Press, 1995).

TITHE SURVEYS
for Historians

Roger J. P. Kain & Hugh C. Prince

Phillimore

2000

Published by
PHILLIMORE & CO. LTD.
Shopwyke Manor Barn, Chichester, West Sussex

© Roger J.P. Kain and Hugh C. Prince, 2000

ISBN 1 86077 125 4

Printed and bound in Great Britain by
BUTLER & TANNER LTD.
London and Frome

Contents

List of Figures

PREFACE

The Tithe Commutation Act of 1836 was an important measure of ecclesiastical, political, social and economic reform that commuted arbitrary and uncertain levies of tithes in kind into varying annual rent-charges regulated on a uniform national basis. Parliament appointed a three-man commission to direct a staff of assistant commissioners, valuers and surveyors who mapped, valued and apportioned rent-charges among hundreds of thousands of separate parcels of titheable land in different states of cultivation. The tithe surveys were carried out expeditiously and with minute care under vigilant eyes of tithe owners, tithe payers and parliament. They provide local historians with enormous quantities of information for England and Wales in the 1840s concerning parish boundaries, field names, rights of way, land use, farming, landownership, and farm and house occupancy.

This book builds on the foundations of an earlier study of *The Tithe Surveys of England and Wales*. We are grateful to the Cambridge University Press for permitting us to reproduce passages from that book. The present work incorporates results of research conducted at the University of Exeter since 1985 on the contents of tithe files, tithe maps and schedules of apportionment. Relevant material has been drawn from *An Atlas and Index of Tithe Files of Mid-nineteenth-century England and Wales* and *The Tithe Maps of England and Wales*. Permission from the Cambridge University Press to reproduce illustrations from these books is gratefully acknowledged. This work also extends the field of inquiry into the historical background to the tithe surveys, relating structural changes in agriculture and rural society to concurrent changes in local government, population movements, industrialization and world markets. Information from tithe maps, apportionments and files is examined in greater detail than in our earlier study and the last chapter discusses more fully the relevance of this information for broader questions addressed by historians.

Many people have helped us in collecting material and suggesting new lines of thought. We are particularly grateful to past and present members of University College London and the University of Exeter for the inspiration, support and generous assistance they have given us. We owe special debts of gratitude to H.C. Darby who directed our early researches and remained a constant source of help and encouragement; to fellow students of the tithe surveys, in particular, Elizabeth Burrell, John Chapman, Elwyn Cox, Brian Dittmer, Tom Dormer, Wynn Edwards, David Gramolt, David Hartley, Harriet Holt, Michael Naish, Richard Oliver, Malcolm Postgate, Roger Sinfield and Sarah Wilmot, who have provided many valuable reflections on their work and over many years have kept us informed about new publications and research in progress. During the past thirty years, we have received helpful letters and much useful advice from Maurice Beresford, Robin Butlin, Harold Carter, Andrew Charlesworth, Ted Collins, Martin Daunton, Richard Dennis, John

Dodgson, Jim Dyos, Frank Emery, Eric Evans, Harold Fox, Barrie Gleave, Alan Harris, Janet Hooke, Glanville Jones, Paul Laxton, Grant Longman, Clare Lukehurst, Gordon Mingay, Dennis Mills, Mark Overton, Alan Parton, Robert Perry, Tony Phillips, William Ravenhill, Terry Slater, Colin Thomas, Michael Thompson, Michael Turner, and Jim Yelling. Many others have supplied information, replied to letters and answered questions. We deeply appreciate the kindness of Christie Willatts and Harry Henderson who commented on and amplified accounts of their pioneering studies, and we thank Tony Cartwright for discussing the contribution of John Mosby.

We are grateful to all county archivists, who without exception answered questionnaires on the custody of tithe documents. We owe special thanks to F.G. Emmison, K.C. Newton, Felix Hull, and Hugh Hanley for help in directing us to relevant manuscripts. We remain greatly indebted to Charles Smith in the Inspection Room at the former Tithe Redemption Commission offices in Finsbury Square for his friendly guidance and amazingly detailed knowledge of the contents of the original maps, apportionments and files kept by the Commission. At the Public Record Office, Geraldine Beech, Margaret Condon and Rose Mitchell have always been helpful and supportive.

We wish to record our thanks to the editors of the *Agricultural History Review*, the *Cartographic Journal*, the *East Midland Geographer*, the *Geographical Journal* and the *North Staffordshire Journal of Field Studies* for permission to reproduce illustrations and passages from articles they have published and to thank Michael Reed, editor of *Discovering past landscapes*, for permission to draw upon material from a chapter on the tithe files.

We gratefully acknowledge financial help given by University College London, the University of Exeter, the British Academy, the Leverhulme Trust and the Social Science Research Council towards bibliographic and cartographic work. We thank Helen Jones at Exeter University who drew the maps and Chris Cromarty and Andrew Teed for their care and skill in photographing cartoons and fading documents.

Alan Baker and Brian Harley have been guides, philosophers and friends to both of us for longer than we care to remember. We are grateful for their patience and understanding. Beyond all others, our wives have borne the brunt of trials and tribulations attending research and writing. Their gentle encouragement has sustained us.

INTRODUCTION

The first half of the 19th century was an age of statistical enquiries and cadastral surveys. Political and social problems were approached by select committees collecting facts and figures, parliament legislating reforms, commissions securing local agreements or confirming local awards, and surveyors mapping and scheduling results. In response to threats of war and, after 1815, in seeking solutions to problems caused by agricultural depression, industrial reorganisation, migration of people to towns, crowding and disease, volumes of statistical information were collected and hundreds of parliamentary acts were passed. Surveyors and valuers were kept busy measuring and redrawing maps of villages that had been enclosed, surveying lines for proposed canals and railways, drawing plans for housing estates, and laying out parks and gardens. In other countries, where smallholdings were exchanged and consolidated, where feudal properties were partitioned and where land passed from a public domain into private ownership, large-scale cadastral surveys were carried out: in Ireland, the Townland Survey; in France, the *ancien cadastre;* in the United States, the Original Land Survey.[1] In England and Wales, the largest and most detailed survey was that carried out under the Tithe Commutation Act of 1836.

Why in the eyes of the government did the tithe question loom so large and so menacingly in the 1830s that it called for draconian remedies by compulsory commutation requiring a large-scale nation-wide survey? In most parishes, tithes had been paid grudgingly but regularly for a very long time, and in a few places their payment may be traced back to the ninth century. During much of that time they had been regarded as continuing sources for grievance. Local disputes erupted from time to time when new incumbents or tithe owners demanded increased payments or when Quakers or other dissenters refused to pay customary charges. The nature of tithes and the deep-seated causes of recurrent conflict are discussed in Chapter 1.

Not until the 19th century did governments consider the tithe question as a serious or potentially serious threat to the maintenance of public order, but fears of widespread unrest were aroused by disturbances in 1830-2. To a prevailing dread of Jacobinism was added the spectre of chateau burning, peasant uprisings in many European countries and worsening agrarian troubles in Ireland that had sectarian as well as social and economic causes. Closer to home, Luddite violence and frame-breaking disturbed woollen manufacturing districts, crowds of angry demonstrators assembled on the outskirts of London, Manchester and Birmingham, and apprehension was growing that discontent was being fomented by secret people in remote spots deep in the countryside, plotting vast, shapeless, uncontrollable revolts that would spread like fire among ricks and barns in rural England. When flames lit night skies over Norfolk, Suffolk, Kent, Sussex, Hampshire,

Wiltshire and Dorset in 1816-17 and again in 1830-2, the government was alarmed.[2] A new sense of urgency animated debates on tithes, and tithe owners felt impelled to find a quick solution to their problems.

The tithe question had deep economic causes. Tithes were a burden that fell most heavily upon land undergoing agricultural improvement. Tithe owners enjoyed unearned increments from higher yields obtained through investments made by tithe payers in enclosures, farm buildings, improved livestock, new crops, fertilisers and machinery. In the depression which followed the Napoleonic wars, prices of farm produce fell. Wheat prices were particularly affected and wheat was subject to a great tithe. Returns from capital in land and improvements also fell, farm rents were remitted, but tithe owners were still entitled to, and some collected in full, their tenth. Political economists considered the imposition of tithes a disincentive to investment and an obstacle to improvement.

Tithe payers felt discriminated against as countrymen, since they not only suffered agricultural distress but, through their tithes, bore a disproportionate share in the cost of maintaining an established church. Urban land paid little tithe but earned high rents and carried increasing numbers of people, including churchgoers. Farmers, especially enterprising capitalists, regarded the manner of collecting tithes in kind peculiarly archaic and humiliating. No other group of producers was required to set aside a proportion of their actual produce for a tithing man. In most parishes, the odium of rendering tithes in kind had been removed by commutation before the 19th century, but that highlighted the anomalous position of parishes where tithes remained uncommuted. Farmers reacted as a beleaguered minority group, oppressed by landlords, harassed by labourers and in conflict with urban masses demanding cheap food.

By 1830, most tithe payers and tithe owners were ready to surrender some benefits or claims to benefits for the sake of convenience, conformity and peace. Arguments for and against every possible measure of reform had already been rehearsed and it only remained for a reformed parliament to put together a bill that would render a fair money payment to tithe owners while freeing tithe payers from an encumbrance on their enterprise and removing a slight to their self-respect. Eric Evans discusses at length, and also in an abbreviated account, the political and ecclesiastical history of tithe commutation.[3] Here, in this book, Chapter 2 traces the steps leading to the passing of the Tithe Commutation Act of 1836 and reviews details of its provisions. That after 1836 no essential changes were made in the mode of assessing or paying commuted rent-charges is an indication of the success of the settlement. The implementation of the Act progressed swiftly and without much resistance. Between 1836 and 1845 the tithe commissioners completed 90 per cent of their work and almost all the rest was finished by 1855. Extensively enclosed midland counties are scantily covered by tithe surveys as are Westmorland, Lancashire and Gloucestershire, where large tracts of land were exempt from tithe payments (see frontispiece map).

For each tithe district, usually a parish in southern England or a township in northern counties, three documents were prepared: a map, an apportionment and a file. Methods of compiling these documents, their contents and their present whereabouts are described in Chapter 3. Chapter 4 analyses and evaluates the comprehensiveness and accuracy of different classes of information provided by the surveys. In an important respect, much evidence has been tried and tested by contending parties: tithe owners jealously guarding their rights, tithe payers striving to rid themselves of burdensome imposts, and assistant commissioners discharging their duty to adjudicate a fair and equitable rent-charge. The minutes of parish meetings testify to the zeal with which tithe owners pursued their claims whereas farmers and landowners sought to reduce their liabilities as far as possible. In all local enquiries, the most important evidence was that observed in the field. Acreages recorded in most surveys provide reasonably reliable guides to the extent of different categories of land use and crop yields. Acreages may be checked both internally and independently with other sources. When this is done, it is clear that some figures, especially for areas of low agricultural or titheable value, are rough estimates. Rounded figures for heathland, moorland and other marginal land are suspect, but checks do not point to a consistent direction of error. The great strength of the tithe surveys is their uniformity in compilation, permitting data from one tithe district to be compared with those from neighbouring districts in regional and national studies.

From the moment tithe surveys were deposited in the Tithe Commission archives, and copies were placed in parish chests and in diocesan record offices, they began to be inspected by searchers for many different kinds of information. For over one hundred years they were consulted by lawyers searching for evidence of parish boundaries, property boundaries, rights of way and liabilities to tithe payments. Their value as historical records was recognised as early as 1856, when R. Dymond used tithe maps to trace lines of hedgerows in Devonshire parishes.[4]

Tithe surveys provide a definitive record of parish and township boundaries before those boundaries were altered or merged and before the powers of parishes were removed by local government reorganisation. Ecclesiastical and political historians are interested in inquiries conducted by assistant commissioners into disputes over boundaries and jurisdiction. Social and economic historians are interested in the functions of parishes, particularly in the administration of poor laws, in the 1830s and 1840s. Tithe maps portray field boundaries at the end of a period of active parliamentary enclosure. A few scattered remnants of unenclosed strips and early field names are recorded. These traces have been used to throw fresh light on open-field husbandry in western Britain and survivals of infield-outfield cultivation in eastern England. Tithe maps record villages and hamlets in their final stages of development as agrarian settlements. Effects of urbanisation and industrialisation are evident in many places. Turnpike roads paved with smooth, hard surfaces carried wheeled traffic from town to town, but at the time of the tithe surveys, four out of five miles of roads were still maintained by parishes. They were dusty in summer and most were so deeply muddy in winter that they were impassable by heavy wagons and coaches. Tithe surveys are useful as evidence for the existence of roads and rights of way. They are also the fullest and most accurate source of information on land use around

1840. Sir Dudley Stamp's Land Utilisation Survey was fortunate in having as its secretary Christie Willatts who, almost at the same time as Harry Henderson, learned of the value of tithe surveys for reconstructing land use maps on a field-by-field basis for about 1840. These pioneer studies provided models for many detailed investigations illuminating the county reports of the Land Utilisation Survey. Research on the tithe records was continued and expanded by students of Sir Clifford Darby. At University College London three advances were made: swifter methods of abstracting data developed by David Hartley and Elwyn Cox enabled larger areas to be mapped; examination of the tithe files by Elwyn Cox, Brian Dittmer and their contemporaries has extended our knowledge of mid-19th-century farming; sampling and computer mapping of the data make possible the analysis of a large number of relationships between land use, ownership, farm size and distance from markets. At about the time the tithe surveys were completed, technical advances in agriculture culminated in a period of high farming, in which arable farming on light soils produced very high yields. Tithe files contain a wealth of information on local farming practices and form a basis for assessing agricultural productivity in every part of the country. Studies of landownership and occupancy are still in their infancy and relative to research on land use and farming, substantive studies on sizes and composition of estates and farms await analysis with the aid of computers. A very recent advance has been made in using tithe surveys for house repopulation and community reconstitution.

A few problems concerning the reliability of the source remain unresolved, but what is daunting about the tithe material is its sheer bulk. Maps, apportionments and files for 11,785 tithe districts may be inspected. Within each there may be as many as 4,000 or as few as one parcel of land or tithe areas. In total, there may be possibly something of the order of 10^7 separate data units, and for each of these information on land use, owners, occupiers, acreage and tithe valuation may be available. A locational coordinate reference and also, to be wished for, some index of soil character should be added for purposes of identification and retrieval. A search may yield up to $10^7 \times 7$ items of information. To examine the interrelations between land use and farm size or between farm size and estate size, for example, many millions of computations are required. In addition, several topics may be examined at a parish scale from the contents of tithe files, from the census returns and from rate books. Some suggestions about how this work may be done are outlined in Chapter 5.

This book attempts to provide an up-to-date guide and work of reference for users of the tithe surveys. It explains the history and usage of terms in the tithe documents that may serve as an aid to reading and interpreting the data. It reviews research using tithe surveys and suggests where further research might profitably be pursued. Finally, this volume is intended as a general introduction to the detailed material that forms the basis of Roger Kain's *Atlas and index of the tithe files of mid-nineteenth-century England and Wales* and his and Richard Oliver's *The tithe maps of England and Wales: a cartographic analysis and county-by-county catalogue.*[5] It is hoped that these studies will lead to a broader understanding and deeper appreciation of the English countryside in the mid-19th century.

THE NATURE OF TITHES

THE BURDEN OF TITHES

For almost a thousand years, to the passage of the Tithe Redemption Act in 1936, tithes were the heaviest direct tax on farming, and from their mode of collection the most repugnant. To be compelled against the dictates of conscience to contribute towards the maintenance of an established church was offensive to many dissenters and was resented by the poor whose condition was worsened while the clergy grew rich. But the strongest hostility was felt by farmers charged with the support of a sleeping partner who put nothing into their business but harassed them at lambing time, at haymaking and at harvest, at the very moment when the rewards of their efforts were being reaped (Fig. 1).[1] Before the introduction of graduated scales of income tax and the imposition of excess profits tax, tithes were not unjustly regarded as discriminating against those who wrested a living from the land, a burden not shared by tradesmen, manufacturers, wage-earners nor by foreign competitors. They were a tax on gross output, a form of share-cropping, increased by skilled management, diminished by incompetence, bearing most heavily on the additional gains obtained from extra investments of capital and effort. In short, they inflicted a penalty on enterprise and acted as a check upon improvements. Arthur Young condemned tithes as 'the

1 'The Vicar': a political satire (after Woodward) published by W. Holland, London, 1790. Beneath the picture is written:

> Then the Vicar
> Full of fees customary, with his burying gloves;
> Jealous of his rights and apt to quarrel;
> Claiming his paltry penny farthing tithes
> E'en at the Lawyers price

greatest burthen that yet remains on the agriculture of this kingdom; and if it was universally taken in kind, would be sufficient to damp all ideas of improvement'.[2] It is, however, abundantly clear that during Young's lifetime agriculture made spectacular advances in spite of the continuing imposition of tithes. It is also true that payments in kind were abolished in many districts where improvements were carried out but commutation to a money rent-charge was not enforced by law throughout England and Wales until 1836, following a period of retrenchment and falling corn prices. The reform, when it came, was intended not so much to remove an impediment to further investment but to relieve agricultural distress. The depression of the 1830s proved that the incidence of tithes was at least as onerous when the profit margin in farming was reduced as it had been when expenditure on improvements was high. The problem that parliament then had to face in devising a monetary equivalent for the fruits of the earth was one of bewildering complexity and it is to the lasting credit of those who framed the Tithe Commutation Act of 1836 that a workable solution was found.

PREDIAL, MIXED AND PERSONAL TITHES

What exactly were tithes? Customarily they represented a tenth of the annual increase of the produce of the soil and were of three kinds: predial tithes, payable on the fruits of the earth, such as corn, hay, wood, fruit and other crops; mixed or agistment tithes, payable on animal products, such as lambs, colts, calves, wool, milk, eggs and honey; and personal tithes, payable on the clear gains of a man's labour and industry, generally levied only on the profits of milling and fishing.[3] Attempts to impose tithes on servants' wages, on milled grains or on catches of fish rarely succeeded. Tithes on grain, hay and fruit were generally more valuable than those on other produce; the former frequently being worth as much as one-fifth of the annual rent of arable land, the latter amounting to about one-ninth of the rent of grassland. Liability might be reduced or avoided by fallowing arable land, by converting arable or meadow to grazing land, thereby substituting an agistment tithe for a predial tithe, by converting productive land to park or warren or allowing it to revert to waste, or by planting fields with trees. Commercial crops such as woad, hemp, flax, saffron, hops and tobacco were gradually subjected to tithes, but the introduction of fodder crops associated with new methods of convertible husbandry created special difficulties. In Suffolk in the 17th century turnips were tithed only when grown expressly for feeding beef cattle or for fattening mutton. When, as was more usual, they were fed to milking cows or to store sheep, tithe was taken not in roots but in dairy produce or in lambs.[4] Similar questions arose as the cultivation of sainfoin, clover, ley grasses, kale, carrots and potatoes became widespread. When cut for hay, clover and temporary grasses were included as predial tithes, but when they stood for seed a mixed tithe was paid. By common law, tithes were not payable on minerals or on anything that formed part of the freehold, although an ingenious Derbyshire parson argued that lead was subject to tithe, because it was believed that the veins increased annually![5] Deer, rabbits, partridges, pheasants, fish and wild-fowl were titheable by special custom only, while the methods of tithing woodland produce differed widely from one locality to another. The liability of day labourers to pay tithes was abolished by statute in 1549 but some customary payments in lieu of personal tithes survived into the 18th and 19th centuries.[6] In general, however, payments levied on individuals became insignificant after 1549 leaving only two main categories of tithe: predial and mixed, each further sub-divided into great and small tithes.[7]

The following categories of land were customarily exempt from tithe payments:

(1) Lands naturally barren.
(2) Barren heath or waste improved or converted into arable or meadow for a period of seven years after improvement.
(3) Forest lands while in the occupation of the Crown or its lessee or tenant, but not if granted by the Crown in fee.
(4) Glebe lands in the occupation of the parson.
(5) Lands owned before 1215 by the Cistercians, Templars or Hospitallers.
(6) Lands which formerly belonged to one of the greater monasteries and which had not paid tithes at the time of the dissolution.
(7) Lands which had paid no tithes from time immemorial.
(8) Lands in respect of which tithes were barred under the Tithe Act of 1832, which specified some lands which had not paid tithes for a very long time, the original cause of exemption being unknown.

GREAT AND SMALL TITHES

In the first instance, tithes were paid to the rector of a parish, who might be a resident incumbent or an ecclesiastical appropriator such as a bishop, prior, prioress, monastery, nunnery or college. An absentee rector normally appointed a vicar to perform his parochial services and allotted to him a portion of the revenues of the benefice, usually the small tithes. The small, or vicarial, tithes included all the tithes except those of grain, hay and wood which constituted the great tithes, generally reserved for the rector. But the division between the great and small tithes was by no means fixed and unalterable. Ancient treatises classify hay as a great tithe, but in 23 of 34 parishes in Staffordshire studied by Evans, tithe hay, or its monetary composition in lieu, was collected as a small tithe.[8] Even corn tithe, usually guarded most jealously because of its value, was not always collected as a great tithe in 18th-century England.[9] In all matters concerned with tithing in England and Wales, not least the definition of what constituted great or small tithes, the ultimate arbiter was the 'custom of the parish'. The best source for unravelling the complexities of these local practices are the parish tithe files (PRO IR18). There is a file for each of the 14,829 tithe districts of England and Wales; their contents vary (see Chapter 3) but those for some districts contain long and detailed accounts of the history of tithing practices which summarise assistant tithe commissioners' researches among glebe terriers and other parochial documents.[10] A number of historians have also consulted parochial documents and episcopal registers and have published descriptions of local tithing customs.[11]

IMPROPRIATION OF TITHES

At the time of the dissolution of the monasteries, rectories and tithes belonging to dissolved houses were vested in the Crown, and most were subsequently sold to laymen.[12] Instances of laymen appropriating tithes for their own are recorded as early as the 12th century, but, after the sale of tithe forfeited to the Crown in the 1530s, about one-third of all great tithes was held by lay impropriators.[13] Impropriate livings were not evenly distributed over the country. In Kent, 140 out of 252 parishes were impropriate, while in Yorkshire the figure was as high as 63 per cent.[14] Lay impropriators still held nearly a quarter of the net annual value of all tithes at the time of commutation.

TITHE PAYMENT IN KIND

Until tithe was permanently commuted perhaps by an enclosure act or eventually by the Tithe Commutation Act of 1836, a tithe owner had the right to claim payment of tithe in kind (in actual produce from the fields at harvest, from the dairy, sheep pens and pig styes) and he was also entitled to enter farms to exact his claim. Tithe barns were built to store the great tithes of corn (Fig. 2). Most great tithe was rendered in kind until the mid-17th century from which time it was gradually supplanted by a variety of monetary payments, negotiated and arranged locally and which in time came to have the force of parish custom.[15]

2 The tithe barn at Abbotsbury, Dorset. These great barns, often the largest building in a parish apart from the church itself, were looked on by land owners as potent symbols of the oppressive tithing system. Photograph by A. Teed.

If somewhat eclipsed as the norm by the 18th century, tithing in kind did not disappear. In Eric Evans' opinion, R.E. Prothero (Lord Ernle) was wrong to state that, at the close of the 18th century, comparatively little tithe was collected in kind.[16] Prothero's view was based on the Board of Agriculture Reports, and passages from the reports referring to tithe in kind are abstracted in Appendix V of his *English farming past and present*. The Board's reporters did, however, correctly identify the 'heartlands' of tithing in kind as the north-west and south-east of England. Tithe owners in both the metropolitan south-east and in the manufacturing districts of south Lancashire and north-east Cheshire were among those who clung most tenaciously to their ancient rights to tithe in kind. The three northern counties of Northumberland, Cumberland and Westmorland, the collegiate estates in Cambridgeshire and the southern counties of Middlesex, Kent, Surrey, Sussex and Hampshire retained more than their share of tithes in kind, though the Board's reporters were wrong when they stated that collection in kind had ceased in the midland and western counties. Evans' analysis of evidence contemporary with the Board of Agriculture reports for 115 places recorded in F.M. Eden's *The state of the poor* (1797) and that produced by William Pitt's questionnaire on tithe reform in 1791-2 reveal that the collection of tithe in kind was by no means uncommon elsewhere.[17] Evidence in the tithe files corroborates this view; tithing in kind is mentioned in 675 files.

COMPOSITIONS AND MODUSES IN LIEU OF TITHE IN KIND

Tithes were rendered in cash before 1836 by annual payments known as compositions, which might be adjusted from time to time or be terminated by either party, or alternatively by a modus which was a permanent charge on an article of titheable produce or on a piece of land.

Methods of assessing the level of compositions varied a good deal and contributed to the multiplicity of tithing customs which confronted parliament when framing permanent commutation legislation in the 1830s.[18] The wide variation in the manner of assessment meant that some tithe owners got much closer to the 'tenth' than others. Those who could afford it might commission annual valuations of the growing crops as a basis for a cash composition each year, but this was expensive. A cheaper alternative was for the tithe owner to set a composition value per acre of each crop. But a fixed money payment was not strictly equivalent to a tithe which varied from year to year according to the amount and value of farm produce. For this reason, some composition agreements stipulated that a fixed sum be paid for an agreed number of years, some provided for the periodic revision of the payment, while others specified that the sum should fluctuate from year to year with the prices of some commodity, usually wheat, sometimes other cereals, in a few cases oats and barley jointly with wheat. The clergy were also reluctant to enter into arrangements that might bind their successors or that might permanently deprive them of the prospective benefits arising from improvements. Agreements to alter the methods of paying tithes were generally accompanied by full valuations of the amounts collected, together with schedules of the titheable lands and sometimes large-scale plans.

If payment of his tithes in kind was the most repugnant method for a farmer, then modus payments were the least satisfactory from a tithe owner's point of view. The existence of a modus in his parish was probably the greatest single obstacle to the full realisation of an incumbent's income. Moduses were small (certainly by the 17th century) payments made in lieu of the actual value of titheable produce. In the words of Lord Chief Justice Hardwicke in 1747, 'a modus is nothing more than an ancient composition between … the owners of land in a parish, and the rector, which gains strength by time'.[19] Some parochial moduses applied throughout a parish for a particular crop or animal. The tithe files reveal that in Somerset twopence an acre was paid in many places in lieu of tithe hay, while in south-east England moduses of a shilling an acre covered grass tithes in some marshland areas. Alternatively, farm moduses might exonerate all the lands of a particular farm for a sum of money fixed by the force of custom for all time. Not all moduses were rendered in cash, though this was the most usual. The modus in lieu of hay tithe from Tyddyn Mawr farm in Llanfihangel Esgeifiog parish in Anglesey consisted of a dinner every alternative Sunday for the officiating minister and a feed of corn for his horse. On the other Sundays they were both fed at Hendrefaig farm in Llanffinan parish where a similar modus applied![20]

The economic iniquity of a modus is clear enough. The modus was intended to be a rough equivalent of a tithe but as most moduses were fixed by the mid-16th century at the latest, and generally earlier, the sums were clearly derisory some two or more centuries later. While some moduses were overturned by litigation, particularly in the course of the struggle by 18th-century clergy to increase their incomes, tithe files reveal that moduses still applied in at least 2,571 tithe districts c.1840. They were most numerous in the north and west of the country and most usually replaced tithe on hay and animals, particularly dairy cows and their milk. Though collection in kind could be very expensive in upland England and Wales (up to 40 per cent was deducted from the gross produce of tithe when it was valued for commutation after 1836), a modus set aside could, as Eric Evans has shown, perhaps quadruple tithe income at a stroke.[21]

TITHE DISPUTES

Payment of tithes in kind was a cause of endless disputes between farmers and tithe owners. It would, indeed, be an enormous task to compute the amount of time and effort diverted from the practice of husbandry and from pastoral care by these incessant quarrels over trifling matters and it would be even more difficult to discover how parsons and farmers obtained the money to pour into protracted legal battles, especially as the most persistent litigants struggled for the possession of nothing more than the value of the small tithes. Very costly proceedings were entered upon to determine which courts should hear such suits, who was liable to pay, how payments should be assessed and how or to whom they should be paid.[22] Frequent disputes arose concerning the nature of titheable produce. It was once decided that partridges were *ferae naturae* and therefore exempt from tithe, and a precedent was established for exempting domesticated turkeys.

On another occasion, wild ducks were declared tithe-free, but eggs laid by tame ducks used to decoy them were held to be titheable. Not even the herbage on balks and headlands, nor the stubble left after a corn crop had been cut, nor wild cherries, nor fallen apples escaped the attention of some claimant, and the question of whether to tithe perry and cider was a cause for lengthy disputations. But the most difficult cases of all were those involving the produce of woodland. In some areas such as north Wales and the Weald all woodlands were exempt, in others only certain trees (such as beeches in the Chilterns), in yet others the trunks and branches were exempt, but acorns, mast, foliage and even charcoal were titheable. In one such case timber trees of over twenty years' growth springing from the stools of older trees were adjudged to be subject to tithes.[23]

When tithes were allotted to more than one owner further litigation began, and tithes payable on Lammas lands and half-year commons had to be apportioned between different occupiers and then perhaps also assigned to different tithe owners. It was asked what constituted the vicar's tithe and how much belonged to the rector or lay impropriator. In the common fields at Cambridge different strips were tithed by different churches without regard to parish boundaries.[24] Were tithes to be collected by the owners and, if so, when? Must the farmer await the arrival of the tithe collector before carting his harvest, so risking a heavy loss in wet weather, or might he summon the collector on the pretext of gathering his harvest, then lift ten roots of turnips and send the man away with only one? Or should tithes be delivered to the owner, and if so to what place? Should milk be taken each day or every tenth day; should it be laid in the church porch or presented to the vicarage; and at what age should lambs be selected for tithing?

Both tithe payers and tithe owners were guilty of pettiness and sharp practices but Arthur Young considered the clergy the worse offenders. Even in France in the last year of the *ancien régime*, he observed that tithe 'was never exacted with that horrid greediness as is at present the disgrace of England'.[25] There is certainly evidence that, at the time when Young was condemning tithe owners, the English clergy were engaged in a campaign to reassert their right to a full 'tenth' because they perceived that tithe revenue was static while agricultural productivity and output were increasing.[26] But, as Eric Evans asserts, 'tithe disputes were endemic in British society, and litigation was instituted by all manner of tithe owners'.[27] Many disputes were over rights to increase compositions, and many were over what had become, from a tithe owner's point of view, that least satisfactory money payment, the prescriptive modus.[28] Other disputes were occasioned by antipathy towards the established church. In the vanguard of early opposition on these grounds were the Quakers, though their carefully orchestrated propaganda may give a somewhat exaggerated picture of their grievances, at any rate by the 18th century.[29] But in the 17th century it was a real problem for this sect. A.B. Anderson, who has analysed 1,234 separate incidents in which Lancashire Quakers suffered between 1650 and 1690, finds that seizure of goods for non-payment of tithes increased from about two incidents a year in the first half of this period to an average of thirty per annum in the 1670s and 1680s.[30] By the time of their great campaign against tithes in 1736, the number of prosecutions of Friends for non-payment of tithe had markedly declined by comparison with the second half of the 17th century. Tithe owners cooperated by obtaining payment through distraints granted by the courts or sanctioned payment by Friends through third parties so avoiding them the embarrassment of paying directly to the established church.[31]

TITHE AND AGRICULTURAL IMPROVEMENT

It can be argued, however, that the moral dilemma which non-conformist groups faced when paying tithes was overshadowed in the 18th century by grievances arising from economic considerations. Tithes were a regressive tax which bore most heavily on lands whose yields were great but whose costs of production were also high. In areas where the profit to be gained was likely to be small, potential investors might have been deterred from venturing their capital because of the incidence of tithes. F.M.L. Thompson argues that the incidence of tithes would be taken into consideration when calculating an economic rent and it therefore added nothing to the charges paid by a tenant. But a tithe levied on profits made by a farmer's additional investments would fall on him alone and might be equivalent to a tax of 30 per cent. Assuming a return of 10 or 12 per cent on an investment, a farmer might expect to receive, after payment of tithes, between 7 and 8.5 per cent, which would still be a worthwhile reward.[32] It would be extremely difficult to ascertain how far investment was discouraged by tithe payment, but clearly it should have militated most severely against undertaking such costly improvements as moorland reclamation, fen draining, marling and enclosing. The reports to the Board of Agriculture around 1800 found little specific evidence of schemes of this kind having been abandoned but were loud in complaints of a general character. In Somerset, Norfolk and other counties that had brought large areas of unproductive land into cultivation, tithes were not considered immoderate.[33] In Gloucestershire, where substantial improvements had been made, Thomas Rudge found that 'a solitary instance may possibly be produced, where a small quantity of land has been suffered to lie in a neglected state to defeat the demands of the tithe owner'.[34] On the other hand, John Boys claimed that in east Kent, 'there are immense quantities of poor land, which experience has proved might be made to produce good crops of turnips and clover' but for the discouragement of paying tithes in kind.[35] In Hertfordshire, it was observed that those parts subject to a reasonable annual money payment in lieu of tithes were generally farmed on improved methods, whereas lands liable to pay tithes in kind were often abandoned to almost total neglect.[36]

As practices of assessing and collecting tithes were prescribed by local customs, farmers in neighbouring parishes or townships were required to pay widely differing amounts of tithe.[37] Many tithe files noted how farmers, out of frustration with the unreformed tithe system, had practised evasive land-use management to minimise tithe payments. Yorkshire farmers seem to have been remarkably adept at farming in a manner that yielded the smallest amount of titheable produce. At Nidd in the West Riding, farmers took their ewes out of the parish immediately before lambing and again before shearing for the express purpose of depriving the vicar of his tithes of lambs and wool.[38] A farmer at Stutton also held land in Hazlewood, where a modus was payable in lieu of all small tithes. He milked and clipped his animals and had his mown meadows in Hazlewood so that he only paid agistment tithe in Stutton.[39] At Sherston Magna in Wiltshire the Tithe Commission's George Bolls found circumstances which were by no means unusual where parliamentary enclosure had extinguished tithes in part of a parish and replaced them with an allotment of land. As the titheable and tithe-free lands in this parish were intermingled, occupiers would grow most of their corn crops in the tithe-free fields and feed their stock in those that were titheable.[40] Scottish teinds were abolished by act of parliament in 1633 so farmers such as those at Longridge (now in Northumberland) with land in both England and Scotland summered their stock on the Scottish side of the Tweed to reduce tithe liability.[41]

The tithe files also contain evidence of the effect of tithe on agricultural improvement in the 1820s and 1830s as assistant tithe commissioners had to take account of any changes in the gross produce of a tithe district that might directly result from the general commutation of 1836. If they thought improvement or change affecting output would follow immediately, they could make an additional charge to protect the tithe owners' interests. Tithes were usually worth about one-fifth of the arable rent and about one-eighth or one-ninth of the grassland rent. The difference in value of grassland and arable tithes thus amounted to about a tenth of the rent. In marshland areas this difference was sometimes even greater, as traditionally extensive tracts were subject to a nominal modus of a few pence per acre regardless of quality or produce while they remained down to grass. Where differences in the value of arable and pasture tithes were large, assistant tithe commissioners, assessing global rent charges, had to consider the probability of some grassland being ploughed up as a direct result of commutation. Tithe payers presented them with evidence to support the view that pasture would be little affected by tithe commutation while representatives of tithe owners forecasted phenomenal yields of grain from ploughed-up pastures once a commutation for tithe was effected. This topic is discussed at particular length in the tithe files of Cumberland, Northumberland, Yorkshire, Staffordshire, Oxfordshire and Lincolnshire, but nowhere in England was this question more fiercely debated than in the Romney Marsh district of Kent where there was a great difference between the nominal modus of one shilling per acre on grass and the tithe of highly productive arable.[42]

With the rising corn prices of the 1840s there can be little doubt of the extra profit to be obtained by breaking up some pasture. For reasons of prejudice and vested interest the desirability of this was not always acknowledged at commutation meetings. By about 1875 farmers had experienced a generation of high corn prices and the acreage of pasture in Kent, for example, had greatly decreased. The tithe apportionments show that, c.1840, as much as 32 per cent of the county was down to grass. A sample of 55 Books of Reference to the first edition Ordnance Survey 1:2500 plans shows that by c.1875 only 24 per cent was under permanent grass.[43] Eric Evans has approached the factors affecting landowners' decisions to invest in improvements more directly by examining estate papers. This led him to infer that 'improvement was more readily put in train on land which was either tithe free or covered by small moduses, despite the fact that it was invariably subject to a higher rent. Tithe free land which came on to the market was advertised prominently as such, being considered a clear selling point'.[44]

The tithe commissioners in their annual reports to parliament also lost little opportunity to proclaim the beneficial effects of the Tithe Commutation Act whose provisions they administered. And, of course, there was much investment on drainage schemes, artificial manures and new farm buildings between 1836 and the onset of the great depression in the 1890s. But, as Eric Jones has demonstrated, there was at least as much investment in livestock fattening and mixed farming as in arable enterprises.[45] Grassland tithes were much lower than those of arable and in many places were reduced still further by the presence of a modus so that the case for tithe restraining the improvement of purely livestock farms is much weaker. But, as Evans concludes, 'agricultural England as viewed by Arthur Young in 1790 and James Caird in 1850 were very different places. Although Young and some of his followers overstated their case, it is clear that a national commutation in, say, 1800 would of itself have stimulated still more improvement on the less naturally fertile arable lands, particularly where tithe had been paid in kind. After 1836, the situation was more complex, the requirements more diverse. Far heavier injections of capital were required which made tithe calculations less crucial to the improvement equation in Caird's day than in Young's.[46]

ALLOTMENTS OF LAND IN LIEU OF TITHES

When tithes were dealt with under a parliamentary enclosure act, they were generally extinguished in exchange for allotments of land. Under the terms of many acts, tithe owners had the power to nominate a person to represent their interests as one of the commissioners appointed to administer the act, and in all cases where tithes were disposed of the agreement of the owners had to be sought and freely given. In every enclosure award which dealt with tithes, they secured compensation on a very generous scale, and under later enactments they obtained what can only be described as remarkable bargains.[47] There was no question of receiving allotments of as little as one tenth of the titheable land. At the end of the 18th century one-fifth of the arable land and one-ninth of the pasture was normally ceded to them, practices which add weight to the argument that tithe was in fact a disincentive to improvement, and farmers and landowners were evidently keen to find a method of extinguishing tithes less costly than surrendering land.[48] During the Napoleonic wars the size of allotments increased and in 1792 in an exceptional parish, Shipton in Hampshire, the tithe owner acquired no less than three-tenths of the land and retained the right to collect vicarial tithes. In a study of the results of this procedure, based on an examination of 20 enclosure awards covering the period from 1793 to 1815, Vladimir Lavrovsky concluded that almost without exception, 'tithe commutation led to a diminution in the area owned by the peasantry'.[49] On a broader scale, the findings of W.R. Ward suggest that 'the effect of commutation was to multiply the average glebe by a factor of 2 or 3'.[50] But, as E.C.K. Gonner has pointed out, there were marked regional as well as social differences in the manner of commuting tithes under parliamentary acts.[51] In some areas they were entirely extinguished; in others, moduses and compositions prevailed. Figure 3 is a map of the number of places where at least part of the tithes was commuted under the terms of enclosure acts between 1757 and 1835. As can be seen from the map, the redistribution of property associated with commutation was

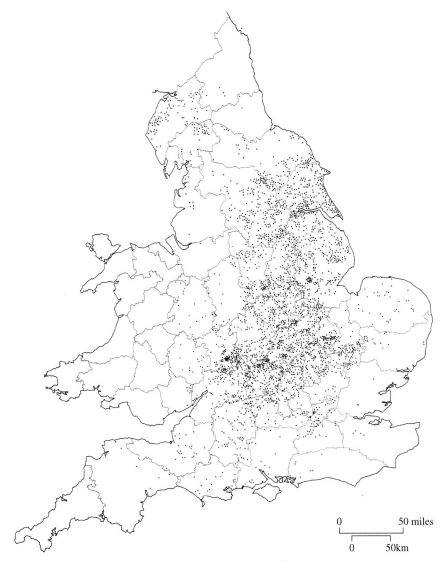

0 _____ 50 miles

0 _____ 50km

3 Commutation of tithes by enclosure acts in England, 1757-1835. The map is very much a mirror image of the map of tithe coverage (see frontispiece). Source: BPP (HC), 1836, XLIV, 'A return from the inclosure and other private acts in which provisions are included for the commutation of tithes, of the proportion in land, yearly money payment, or corn rent, allotted in lieu of tithe', 344pp.

concentrated in particular areas. In the counties of early enclosure this was an unimportant process but in Yorkshire, for example, part at least of the tithes of 628 places was commuted, much being for land.[52] 'Thus, at the very time when churches within reach of revolutionary France were losing property wholesale, the Church of England was gaining it on a considerable scale throughout the midlands and the east.'[53] About 2,230 enclosure acts passed before 1835 provided for the abolition of the payment of tithes in kind.[54] In 1,510 of these, all tithes were extinguished by allotments of land made to the tithe owners; in 550, tithes were partly extinguished by allotments of land and partly converted into annual money payments; in only 170 acts were tithes entirely converted into annual money payments.[55] That so high a proportion of the acts provided for the abolition of tithes and that compensation was fixed at levels that are, by any measure, very high, suggests that tithe payers were prepared to pay almost any price to be relieved of the burden, and it also indicates that the clergy held very powerful bargaining positions. By threatening to withhold their approval, tithe owners were able to dictate the terms on which enclosures might be proceeded with.

After the Napoleonic wars, crippling taxes, rates and tithes, uncertain corn prices, a succession of poor harvests, and a decline in domestic industry brought distress to many farmers and hunger to many labouring families. Hardship was greatest in south-east England where poor rates reached unprecedented levels and the exactions of tithe collectors were much harsher than elsewhere. Labourers begged for wages that would enable them to feed their families without having to apply for poor relief, while farmers clamoured for reduction in rents, for an easing of the burden of poor rates and, above all, for abolition of tithes in kind. William Cobbett, in speeches throughout the southern counties, repeatedly reminded farming audiences that privileges enjoyed by the clergy could not last much longer: 'there must be a *settlement of some sort*; and that settlement never can leave that mass, that immense mass, of public property, called "church property", to be used as it now is'.[56] When violence erupted in Kent and in other southern counties in the autumn of 1830, it was directed not only against farmers' ricks and workhouses but in many parishes angry mobs attacked their parson.[57] In the uneasy peace that followed, the clergy themselves began to deliberate on ways and means of bringing to an end abuses of the tithing system, and a measure presented to parliament finally became law in 1836.

2

THE TITHE COMMUTATION ACT OF 1836

For many centuries tithes had been paid grudgingly in most parishes and in a few this payment may be traced back over 900 years. During much of that time they had been a cause for grievances and had been regarded as a continuing source of irritation. From time to time additional demands by a new incumbent or by an assertive tithe owner had provoked outbursts of resistance, but for the most part it was possible to blame deviant groups of Quakers or more militant dissenters for stirring up trouble. Magistrates confidently dealt with such outbreaks as if they were fomented by a minority of activists who could be ostracised as religious cranks. On few occasions and in few localities were tithes seen as serious or potentially serious threats to the maintenance of public order, and not until the beginning of the 19th century did the government feel that the survival of the regime in any way depended upon a reform or abolition of the age-old practices of collecting them. The tithe question did not seem to be a rallying point for widespread popular uprisings and, indeed, it might well have been ignored even later had not other more pressing sources of discontent arisen.

TITHE IN THE POST-NAPOLEONIC DEPRESSION

Teinds had been abolished in Scotland in 1633 and with the passage of the Irish Tithe Composition Act in 1823 their retention in England and Wales became an undesirable anachronism.[1] By this time the established church was no longer in a position to negotiate a tithe settlement on terms as favourable as those conceded under enclosure awards. In the recession following the Napoleonic wars, further territorial expansion of ecclesiastical estates by additional tithe allotments was unlikely to be countenanced either by parliament or by a large section of the tithe owners themselves. Another more generally acceptable solution had to be found without delay. The agricultural depression had two direct consequences that made demands for tithes especially hard to bear. First, the collection of tithes in kind presented an all too obvious spectacle of clerical oppression when crops and livestock were taken from the fields of farmers on the verge of ruin, under the eyes of famished labourers. The incidence of the collection of tithe in kind fell heaviest in the distressed southern counties and to a lesser extent in the north-west. Secondly, more than half the cultivated land of England and Wales was subject to money payments, many of which had been fixed when corn prices were high and, on the recommendation of a Select Committee on Tithes in 1816, many such charges had been made binding upon the parties concerned and on their successors by leases entered into for periods of up to fourteen years.[2] When farm incomes fell these covenanted commitments became intolerable imposts, contributing to numerous insolvencies. These, in turn, increased difficulties experienced by landowners in finding tenants for vacant farms, even at greatly reduced rents. From the clergy's point of view, the most menacing aspect of the disturbances of 1830-2 was that farmers took little or no action to restrain the violence of the rioters, and at Benenden, Horsham, Mayfield, Brede, Selborne and other places in the Wealden districts of Kent, Surrey, Sussex and Hampshire they invited or offered encouragement to mobs to press demands for the abolition of tithes. The riots were quelled, six men and boys were hanged and 457 were transported to Van Diemen's Land and to New South Wales, but resentment remained as deep as before.

A final legislative solution to the tithe problem had to wait until parliament was itself reformed. John Christian Curwen, Whig MP for Carlisle and a practising farmer, was one of the principal agitators for reform in the immediate post-Napoleonic-war period. It was he who secured the appointment of a Select Committee in 1816 to consider the many petitions against tithes being placed before the House. The following year he won a debate on moduses and the claims and counter-claims arising from these customary payments.[3] The next important parliamentary debate on tithes did not take place until 1828 when Thomas Greene, MP for Lancaster, introduced what was effectively the first bill to procure a national commutation. Greene's solution was to authorise the establishment of corn rents in lieu of tithe. His bill was lost, largely as a result of arguments put forward by the tithe-owning interest in defence of their own claims to a share in the fruits of agricultural improvement.[4]

After being blamed in 1831 for the failure of the first parliamentary reform bill, the church found itself subjected to massive anti-clerical demonstrations. As Evans asserts, 'in the period 1831-4, it seems safe to say, the Church of England stood in more imminent danger of disestablishment than at any time before or since'.[5] The question facing the government was how to remove or greatly diminish the danger of continued strife and how to bring about a lasting settlement. It was clear that expropriations of land would only inflame a tense situation and that imposition of permanent charges unrelated to changing prices would be equally unacceptable. It was also evident that compositions based on the quantity and value of land, in effect surcharges on rents, provided no answer. What was required was a variable tax on farm output, regulated according to prevailing price levels. A corn rent, adjusted to current market prices of wheat or of other cereals, went some way towards achieving this objective, and from this simple device were derived the underlying basic principles of several proposed reforms. Between 1833 and 1836 no fewer than four attempts, three Whig and one Tory, were made to secure the passage of bills to commute tithes.

THE TITHE COMMUTATION ACT OF 1836

On 9 February 1836 Lord John Russell introduced his bill for the commutation of tithes in England and Wales. He reminded the House that various plans had been submitted to parliament, that none of them had been completed, yet none had really failed. He saw that tithe commutation had to be effected quickly, not only because of the abstract objections against tithes pointed out more than fifty years earlier but because 'tithe was now, as it was then, a discouragement to industry—a penalty on skill, a heavy mulct on those who expended the most capital and displayed the greatest skill in cultivating the land'.[6]

When the bill was debated in the House the middle ground of both Whig and Tory parties saw the prospect of getting at last a measure for tithe commutation on to the statute book. As Russell himself contended during the debate on the second reading of the bill, the fact that it was opposed by extremes on both sides of the House was proof that those like himself who steered a middle course had devised a measure which ultimately would satisfy all parties.[7] A repetition of the Irish tithe debacle could not be countenanced by either side.[8] Parliamentary debates on the tithe question in the 1830s usually divided along party lines: landowning Whigs favouring coercion, church-going Tories championing voluntaryism. Russell's bill allayed Tory concern about coercion by extending the period to reach a voluntary agreement from six months to over two years.[9]

The act passed on 13 August 1836 commuted all tithes in kind and substituted a fluctuating money payment known as a tithe rent-charge adjusted each year on the basis of the seven-year average price of wheat, barley and oats.[10] The amount of the tithe rent-charge was to be obtained by dividing £100 of tithe into three equal portions of £33 6s. 8d., calculating how much wheat, barley and oats could be bought with each portion, and multiplying these quantities by the average price in succeeding years. In 1836 the septennial average price of wheat was 7s. ¼d. per bushel, of barley, 3s. 11½d. per bushel, of oats, 2s 9d per bushel. At these prices £33 6s. 8d. bought 94.96 bushels of wheat, or 168.42 bushels of barley, or 242.42 bushels of oats. Each succeeding year the tithe rent-charge on £100 of tithe was to be the sum of the septennial average prices of these quantities of grain, and tables were to be published annually to enable the precise amount of any rent-charge to be calculated. In this way the relationship between the prices of the three cereals and the value of the money payment for which tithes were commuted was to be preserved.[11]

THE TITHE COMMISSION IN LONDON

Responsibility for tithe commutation was vested in a Tithe Commission set up on the model of the earlier Poor Law Commission.[12] Three commissioners—William Blamire, Reverend Richard Jones (Fig. 4), and Captain Thomas Wentworth Buller—were appointed under the provisions of the 1836 Act. William Blamire, the Commission's chairman, was a Cumberland landowner and farmer who represented his county in parliament as a Whig from 1831 to 1836 when he was required to resign by virtue of his tithe appointment. He was not a frequent speaker in the House and confined himself in the main to subjects concerning the Cumberland rural interest. In that part of the country tithe was very much a live issue during his years in parliament and, with experience he gained from Kendal and other tithe disputes, Blamire probably knew as much as anyone in the country about the practical difficulties associated with the unreformed tithe system.[13] From 1845

4 A likeness of Rev Richard Jones, tithe commissioner, reproduced from the frontispiece of his *Literary remains consisting of lectures and tracts on political economy, edited with a prefatory notice by Rev. William Whewell* (London, John Murray, 1859). Reproduced by permission of the British Library Board.

he combined the job of tithe commissioner with that of commissioner for copyhold enfranchisement. His 19th-century biographer, Henry Lonsdale, speaks of his prodigious labours embodied in statutes and official reports. But, as Professor Spring observes, William Blamire's work was not only a paper contribution but also 'helped to re-make the face of rural England'.[14]

Rev Richard Jones was nominated to the Tithe Commission by the archbishop of Canterbury. Son of a Tunbridge Wells solicitor, Jones graduated from Cambridge and was ordained in 1816. While serving as a curate in parishes in Sussex and Kent, he studied relations of population and production, wrote a treatise on rent and, in 1833, was appointed professor of political economy at the newly-founded King's College, London[15] His attention turned to the question of tithe commutation and he published tracts on the subject in 1833 and 1836.[16] In 1835 he moved to the East India College at Haileybury to take up the chair of economics left vacant by the death of Thomas Malthus. Though a church appointment, his work for the Tithe Commission showed 'no greater partiality to the interests of the church than Blamire's did to the farming interest'.[17] The third commissioner, Captain Buller, benefited from Lord John Russell's patronage. He was a landowner in Northamptonshire and Devon and was an active promoter of the Whig cause in the South West.[18] The three tithe commissioners were based in London where they were supported by a secretary and assistant secretary and more than 30 clerks and 20 draughtsmen. Also working in the London office was the first assistant tithe commissioner to be sworn in, Lieutenant Robert Kearsley Dawson (Fig. 5).

Dawson was seconded to the Tithe Commission from the Royal Engineers on 27 August 1836 and was given the task of organising and superintending the land surveys on which the permanent commutation was to be recorded. R.K. Dawson was the son of Robert Dawson (1776-1860), a celebrated topographical artist and surveyor. He was commissioned into the Royal Engineers in March 1816, from 1819 he worked as assistant to Thomas Colby on the triangulation of Scotland, and in 1825 accompanied Colby to Ireland. Here in 1829 he was put in charge of a staff of civil assistants engaged in sketching hills for the one-inch map. His men also collected material for county memoirs to the six-inch survey. Under his guidance and critical eye some notable talents emerged from the body of civil assistants and some excellent memoirs were produced.[19] In 1831 Dawson was called back to England and appointed a commissioner under the Reform Bill to settle and map the boundaries of parliamentary boroughs.[20] Of all the varied survey activities with which Dawson was concerned before 1836, his association with the Irish Survey had the most profound influence on his approach to the organisation and specification of the tithe surveys. In particular he used the need for tithe maps as a reason for beginning a full cadastral survey of England and Wales on the Irish model (see Chapter 3). His work with the tithe survey established him as an authority on cadastral mapping, and, at the same time as superintending the tithe survey, he was employed as surveying consultant to the Wakefield settlements in Australia and New Zealand.[21]

5 Robert Kearsley Dawson, assistant tithe commissioner and superintendent of the tithe surveys, pictured in about 1841. Reproduced from a miniature in the possession of G.A. Dawson by his kind permission.

ASSISTANT TITHE COMMISSIONERS AND LOCAL TITHE AGENTS

The Tithe Commutation Act required the tithe commissioners to confirm such voluntary agreements to commute tithes that were reached before 1 October 1838 and to impose awards in those districts where agreements could not be reached or where the commissioners considered the terms unfair to one or other party. In practice these powers were delegated to assistant commissioners and local agents whose recommendations were usually accepted in London. The duties of local agents were restricted to reporting on draft agreements and advising the tithe commissioners whether they should be confirmed. Assistant tithe commissioners also conducted this business but in addition had the more responsible duty of framing awards.[22] In Eric Evans' words, these men 'became the "restless shuttles" of the commutation machinery, as they scurried from one parish to another, offering advice, settling disputes, confirming agreements and effecting compulsory commutation' (Fig. 6).[23]

Applications for full-time posts as assistant commissioner were closely scrutinised. Among the earliest applicants was Joseph Townsend, a surveyor and owner of a small

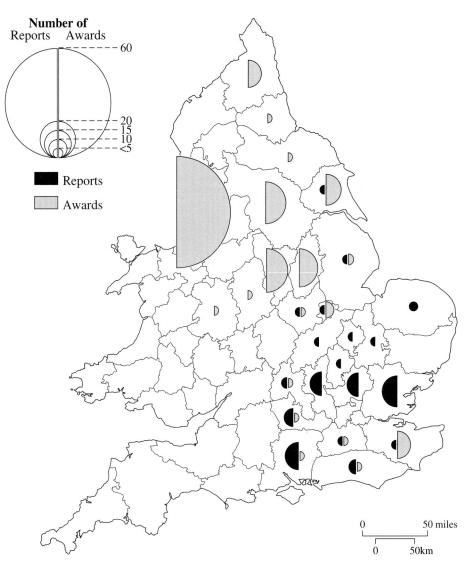

6 Places where assistant tithe commissioner Joseph Townsend of Medmenham, Buckinghamshire reported on agreements for commutation of tithe and drafted tithe awards. Source: R.J.P. Kain, *An atlas and index of the tithe files of mid-nineteenth-century England and Wales* (Cambridge, Cambridge University Press, 1986), 15.

estate on the borders of Buckinghamshire and Oxfordshire. He had gained 21 years' experience in dealing with tithes as commissioner and surveyor for many enclosure acts. The Tithe Commission called for testimonials concerning his commissions in different counties and sought evidence concerning his character. On becoming a full-time public servant, Townsend was required to reside near London, give up most of his private business interests, conduct official inquiries with absolute impartiality and integrity, and obey directives from the commissioners. Townsend's life as a country gentleman was restricted by his public employment. There was long hesitation before he was enrolled as a Justice of the Peace. In 1851, as the work of the Tithe Commission neared completion, Townsend was made redundant and efforts to find him other official employment failed. He received neither compensation for loss of earnings nor a pension.[24] The Commission was a harsh and demanding master.

The volume of work that some assistant commissioners and local agents accomplished was quite prodigious. Henry Pilkington completed 422 reports on agreements in 16 counties between 1837 and 1846, writing 94 in 1839 alone.[25] From 1840 when he was appointed assistant commissioner he also attended many award appeal meetings. In some individual weeks in 1839 he visited and reported on 10 districts; on the single day of 17 June he wrote four reports and another six on 9-10 July. Even this workload pales in comparison with Thomas Hoskins' 538 reports written between 1838 and 1844 with no fewer than 203 completed in 1839 alone. With several townships to report on in a single day it is hardly surprising that the language of their accounts is sometimes terse and hastily penned.[26]

Most local agents were practical men, well-versed in the farming and landscapes of one or two counties in which they undertook reports for the Tithe Commission. The more educated and able, who from an early date were appointed full-time assistant commissioners, such as Thomas Smith Woolley of South Collingham near Newark in Nottinghamshire, conducted work over a large geographical area.[27] Inevitably this meant that they were less familiar with the agricultural systems of some areas in which they were reporting. They were all by dint of experience, if nothing else, practical valuers and required to be skilled negotiators. Without their careful handling of local disputes and the energy and diligence they brought to their work, the Tithe Commutation Act might have foundered.

ESTABLISHING TITHE DISTRICTS

The first task to be performed by the three commissioners appointed under the provisions of the Act was to establish boundaries for every district in which tithes were paid separately. This was known as a tithe district to distinguish it from a parish or township. In the meaning of the Act, districts included every place for which an overseer of the poor was appointed. The commissioners first sent written enquiries to all places listed as parishes and townships in the census returns but could and did, if necessary, form separate districts. This was sometimes necessary where tithe was paid separately in parts of parishes or townships. Occasionally, two or more townships or parishes were combined, a procedure which resulted in economies all round.[28] In all, 14,829 tithe districts were recognised containing in total 36.2 million acres and most are parishes or townships; the latter are usual in north-east Wales and in most of England on the north and west side of the Trent. A minority were tithings, chapelries, manors, hamlets, extra-parochial places and such like, many of which districts enjoyed separate status solely for tithe commutation purposes. A tithe file was opened for each tithe district and into that file correspondence relating to the district was placed. For some 3,044 of these tithe districts the commissioners' labours involved no more than recording replies to their enquiries which confirmed that tithe was no longer payable in 1836. At this date exemption was usually by virtue of a complete enclosure commutation, or else tithe had been redeemed by direct merger in the land, most commonly where a tithe owner and tithe payer were one and the same person.

The existence of districts was usually not contested but what was frequently disputed was the exact configuration of boundaries. The demarcation of a boundary was particularly important for a person who was a tithe owner in one parish and a tithe payer elsewhere. Again, tithe payments themselves differed from parish to parish both in their nature and amount, so that a particular piece of land might carry a higher rent-charge if it were included in one parish than in another. Land subject to tithes on one side of a boundary might even be exempt on the other. Such was the case in those Kent parishes situated along the line of the Pilgrim's Way. Woods were subject to tithe in parishes to the north of the line but exempt by prescription to the south.

Where boundaries were uncertain, the owners of two-thirds (by value) of the land could require the tithe commissioners to enquire into and set out the boundaries of their district. This always preceded the commutation of tithes as the value of tithes would be affected by the extent of the district. Without the help of large-scale Ordnance Survey maps, the commissioners had to rely on the best available maps and documents and on local knowledge. The procedure was for the assistant commissioner appointed to decide a dispute to receive from landowners written descriptions and sketch plans of the claimed boundary line. Landowners were required to support their claims with evidence from witnesses and documents. Representatives of landowners from the adjoining district also attended the hearing prepared with counter descriptions, sketches, documents and witnesses, after which the assistant commissioner decided the line on the preponderance of the evidence.[29]

AGREEMENTS FOR TITHE RENT-CHARGE

Having discovered where tithes remained uncommuted and having set in train machinery to resolve disputed boundaries, the commissioners proceeded to their main tasks of, first, confirming rent-charges and, secondly, apportioning the global sum over various types of land in the district. The Act enabled tithe owners and tithe payers to agree a value for the rent-charge at any time before 1 October 1838. Although the voluntary option was backed up by compulsory powers which could be invoked in deadlocked or dilatory districts after that date, it was the express policy of the tithe commissioners to encourage voluntary agreements. In following such a policy they were respecting the spirit of the Act and the tenor of parliamentary debate.

To help landowners and tithe owners achieve a just and fair agreement, the Tithe Commission made available a mass of printed information sheets providing procedural guidance.[30] One of the most valuable of these was a *pro forma* indicating an acceptable form of words which could be used when drafting an agreement. Parochial meetings to investigate the possibility of achieving an agreement could be called by owners of not less than a quarter of the land *or* tithes and if the owners of two-thirds (by value) of the land and of the tithes could agree a rent-charge in lieu of tithes, this would be binding on the remainder. 'Thus, as at enclosure, a few substantial property holders could dictate terms to the many whose collective stake was smaller.'[31] Once a draft agreement was prepared it was sent to the tithe commissioners who instructed an assistant commissioner or a local tithe agent to visit the district and charged him with writing a report advising whether the agreement was fair to all parties and suitable for confirmation prior to apportionment. To help the Tithe Commission's local representatives judge these agreements and to organise and standardise their reports, they were issued from November 1837 with forms on which a number of questions were printed with spaces provided for answers. These answers provide much information on local landscape, farming practices and the output of agriculture and for historians are perhaps the most important source documents remaining in the tithe files (see Chapter 3). Two basic types of form were printed but in any one county only one type of form was issued. Exceptions to this rule are so rare as to be explained by an agent or assistant commissioner not having any of the correct forms to hand and suggest, in the absence of the letter books and papers of the tithe commissioners, that commutation was probably organised on a county-by-county basis.[32]

During the first year of commutation the small number of agreements made did not require the employment of assistant commissioners and local agents on anything approaching a full-time basis. During this early period officials were sent to far-flung areas of the country. J.D. Merest, for example, reported on a number of agreements reached in 1837 in districts in Staffordshire, Shropshire and Lincolnshire but thereafter he worked only in East Anglia. In any one county, one agent reported on a clear majority of districts. Over 80 per cent of reports on agreements for Somerset districts were completed by Robert Page; John Farncombe officiated at 158 of the 188 Sussex agreement enquiries. Charles Howard of Melbourne, Yorkshire, worked mainly in northern England; Henry Gunning of Whittlesford, Cambridgeshire, in East Anglia; James Jerwood of Teignmouth, Devon, in south-west England. John Fenton and Aneurin Owen were entrusted with most of north Wales and Thomas Hoskins and John Johnes with south Wales.[33] Agricultural practices, land values and tithing customs varied from one part of the country to another so that there was clearly some advantage in employing men with specialist regional experience who would be quick to spot attempted transgressions by one party and who with their local understanding would perhaps better gain the respect and confidence of tithe owners and landowners than would a stranger.

Some 6,740 reports on draft agreements by assistant commissioners and local agents are preserved in the tithe files. An overwhelming majority of these agreements were confirmed by the tithe commissioners even in cases where the man on the spot had some reservation about the level of rent-charge agreed. It was also rare for a local agent to challenge an agreement even if his own valuation of the tithes departed quite considerably from the agreed rent-charge, providing he was confident that each 'side' was aware of how their situation related to neighbouring districts. As Eric Evans notes, the Tithe Commission took an agreement voluntarily entered into as *prima facie* evidence of reasonableness.[34]

The deadline established in the Act for arriving at an agreement was 1 October 1838. In the event, pressure of work during 1838 was such that the Tithe Commission accepted a number of agreements for confirmation between 1839 and 1841.[35] In the autumn of 1838 the process of compulsory commutation began in districts where attempts to come to an agreement had failed. Moduses, a common cause of lawsuits in the pre-1836 period, were also a frequent cause of tithe owners and tithe payers failing to achieve a voluntary agreement for commutation after 1836.

COMPULSORY AWARDS OF TITHE RENT-CHARGE

If agreement could not be reached, an assistant tithe commissioner representing the tithe commissioners was empowered to hold a local enquiry, to frame a draft award, hear objections, make amendments where necessary, and finally recommend confirmation of an award which then became binding on the tithe owners and tithe payers. Though there was a sense of inevitability about this process once the commissioners had been invited to proceed to an award (before 1840) or had decided that events required them to intervene and impose an award (after 1840), every opportunity was provided for various parties to put their cases fairly to an assistant commissioner. The Tithe Commission informed the incumbent by letter of its decision to proceed to an award and notified the date on which an assistant commissioner would hold an award meeting in the tithe district. This meeting had to be advertised 21 days in advance by a notice affixed in a prominent place, usually by the minister on the church door. A copy of this notice had to be sent to the Tithe Commission as confirmation that due notice had been given. Tithe owners and tithe payers were also sent an outline of the order of proceedings the assistant commissioner would follow on his visit.[36] In particular, this indicated to tithe owners and landowners what facts the assistant commissioner would require and at what point in the proceedings they would be able to present their cases.

Assistant commissioners based their award on the average value of tithes over the seven years from Christmas 1829 to Christmas 1835 (Clause 37). If a monetary composition had been in effect and good records had been kept, this initial task was straightforward. Problems usually arose where moduses were claimed by farmers or where tithe had been collected in kind. In the latter case, deductions could be made to allow for costs of collection. These were normally 20-25 per cent but might rise to 40 per cent in hilly districts with poor roads, remote from a tithe barn. In many parishes not only were tithes paid to several different tithe owners but payments were made in several different ways, and it was not always certain what constituted a tithe payment. Excluded from the provisions of the Act, except in special circumstances to be decided by the commissioners, were Easter offerings, mortuaries or surplice fees, tithes of fish or fishing, personal tithes other than those of milling, mineral tithes, payments in lieu of tithes in the City of London, fixed annual rent-charges in cities or towns and lands whose tithes had previously been commuted or extinguished by acts of parliament. By far the largest number of exemptions were those covered by enclosure awards.

The essential principle enshrined in tithe awards was that commutation was based on the *actual value* of tithes paid in immediately previous years, not on what an assistant commissioner thought their value ought to have been. Assistant commissioners were allowed to make some concession where they considered that the actual produce of the land had been affected by extraordinarily high or low farming. A draft award might be challenged by tithe payers or tithe owners on grounds of error or dissatisfaction. An appeal meeting would then be held and a supplementary award drafted, if the assistant commissioner upheld the appeal. Once the awarded rent-charge was confirmed by the tithe commissioners it was binding on all parties. About 43 per cent of districts were subject to awards; the national extremes are represented by Denbighshire at 13 per cent and Leicestershire, where awards were imposed in 78 per cent of districts.

THE APPORTIONMENT OF TITHE RENT-CHARGE

Once an agreement or an award was confirmed by the commissioners, the rent-charge could be apportioned over the parish lands. Landowners had a right to agree upon the principles of apportionment but, if none was agreed upon, rent-charge was apportioned according to the average titheable produce and the productive quality of the land (Clause 33). This clause in the 1836 Act gave landowners a right to apportion rent-charge property-by-property or field-by-field. Landowners could also choose between one gross sum for their whole estate or could assign rent-charge in portions to each farm or occupation. Without instructions to the contrary, a valuer carrying out an apportionment would be inclined to adopt the simplest method, namely apportioning in gross upon estates. However, advice given in contemporary guides and legal manuals favoured a field-by-field apportionment which, if a little more expensive in the short-term, would be beneficial to landowners in the long-term when land was sold. For example, G. H. Whalley stated in his commentary on the Tithe Commutation Act, 'there are, of course, cases in which the first and simplest mode may be preferable, and hence the latitude of discretion accorded, but these are exceptions, and every landowner should satisfy himself that his case is such an exception, before he permits the apportionment to be so completed'.[37] Whichever method was used, and a wide variety or combination of practices might be adopted, an apportionment was recorded on a map and in a written schedule. These maps and schedules of apportionment together constitute what is usually termed by historians 'the parish tithe survey'.

It was inevitably difficult to apportion the rent-charge equitably among lands of differing quality and differing utilisation, not because the actual use of the land was difficult to determine, but because its titheable produce was likely to change from time to time. In practice, there was no way of assessing the probability of lands being converted to other uses, and the only alternative to rating all lands alike at the same value was to differentiate them on the basis of their observed state of cultivation.

The specifications of tithe maps and the detailed nature of apportionment documents are discussed in Chapter 3, but the essential purpose of a survey was to provide an accurate measurement of the acreage of each parcel of land, or tithe area, and to record its observed state of cultivation. For the purpose of valuation, the state of cultivation was entered as 'arable', 'grass', 'meadow', 'pasture', 'common', 'wood', 'coppice', 'plantation', 'orchard', 'hop ground' or 'market garden'. There were, of course, different interpretations of these categories and additional categories inserted in some localities. In general, the most important distinction was between arable land, regularly ploughed and cropped, whose tithes amounted to about one-fifth of the value of the rent, and permanent grassland, whose tithes represented less than one-eighth of the rent. In the west of England and in Wales, 'arable' appears also to have included all ley grasses. In many parishes no distinction was made between meadow that was mown for hay once a year or more, and pasture that was normally used exclusively for grazing, yet the assessment of an acre of meadowland might be as much as eight times that of pasture. Woods, coppices and plantations were not always separately distinguished and were omitted in many parishes where they were tithe-free. Lands devoted to orchards, hop grounds or market gardens were usually classified according to their actual state of cultivation, but they might be rated as arable or grass and charged with a supplementary or extraordinary rent-charge.

A special problem confronted the commissioners in apportioning the rent-charge of Lammas lands and commons. These were owned in severalty for only a part of a year; from Lammas to Candlemas they lay open to common grazing. At High Wycombe in Buckinghamshire the rent-charge was apportioned among two or more owners of the same plot of land in such circumstances. Similar considerations affected apportionments on gated or stinted pastures.

In districts with large acreages of unimproved land, such as moorland, which generated little titheable produce, or extensive tracts of modus land, landowners could save some expense of surveying and valuing by apportioning the rent-charge due to these lands on other land owned by them, usually improved farm land around their farm house, provided that the total rent-charge on that land did not exceed one-third of its annual rent. The residue (but perhaps the greater area) of their holding was deemed nominally tithe free and did not need to be mapped.[38]

Completed apportionments were made available for inspection by landowners who had a right of appeal. Apportionment appeal meetings were held in the parish in the presence of an assistant commissioner and minutes of these meetings are usually preserved in the parish tithe file. To set aside an apportionment, assistant commissioners needed concrete evidence that an apportioner had acted unfairly or incompetently. The only appeals that had much chance of success were those where it could be demonstrated to an assistant commissioner's satisfaction that there was an inequality of charge on lands of similar use and those appeals where it was alleged that there were boundary errors or land-use errors.[39] The compilation of a 'parish tithe survey' was entrusted to private valuers and civilian surveyors appointed and paid for by landowners. The Tithe Commission's role in this final process was one of supervising, checking, arbitrating and confirming.

TITHE VALUERS AND LAND SURVEYORS

Surveyors were employed at two levels in apportioning an agreed or awarded tithe rent-charge: first, as valuers to assess the quality and use of land and apportion proportions of the global rent-charge in accordance with principles established by landowners and, secondly, as land surveyors to construct a map and book of reference of a district to serve as a permanent record of the apportionment. Where adequate maps of a district existed (see Chapter 3), only valuation was required and landowners could dispense with professional help entirely. More usually a new map had to be made or some older survey brought up-to-date. In practice, the normal procedure was for landowners to appoint the same individual or firm for the survey, map and apportionment and the Tithe Commission provided *pro formas* of contractual agreements which landowners and surveyors might use. These agreements specified the principles of apportionment to be employed, levels of remuneration, timetable of work and such indemnities as seemed appropriate.

Lieutenant R.K. Dawson, the assistant commissioner seconded from the Royal Engineers to organise and superintend the tithe surveys, was confident that the mapping as well as the valuation could be carried out by civilian surveyors. He thought that there were sufficient country surveyors immediately available in 1836 to initiate the work and that these could train further recruits as the work proceeded.[40] Dawson's recommendations for civilian control of the tithe surveys flew in the face of a victory for military control of the Survey of Ireland. Colonel Thomas Colby, director of the Ordnance Survey, was not satisfied with the quality of work produced by civilian surveyors while Dawson,,on the other hand, remained impressed with the standards of his own civil assistants on the Irish Survey.[41] But he was also aware of some common failings of country surveyors. His key to successful employment of civilians was a strict system of supervision from London, the issue of sheets of detailed instructions and advice, and careful checking of completed work against field notes (see Chapter 3). Testing the accuracy of survey work associated with apportionment of rent-charge was a fundamental component of the procedure devised by the tithe commissioners for implementing the Tithe Commutation Act.

Apportioners and surveyors were appointed by landowners usually after placing advertisements in the local press.[42] For example, the tithes of the parish of Drewsteignton in Devon were commuted by agreement in 1838 and advertisements for an apportioner and valuer of the Poor Rate and for a surveyor were placed in the *Trewman's Exeter Flying Post* at the end of the year. A valuer was appointed to apportion the tithes in January and he agreed to complete his work within three months of receiving a map of the parish from the surveyor. The landowners' solicitor received at least four offers to map Drewsteignton, one from a London address, but they appointed a local man, William Jole of Plymouth, at the end of January 1839.[43]

The employment of a local surveyor as at Drewsteignton was the usual practice. All but one of the Kent tithe maps which bear the name of their surveyor were produced by men living in London or the county itself. In every part of the country landowners preferred employing local men with local knowledge to apportion their tithe rent-charge and map their lands.

Valuers, as distinct from surveyors, who acted as both apportioners and map-makers, also practised locally.[44] Many were men of wide experience and deep knowledge of local farming. John Farncombe, who considered himself 'extensively engaged in the apportionment of the rent-charges' in Sussex was also 'employed by the tithe commissioners as their usual local agent for the county, in reporting on agreements for the Commutation of tithes'. He had also farmed 'a great many soils and systems applicable thereto' and had been a valuer for 25 years when he wrote the Royal Agricultural Society of England's Prize Essay 'On the farming of Sussex' in 1850.[45] Some experienced valuers such as Robert Pratt of Norwich, who valued 121 tithe districts in Norfolk and Suffolk, or Morris and William Sayce, who valued districts in and around the Welsh borders, must at times have been engaged on tithe work almost to the exclusion of everything else.

THE PROGRESS OF TITHE COMMUTATION

Almost all the 11,800 tithe apportionments and maps for England and Wales were confirmed within twenty years of the Tithe Commutation Act while a majority had been completed as early as the end of 1844. The report of the tithe commissioners to the House of Commons for 1856 records only seven apportionments still in progress.[46] The progress of the commissioners' work can be judged from Figs. 7 and 8, compiled from six-monthly and later annual returns of tithes commuted in each county published in the House of Commons sessional papers.

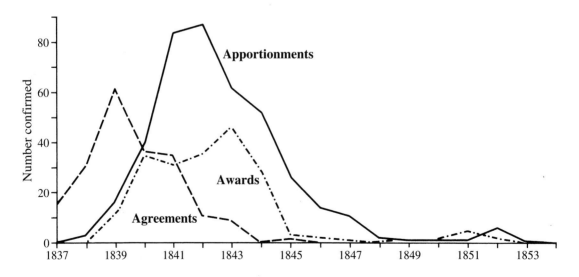

7 Number of agreements, awards and apportionments in England and Wales, 1837-55. Compiled from six-monthly and later annual 'returns of tithe commuted ...' in each county published each year in the House of Commons sessional papers.

The first parochial meeting for commutation of tithes was held on 29 September 1836 and the first agreement was received on 27 October. By the end of February 1837, the tithe commissioners had received 38 voluntary agreements but had been unable to approve any of the maps which recorded the details of apportionment.[47] At this date the

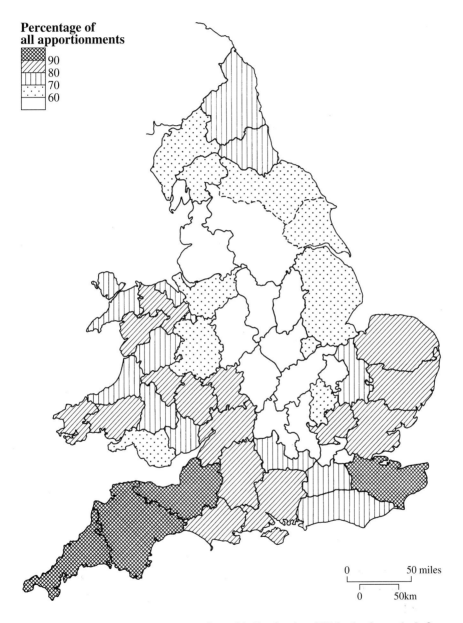

Percentage of all apportionments
90
80
70
60

8   Percentage of apportionments confirmed in England and Wales by the end of 1845.
Source: as Fig.6.

Act was very much a dead letter, although efforts were made to conceal this fact from the public. On 16 February 1837, Sir Edward Knatchbull questioned Lord John Russell in the House about a rumour he had heard that tithe commutation was at a virtual standstill. In his reply, Russell acknowledged the existence of such a rumour but denied that it had any foundation in truth. The tithe commissioners, he said, were quite happy with the Act.[48] But under oath later in the year, William Blamire, chairman of the Tithe Commission, recalled discussing the nature of tithe maps with Lord John Russell who referred him to Mr Spring Rice, chancellor of the exchequer.[49] Just two days after Russell's denial in the House, Spring Rice received a letter from the commissioners putting the problems that they were encountering over tithe maps.[50] The problems centred on the commissioners' uncertainty as to the precise character and especially the accuracy of maps which they could approve for commutation purposes. They felt, on the advice of Lieutenant Dawson, that the maps they had received were insufficiently accurate or drawn at scales too small to permit their acceptance as official records of tithe commutation, even though they had been accepted as suitable by the landowners concerned. A select committee was appointed to investigate this question and a wide-ranging debate ensued about the nature of maps required for commutation and whether they could be combined to produce a general cadastral survey of the kingdom (see chapter 3). In the event, the Tithe Commutation Act was amended in July 1837 to relieve the tithe commissioners of the duty to sanction map accuracy and to enable landowners to present maps at scales and to specifications different from those contained in Dawson's printed instructions to tithe valuers and surveyors.

Uncertainty over the nature of tithe maps put an early brake on the apportionment of tithe rent-charge. This problem affected the whole country but there were marked regional variations in the speed of commutation and apportionment. In 1839, the tithe commissioners reported that 'districts in which tithes have generally been taken in kind or let on annual valuations, contain elements of struggle and litigation, from which the rest of the country is free'.[51] On the other hand, a rapid start was made in East Anglia and the West Country. In Norfolk, for example, 497 out of 660 tithe surveys were made before 1841; in Essex, 272 out of 389. In the opinion of the tithe commissioners the area of slowest progress was south Wales where tithe and tithe commutations were among the grievances which fuelled the Rebecca Riots.[52] Yet more striking is the tardiness of midland England. Fewer than 60 per cent of tithe surveys in these counties had been confirmed by 1845. Though the absolute number of parishes requiring commutation of tithes under the Act was small in this area, the situation was very complicated where only portions of tithe in a parish had been commuted under the terms of enclosure awards. For instance, the township of Great Claybrook in Leicestershire consisted of 1,071 acres and contained 98 houses. All that remained to be commuted were a tithe of pigs worth 20s and a tithe of a mill worth 5s. The tithe commissioners were reluctant to award a rent-charge of 25s and then to proceed by map and apportionment to finish the commutation because of the inordinate expense relative to the value of the tithes.[53] Many similar, if less extreme, cases slowed the final stages of midland commutation.

While voluntary commutation was proceeding rapidly, the tithe commissioners limited the imposition of awards. The apportionment of agreed rentcharges provided at least as much if not more work, 'than can be proceeded with at once by such Mappers and Apportioners as have the confidence of the country'.[54] They would contemplate the imposition of awards at this early date only in districts where litigation was in progress or where tithe had been taken in kind. The commissioners thought that most tithe would be commuted by agreement, and the final figure of some 7,000 agreements proves them to have been right.

The work of commutation built up to a peak in the early 1840s and in general was conducted in an orderly and peaceful manner: 'angry appeals are the very rare exception; contented acquiescence is the general rule', the commissioners noted in 1840.[55] There were some quiet grumblings about the lag of time between commutation and apportionment, which, as Fig. 7 indicates, was considerably more than the six months that the legislature had envisaged. Despite this, the tithe commissioners adhered strictly to their policy of upholding the privilege of tithe payers to have rent-charges apportioned by agents of their own choice.[56] By 1848, with the bulk of their work completed or well under way, the commissioners turned their attention in earnest to problem cases. These were mostly districts where rent-charges were expected to be small, where delay was occasioned by the uncertain state of the law under Lord Tenterden's Act—where moduses had been only partially commuted by enclosure acts—and, finally, the tithes of extra-parochial places to which the Crown had a *prima facie* right. The commissioners spelt out in no uncertain terms the unnecessary expense that inaction might incur, especially as in many instances the matter could be ended by a simple instrument of merger where the tithe owner and landowner was one and the same person.[57]

By July 1849 the end of the tithe surveys was clearly in sight. The commissioners stated, with no inconsiderable pride, that they hoped to complete all the commutations by 1857. But they were less confident that they would achieve an early completion of apportionment. 'The conducting of this operation constitutes the greater part of our Office work at present, and will continue to press upon us until our labours close. Deaths among the persons appointed to apportion, and other causes of delay, may prolong a few of these cases. Still we see ground for expecting that we shall get through this work by August, 1851.'[58]

With but few exceptions they gained their objective. At the beginning of 1863 only five cases were still outstanding: these were Winteringham in Lincolnshire, where a long-running modus dispute was about to be settled; the tiny parish of Llangunnock, Monmouthshire which was overlooked until 1864; Hutton in Lancashire where problems in effecting mergers delayed commutation until 1874; Moulton in Lincolnshire where disputed titheable status of some reclaimed land was complicated by parish boundary uncertainties eventually resolved by a private Act of Parliament so that commutation could be completed in 1880; and a district in Hemingstone parish in Suffolk titheable to Barham which was the last commutation of all in 1883, and which appears to have been overlooked because the Hemingstone tithes were commuted only after those of Barham.[59] The last survey was completed in 1866.

THE ACHIEVEMENTS OF THE SETTLEMENT OF 1836

The achievements of the settlement of 1836 are remarkable if for no other reason than their durability. The provisions of the Act withstood the test of time. Writing in 1854, the clerk to the copyhold and tithe commissioners stated that there was not a single instance on record of an objection to an apportionment ever having been made by a reversioner.[60] With some important modifications, tithe rent-charges continued to be paid on the original basis for one hundred years. Tithe owners chafed under their liability to pay local rates on moneys they received but their responsibility was reaffirmed 60 years after the act was passed. Farmers were dissatisfied with the method of calculating rent-charges but the only remedy applied was a limit on the maximum payment. The proportions of wheat, barley and oats fixed in 1836 gave undue weight to fluctuations in the price of oats which rarely entered the market, while that of wheat, whose price was sensitive to worldwide changes and fell steeply after 1879, was under-represented. Moreover, prices quoted in the *London Gazette* were those of high-quality grains sold to dealers, not values of crops at the farm gate before transport charges were added. Another cause of dissatisfaction, that of extraordinary rent-charges on hop grounds and market gardens, was removed in 1886 by the redemption of the capital value of the charges at a rate of 4 per cent per annum.[61] In 1891 an upper limit was placed on the level of rent-charges to prevent them exceeding the value of rents.[62] They were restricted to no more than two-thirds of the gross annual value of the land. By the same Act responsibility for paying rent-charges was laid squarely on the landowner. In 1918, rent-charges were fixed for the following eight years at their current level, which then stood at £109 3s. 11d. of their 1836 par value.[63] In 1925 new levels were fixed and provision was made for voluntary redemption of rent-charges by means of annual repayments over a period of 60 years.[64] By the Tithe Act of 1936 the capital values of all remaining rent-charges had to be redeemed.[65] A new form of payment, known as a redemption annuity, was to be paid into the funds of Queen Anne's Bounty over a period extending from October 1936 to October 1996.[66] Allowances were made for costs of chancel repairs, hitherto borne by some owners of rectorial tithes, and all other outstanding charges and payments were redeemed.

3
Tithe Maps, Apportionments and Files

The tithe commissioners succeeded in resolving many of the complex problems that had previously embittered relations between tithe payers and tithe owners. In a majority of parishes they were able to secure an agreement within the statutory period of two years; in the remainder they imposed an award. Throughout the country they carried out their task with speed and thoroughness, setting down details of the survey for most parishes in three documents: a map, an apportionment and a file. In spite of the additional work involved in valuation and apportionment, most of the survey was completed in about one-tenth of the time taken by the Ordnance Survey to complete its large-scale plans. Yet speed was obtained without undue loss of accuracy. The reports submitted to the commissioners, surviving minutes of local enquiries, and correspondence in the tithe files testify to the vigilance of tithe payers and tithe owners, each jealously guarding their rights or pretended rights against infringement by the other party.

TITHE COMMUTATION AND A GENERAL SURVEY OF ENGLAND AND WALES

Immediately after his secondment to the Tithe Commission from the Royal Engineers on 27 August 1836, Lieutenant R.K. Dawson began working out details of the technical specification for maps the Tithe Commutation Act required as a record of commutation in each district. From the outset Dawson saw the need for tithe maps of three-quarters of the parishes of England and Wales as an opportunity for obtaining a full cadastral survey of the country. He wrote to the tithe commissioners about this on 8 September 1836, setting out the advantages to be obtained from combining the tithe survey with a general cadastral survey.[1] Dawson was keenly aware that, in the early 19th century, cadastral surveys were playing an important part in the administration of nation states throughout Europe. As well as telling the tithe commissioners about the Townland Survey of Ireland under the direction of his 'friend Colonel Colby', he drew their attention to the cadastral survey of France and to the Swedish system of land registration based on cadastral plans. He noted that similar surveys were in progress in Austria, Bavaria, Savoy and Piedmont, and suggested that, 'in many of the States of Continental Europe, Cadastral Surveys have long been in progress, at an annual expense commensurate with the importance attached to the possession of such documents'.[2]

In the same letter he set out an impressive list of advantages to be derived from a similar survey of England and Wales. These included the resolution of boundary disputes, easier transfer of real property, and identification of the best lines for new roads, railways and canals. The government would also obtain an accurate statement of the 'real capabilities of the country' and be able to decide where investment in improvements might be most beneficial. He concluded this review by saying that, 'the necessity which now exists, for Surveys of nearly the whole country, for a specific purpose presents means for forming a General Survey or Cadastre, at such a cheap rate, that the opportunity cannot be lost without exposing those who ought to represent its importance, to the certainty of future censure, if they fail to perform that imperative duty'.[3] Dawson considered that the survey could be carried out by civilian surveyors under strict supervision and with rigorous checking.

R. K. DAWSON'S SPECIFICATIONS FOR TITHE MAPS

Before the tithe commissioners would lend their support to Dawson's proposal, they requested a detailed report from him on the precise nature, scale and construction of plans required by the Tithe Act. They received this on 29 November 1836 and in it Dawson elaborated further on his idea for combining tithe commutation with a full cadastral survey and specified the type of map he considered the Tithe Act required.[4] He thought that tithe maps should portray both tithe district and tithe area boundaries with absolute accuracy. There was no real case for disputing the first of these points. It was important to know the exact area of a district to enable a fair and just apportionment of rent-charge. However, the accurate representation of field boundaries was not at all necessary for the immediate purposes of commutation though, of course, a vital element in any large-scale, cadastral survey. Dawson put forward two arguments in favour of the exact positioning of field boundaries on tithe maps. First, he stated that the Tithe Commutation Act was designed to provide an enduring settlement of the tithe question. In order to avoid future litigation it was important that fences be accurately portrayed so that particular tithe areas could always be identified. Second, he drew attention to the need for testing the accuracy of other maps which landowners might use to reduce the expense of commutation. He concluded that, 'it so happens, fortunately for the facility and economy of the whole operation, that the means necessary to effect the first of these objects are means which will ensure the attainment of the second'.[5] The means he had in mind were maps at a scale of three chains to an inch (26.7 inches to a mile), constructed by a strict system of triangulation. Dawson thought maps on a three-chain scale the smallest from which it was possible to measure quantities directly. He also considered this the usual scale for estate maps and thought that conformity would facilitate incorporation of these into the tithe survey.[6]

Having decided upon a scale, Dawson then described a system of triangulation for parish surveys. In all cases, construction lines were to be left on the final drawings in red ink to provide a check on map accuracy. An example of the diagrams Dawson produced to illustrate his instructions is reproduced in Figure 9. Dawson's military survey training is quite evident and his recommendations follow very closely those of contemporary military survey manuals: for example, Colby in his 1825 *Instructions for the interior survey of Ireland* required that 'the bearings and distances ... are to be laid down on the plots and penned in with light blue lines, that they may shew the relative accuracy of the work ...'.[7] The only difference in the instructions for the tithe survey was the colour of ink.

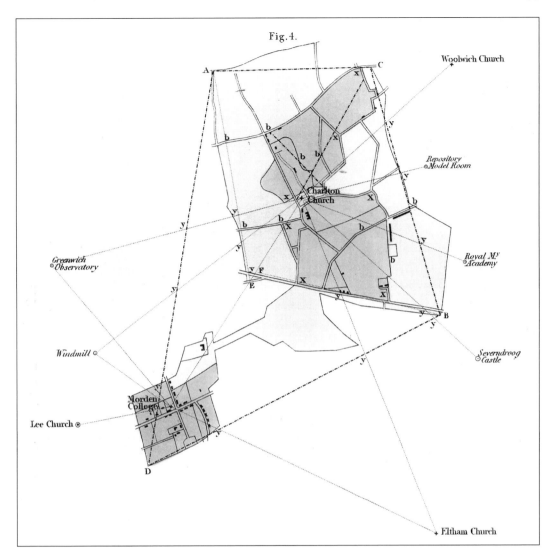

Fig.4.

9 One of a number of diagrams which accompany R. K. Dawson's report on the specification for tithe maps. This one indicates the preferred method of setting out construction lines for a tithe map. Source: BPP (HC), 1837, XLI, 'Copy of papers respecting the proposed survey of lands under the Tithe Act …'.

THE TITHE COMMISSION'S VIEWS ON TITHE MAPS

The tithe commissioners were very pleased with Dawson's report. On 4 January 1837, their secretary wrote to him saying that: 'it appears to the Commissioners to be their duty to require such Plans as will ensure a possibility, and, as far as may be, a facility for ascertaining precisely the extent and position of lands to be declared subject to or free from the rent-charges to be created under the Tithe Act, when the present boundaries of those lands have been altered or displaced. The Commissioners are of the opinion that the Scale recommended in your Report, and the lines of construction proposed to be left marked on the Plans, are essential for this purpose, and they authorize you to communicate this opinion to all parties with whom you are, or may hereafter be in correspondence or communication on the subject.'[8] The commissioners were quite clear about the type of map necessary for tithe commutation. Tithe maps were to be first-class, accurate plans at a scale of 26.7 inches to a mile constructed according to a system of internal triangulation. Such maps would be ideally suited to form a basis for a full cadastral survey of the nation.

The Tithe Act itself contained contradictory clauses on the nature of maps it required.[9] The 35th clause stated that: 'the Valuer or Valuers or Umpire may, if they think fit, use for the Purposes of this Act any Admeasurement, Plan or Valuation previously made of the Lands or Tithes in question of the Accuracy of which they shall be satisfied; and that it be lawful for the Meeting at which such Valuer or Valuers shall be chosen to agree upon the Adoption for the Purpose aforesaid of any such Admeasurement, Plan or Valuation, and such Agreement shall be binding upon the Valuer or Valuers; provided always, that Three Fourths of the Land Owners in Number and Value shall concur therein'. But the 63rd and 64th sections of the Act required the tithe commissioners to sanction the accuracy of every map by affixing their official seal as a final duty when confirming the commutation of tithes in a district. 'If the Commissioners shall approve the Apportionment they confirm the Instrument of Apportionment under their Hands and Seal, ... and every Recital or Statement in or Map or Plan annexed to such Confirmed Apportionment or Agreement for giving Land, or any sealed Copy thereof, shall be deemed satisfactory Evidence of the Matters therein recited or stated, or of the Accuracy of such Plan'. Clearly there were some grounds for ambiguity here. On the one hand, the Act entitled landowners to adopt any plan of their choice, whilst, on the other, the tithe commissioners were required to certify the accuracy of every map before confirming an apportionment.

By the end of February 1837, the tithe commissioners had received 38 voluntary agreements for tithe commutation but were unable to approve any of the accompanying maps.[10] One of the first examples of a grossly inaccurate map being adopted by landowners as a basis for commutation came from the north Kent parish of Tonge. It was drawn at the recommended scale of 26.7 inches to a mile, was accepted by three-quarters of the landowners, and was sent up to Lieutenant Dawson's office for approval in February 1837. Here the sizes of fields were computed from the map and compared with acreages in the book of reference. Errors of up to 100 per cent were found. Further enquiries at Tonge revealed that the map had been enlarged from a small-scale plan more than thirty years old. Dawson maintained that it would be impossible from this map to identify parcels charged with tithe if field boundaries were altered, although in the short term landowners would have saved themselves the expense of a new survey.[11] Richard Jones, the church representative on the Tithe Commission, thought it very likely that similar problems would occur where existing surveys were adopted for tithe purposes. At this date the Tithe Act, as noted in Chapter 2 above, was very much a dead-letter.

A SELECT COMMITTEE APPOINTED

The tithe commissioners remained convinced that accurate maps were necessary for an effective and lasting commutation of tithes. But by pressing for accuracy they were increasing an already considerable cost of commutation for some landowners. In a letter to the Chancellor of the Exchequer, Mr Spring Rice, the commissioners reiterated Dawson's arguments for combining tithe surveys with a general survey of the whole country in the hope that some of the cost of cadastral accuracy might be defrayed from the public purse.[12] They also outlined other tax collection advantages that would accrue from a full cadastral survey. In particular they referred to maps required for assessing poor rates under the new Poor Law. The poor law commissioners strongly supported both the idea of a general survey and the method of producing parish maps described by Dawson. Edwin Chadwick, their secretary, wrote the following note to the tithe commissioners on 5 January 1837: 'the Poor Law Commissioners are sensible of the great advantage which will result, both to owners and occupiers of land and other real property, and to the public in general, from the adoption of the uniform and well-considered system which is suggested in the Report ...'.[13] The tithe commissioners concluded their appeal to Spring Rice by asking whether: 'such maps shall be attained at enormous expense at some future period, or whether the large sums of money which must now be expended on the maps, good or bad, supplied for the purposes of the Tithe Act, instead of being wasted for all other public purposes, shall be so expended as to be the means, as far as it goes, of supplying all the wants of the Nation as connected with surveys'.[14]

These arguments persuaded the Chancellor of the Exchequer to appoint a House of Commons select committee on 16 March 1837 under the chairmanship of Mr Shaw Lefevre: 'to consider the best mode of effecting the Surveys of Parishes for the purpose of carrying into effect the Act for the Commutation of Tithes in England and Wales'.[15] In April 1837, the committee heard evidence from the three tithe commissioners, from Lieutenant Dawson and from John Matson, a Cumberland farmer who acted as commissioner when the tithes of all the Kendal townships were commuted by special act of parliament.

The committee had to decide whether accurate maps were needed for tithe commutation; maps which might be combined into a general survey, and then be reduced, engraved, and published on the six-inch scale in conformity with the Ordnance Survey of Ireland. The committee soon realised that for the immediate purposes of commutation and apportionment it was not necessary to have a map at all. Even the chairman of the tithe commissioners, William Blamire, stated that an accurate schedule would suffice.[16] But it was the future confusion that might result from the adoption of such a system that the tithe commissioners stressed in their evidence. The act of 1836 placed the onus of providing proof of tithe liability or exemption firmly on the landowner, so it was not so much in the church's interest as in the landowners' that titheable plots could be identified for all time. But Richard Jones, speaking on behalf of the church, thought that tithe owners could take little comfort from this. In his evidence he remarked: 'a clergyman goes to drive off a sheep from a particular portion of land; the landowner says, "that is exempt from tithes"; the clergyman says, "it is upon you to prove that"; and they go to law. It will be a poor satisfaction to the church or the public during such litigation to be able to say that the onus lies with the landowner'.[17]

There were three main situations in which landowners might be unwilling to produce new, large-scale maps. These occurred first in areas where large tracts of land were tithe-free, second, where parochial or township maps had been recently produced for other purposes, and, third, where maps of individual estates were available for combination into a parish map. In all these circumstances, the production of new maps specifically for tithe commutation would have imposed extra costs on landowners. William Blamire thought a large number of landowners would say, 'we are entitled to give you a map on any scale we think fit, and you have no right to call into question the accuracy of that map'.[18] During April 1837, while the select committee was hearing evidence, groups of landowners petitioned the House of Commons requesting that the tithe commissioners' proposals for large-scale maps be defeated or that the proposed surveys be made at public expense.[19]

After weighing the evidence, the select committee reported in May 1837 their recommendation that precise, accurate maps were not required for successful tithe commutation. Its conclusion was influenced by matters of cost to landowners and by the spirit of the 1836 Act which was to encourage voluntary commutations wherever possible. The committee recommended some relaxation of the 63rd and 64th clauses of the Tithe Act to relieve the commissioners of the duty of sanctioning map accuracy.

THE TITHE COMMUTATION ACT AMENDED IN 1837

In June 1837, a bill to amend the Tithe Commutation Act was introduced in the House of Commons. It was given a speedy passage through both Houses and became law on 15 July.[20] The maps accepted by the tithe commissioners were on a variety of scales and made at a variety of dates. As a body the tithe maps were quite unsuitable to form the basis for a national cadastral survey.[21] The country, 'lost its last chance of a cadastral system on the continental pattern, with all that means in terms of cheap and simple property transfers'.[22]

The debate over registration of land was to recur time and again. Unnecessary expense and duplication of surveys did occur as Dawson predicted. Dawson was to look back on the government's decision later in life with deep regret. Writing to the registrar general in 1852 he said: 'and had the requirements of that Act [the Tithe Act] been carried out, the deposited Records in the Tithe Office should now have afforded accurate returns of the acreage of about five-sixths of the Parishes in England and Wales, and might have been made the basis, as was indeed at one time contemplated by the Government, of a perfect system of Agricultural Statistics'.[23]

Even the Ordnance Survey was in the end to turn its back on a full survey of England and Wales recording ownership and occupation of land as well as the acreage and land use of individual parcels.[24] But, to the lasting credit of Dawson is the fact that within the space of only a few years his method of surveying parishes on trigonometrical principles was in regular usage by a growing corps of country surveyors. In the words of Butler Williams, professor of geodesy at the College of Civil Engineers, Putney, in 1844, 'the mode of conducting the operations for parish surveys by great lines, embracing the whole of the district to be surveyed, described in Captain Dawson's "Instructions to Tithe Surveyors", is now universally adopted, and no acknowledged surveyor would now proceed with isolated surveys of separate fields, to be afterwards combined into a general map.[25]

FIRST- AND SECOND-CLASS TITHE MAPS

The first section of the amended Tithe Act relieved the commissioners of the need to certify the accuracy of every map accompanying apportionments and permitted them to establish two classes of tithe map. 'First-class maps' are those which the commissioners considered sufficiently accurate to serve as legal evidence of boundaries and areas and can be identified by the certificate of accuracy signed by two tithe commissioners which they bear and also by the impress of the Commission's official seal (Fig. 10). All first-class maps and accompanying field books were carefully checked by Lieutenant Dawson's staff in London (see Chapter 4). The technical specification that Dawson prepared before the amendment of the 1836 Act still applied to first-class maps, with the exception that the

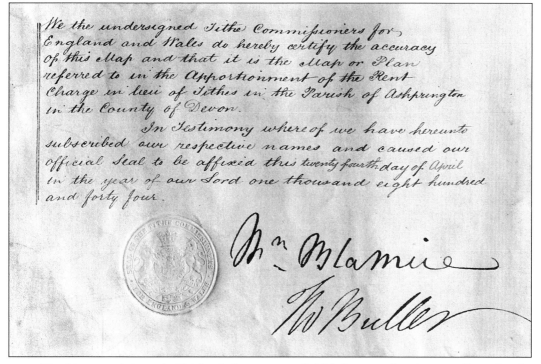

10   The tithe commissioners' official seal, the presence of which denotes a first-class map. Reproduced by permission of Devon Record Office.

commissioners no longer considered it essential for a system of conventional signs to be used. 'The maps which will be most acceptable to the tithe commissioners are the plain working plans, with the lines of construction, names and reference figures shown upon them, and with no other ornament or colour whatever; and the most ready way of obtaining the seal of the commission will be to send up the actual working plan'.[26]

Dawson's instructions were printed by the Tithe Commission and made available to landowners' solicitors so that they could be incorporated into contracts drawn up between landowners and surveyors when the former commissioned a first-class map of their tithe district.[27] The category of second-class maps includes those which were intended to be first-class but which failed Dawson's tests and were not subsequently corrected to the Commission's satisfaction but by far the larger number are those maps 'which three-fourths of the landowners are desirous to use, but which the parties do not mean to submit to the test of the commission'.[28] Not all of these were inferior to first-class maps; some were not eligible for first-class status simply because of their small scale without regard to their internal accuracy because 'maps on a smaller scale than four chains to an inch do not admit of being accurately tested as to quantities; and no map on a smaller scale can therefore receive the seal of the Commission'.[29] While the Commission still retained its full powers to refuse to confirm an apportionment accompanied by a map which Lieutenant Dawson's office deemed wholly unsatisfactory, maps were rejected only in very exceptional circumstances.[30] The published specification for second-class maps contains nothing to ensure planimetric or topographic accuracy but is concerned mainly with the way information on the maps was to be set out and linked to that in the apportionments. Most refusals to confirm on first submission were for reasons of clerical or procedural errors.

Second-class tithe maps were usually based, at least in part, on existing parish or estate maps. Field boundaries and locations of buildings would be brought up-to-date, unsurveyed areas filled in and the whole redrawn to the tithe commissioners' requirements as regards district and tithe area boundaries and reference numbers. For example, in 1844 surveyor John Thorpe of Stenton traced a copy of an 1818 survey of Hinckley in Leicestershire for tithe commutation and resurveyed the town of Hinckley itself. The old and new maps were tied together to constitute a second-class map of the district.[31] Substantial savings in cost to landowners could be made by these methods. For instance, the second-class map of Bilstone parish, also in Leicestershire, was reduced from a working plan at the three chain scale 'corrected and partly resurveyed by Samuel Morris and William Thorpe' in May 1850. For compiling this map, 256 acres derived from the earlier survey were billed to the landowners at a copying charge of 2d. an acre plus 2 guineas for 'examining and correcting old map'. A new survey required for the remaining 436 acres was charged at Dawson's recommended rate of 9d. an acre.[32]

Authors of contemporary textbooks on tithe commutation procedure exhorted landowners to commit the extra expense that a first-class survey entailed. G. H. Whalley argued, for example, that: 'it is often a matter of grave deliberation and doubt amongst the landowners of a parish, whether they will put up with any old map they may chance to possess, or will at once construct for the apportionment an efficient map, which, by receiving the tithe seal, will be evidence in all time to come of quantities and estates. There can be no doubt that a parish which can boast such a map will be better off, in many respects, than its neighbour without one; and a map, with such legal qualifications, can never be procured, unless now as part of the apportionment'.[33]

The cost of a first-class map could vary considerably around Dawson's average figure of 9d. an acre depending on local topography. Moreover, total cost in relation to the rent-charge also varied depending on land value and factors such as the intermixture of titheable and tithe-free land. It could also be prohibitively expensive to survey at three chains to an inch districts with large extents of moorland. The tithe commissioners calculated that 2,333 of the 11,800 tithe maps were first-class category.[34] In fact there are only 1,458 (12 per cent of the total).[35] As might be expected from the above comments, first-class maps are rarer in northern, upland counties and also in the midlands where often only part of a district remained titheable. On the other hand, there are notable concentrations in Kent, Surrey, Sussex, Suffolk, Monmouthshire, Herefordshire and Worcestershire and Cumberland. The concentration in Cumberland may well have been a result of William Blamire's influence in the county. Part of the unevenness is probably also a reflection of successful promotion of first-class mapping by map-makers themselves. For example, maps produced by Richard Barnes of Lowestoft, Suffolk and those of the Kent-based surveyors Alexander Doull of Chatham, Frederick and Henry Drayson of Faversham, and Thomas Thurston of Ashford are almost all first-class.

THE CHARACTERISTICS AND CONTENT OF TITHE MAPS

At three chains to an inch, tithe maps representing large parishes with detached portions, such as Dagenham or North Benfleet in Essex, may cover as much as 10 square metres. James Walker, a civil engineer, estimated in 1854, that a map of England alone at this scale would cover nearly 612 acres and take 46,950 sheets of paper of the same size as the published sheets of the Ordnance Survey of Ireland.[36] Although not all tithe surveys are on the three-chain scale and they do not cover the whole of England, they are extant for most of Wales so an estimate of the surface area of the whole body of tithe maps would not be far short of Walker's figure. For large parishes and townships in upland areas, smaller scales were the only practicable choice. One of the smallest scales used is the 27 chains to one inch for the maps of Nant Glyn, Denbighshire. Often, villages and towns are drawn at a larger scale of one or two chains to an inch and appended to the main tithe map. An extreme instance of this practice is the tithe map of Wiveliscombe, Somerset which is a 6-chain map supplemented by no fewer than 40 enlargements of detail.

All tithe maps, whatever their origin, show the boundaries of the tithe district. The natural unit for tithe commutation was the parish but where these were very large, as in the northern counties, townships were used instead. Also in southern England some villages, hamlets and extra-parochial places were designated as separate districts. This practice was quite common where there was more than one nucleus of settlement in a parish or where detached portions were separated by some distance.

Tithe maps also show the boundaries of the tithe areas within a parish. Tithe areas usually corresponded with fields, but in some instances, as at Rhosbeirio in Anglesey, they constituted whole farms or more rarely, as at Marske-by-Sea in Yorkshire where there was only one landowner, a whole township. In early surveys, where the sum to be apportioned was agreed, it could be considered unnecessary to assign a separate rent-charge to each parcel of land, but re-apportionment when fields changed hands proved so inconvenient that the practice was abandoned in 1840. After that field-by-field surveys were required.

On most maps the boundaries of enclosed fields are represented by continuous lines and those of unenclosed fields by dotted lines. Occasionally, hedges, fences and gates are also portrayed. The amount of other detail shown on tithe maps varies considerably. Most maps mark the courses of streams, canals, ditches, drains, the outline of lakes and ponds and lines of roads and paths. Some, such as the second-class map of Gittisham, Devon (Fig. 11), use conventional symbols recommended by Dawson in his 'Instructions' to identify different types of land. Some maps differentiate between commons, heaths, rabbit warrens, osier beds and undrained marshes. On many maps, coniferous and deciduous tree symbols of different sizes depict mature woodlands, plantations, parks and sometimes coppice and coppice-with-standards. Characteristically, inhabited buildings are tinted red, while barns and other structures are shaded in grey. Brickworks are shown on the map of Frindsbury in Kent while maps of industrial areas, like that of Wolverhampton (Fig. 12), distinguish a greater variety of buildings. On this map chapels are marked and named as are the principal places of manufacture such as the Shrubbery iron works. Indeed, many towns are depicted in exceptional detail on tithe maps because they contained some titheable properties (Fig. 13). A few maps are rendered in full colour, to distinguish tithe-free land or various properties or farms or to show different categories of land use. Hop grounds, orchards and gardens are much more frequently indicated by symbols on tithe maps according to Dawson's convention.

The overwhelming majority of tithe maps remain in manuscript; only 269 maps in the Public Record Office collection (less than three per cent) are printed. Most printed tithe maps are lithographed and most of these were undertaken by Standidge and Co. of Cornhill, London, a leading firm of lithographers. There is no single explanation for the printing of this small minority of tithe maps; the decision to print was made by local landowners moved by a variety of motives requiring more than the statutory hand-drawn copies of a parish tithe map (Figs. 14 and 15).[37]

As a general rule all roads are shown on tithe maps where they run across or form the boundary of titheable land, although there are occasional exceptions. For example, the tithe map of Warlingham cum Chelsham in Surrey omits a number of public roads and paths which re-appear on the tithe maps of adjoining districts. Turnpike roads are generally indicated on tithe maps either by name or by identification of toll gates; it is rare for turnpikes to be shown by boldened road casing and very rare for distinctive colouring to be employed. It is very unusual for rights of way to be unequivocally indicated on tithe maps.

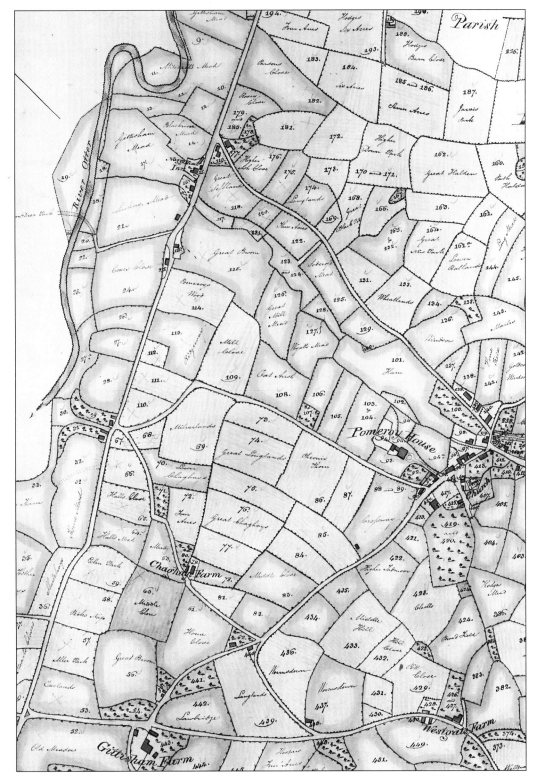

11 Part of the second-class tithe map of Gittisham parish, Devon. Reproduced by permission of Devon Record Office.

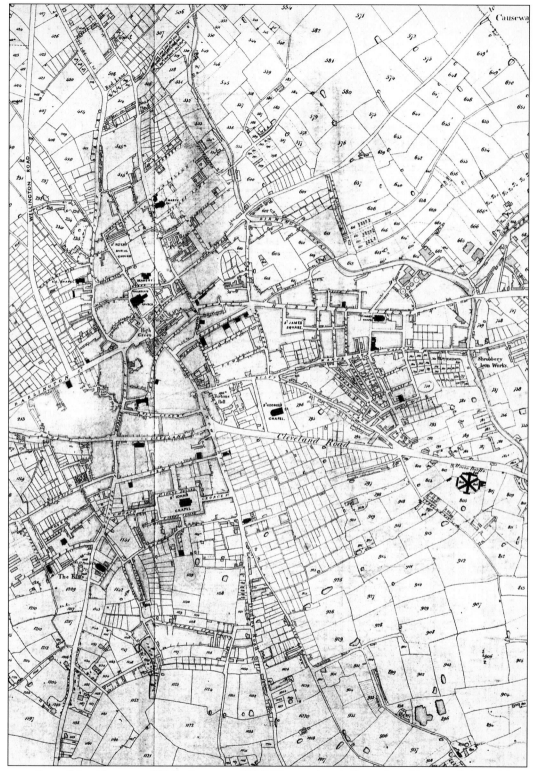

12 Part of the tithe map of Wolverhampton [PRO IR30 32/237]. Reproduced by permission of the Keeper, Public Record Office.

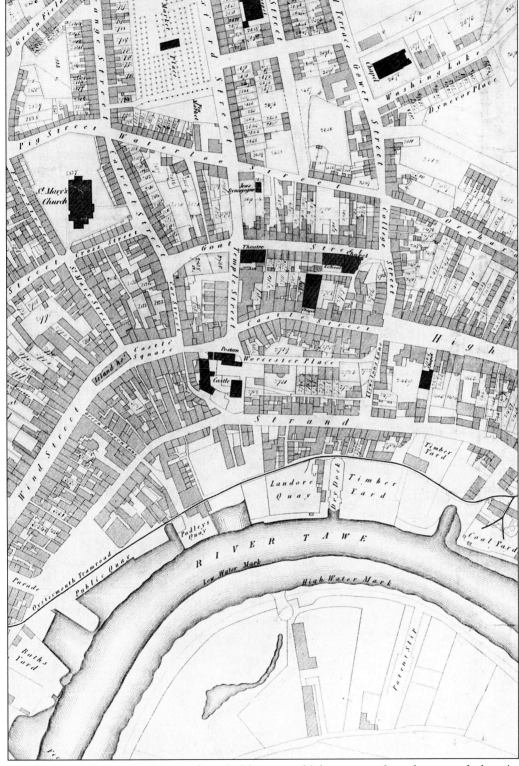

13 Swansea, Glamorganshire, *c*.1842. A tithe map which portrays the urban morphology in exceptional detail [PRO IR30 14/106]. Reproduced by permission of the Keeper of the Public Record Office.

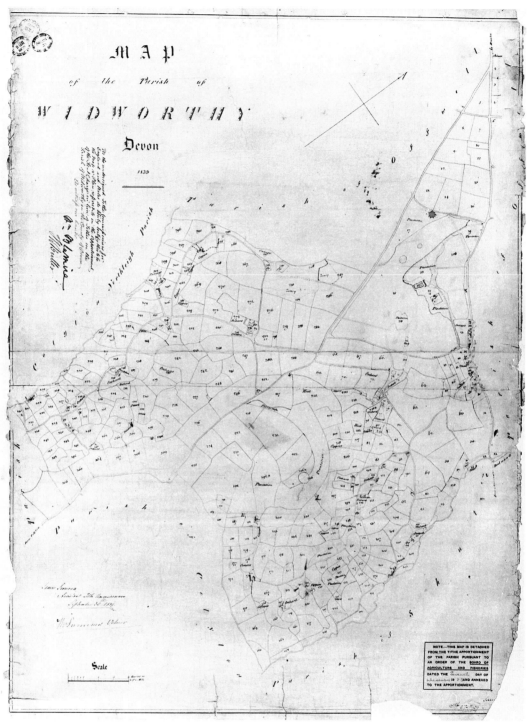

14 Widworthy, Devon, 1839. There are two versions of this map in the Public Record Office collection: this one is in manuscript and woodland and orchards are indicated by annotation [PRO IR30 9/450]. Reproduced by permission of the Keeper of the Public Record Office.

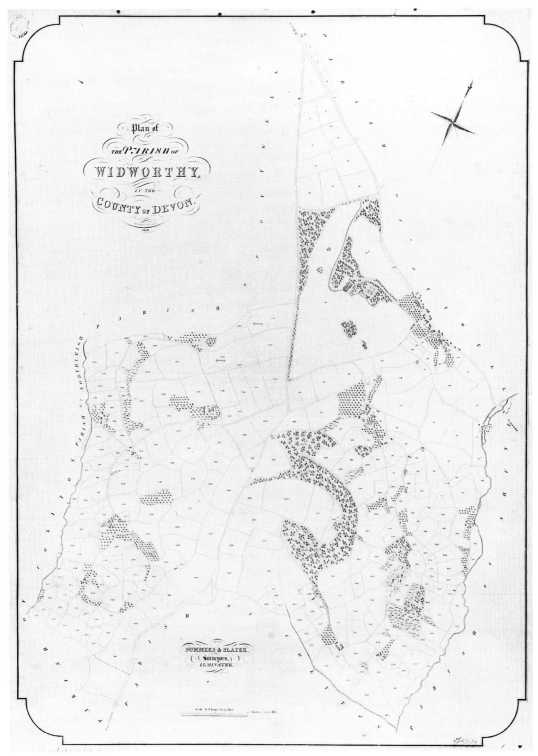

15 Widworthy, Devon, 1839. This is a lithographed version of the map illustrated in Fig. 14. It was lithographed by Standidge and Co. of London and has that company's characteristic border with rounded corners [PRO IR30 9/450]. Reproduced by permission of the Keeper of the Public Record Office.

The portrayal of roads on tithe maps can be understood only by reference to the prime purpose of the maps themselves. The direct and immediate purpose of tithe maps was to serve as an official record of the boundaries of all tithe areas (usually fields or other similar land parcels) on which tithe rent-charge was apportioned in the schedule of tithe apportionment. The portrayal of roads is one matter that is incidental to this prime purpose of tithe commutation and its associated map record. Roads are shown only because their margins very often constituted a tithe area boundary. In general terms, no tithe map provides direct evidence of whether a road was used or not, nor the purposes for which it might have been used unless there is annotation to that effect.

Some roads on tithe maps are coloured in sienna. A convention on large-scale maps at this time was to colour public highways and to leave private and occupation roads uncoloured, though there was no requirement to make this distinction on tithe maps and, as noted above, very few maps do specify which routes were public rights of way. It is difficult to say how extensive the practice of colouring roads was because lighter tints have faded and cannot be distinguished readily from the colour of the paper. However, colouring of roads does appear to have been relatively uncommon on first-class maps and in Wales. At a local level, the practice varied very much. For example, the tithe map of Alderley parish in Cheshire is in three parts. On the parts relating to Over Alderley and Great Warford every road and path is tinted sienna including unfenced paths braced with and crossing single tithe areas. On the third part of the map, that for Nether Alderley, this practice is not followed and some roads and ways are left white.[38]

A few working copies of tithe maps have survived among surveyors' papers deposited in county record offices and occasionally tracings are found in the tithe files. The tithe file of North Ormsby in Lincolnshire contains a tracing of a working plan used by the valuer when making his apportionment of rent-charge and this shows the crops grown in each field and other details. First-class tithe maps are often plainer in appearance than second-class, reflecting the Commission's advice noted above that a plain working plan with construction lines was the kind most likely to be certified first-class (Fig. 16). Sometimes a surveyor produced a 'plain working plan' for retention by the Tithe Commission and produced a more colourful version containing more topographical detail for local deposit.[39] Decorative cartouches are rare, but not unknown but colour is more frequently employed—to highlight titheable land, to differentiate ownership, or to distinguish different land uses.

Figure 17 is an extract of the 1844 tithe map of Winterborne Kingston in Dorset. It shows part of the village and some of West Field. Dotted lines indicate boundaries of tithe areas or strips in the open field while continuous lines bound closes around the village. In 1848 Winterborne Kingston was enclosed and its pattern of fields and landownership totally transformed. Such was the extent of alteration that a complete re-apportionment of the rent-charge over the parish was required. Part of this altered apportionment map is reproduced as Fig. 18. Now all tithe areas are bounded by solid lines indicating their enclosed state. Typically, altered apportionment maps cover only a

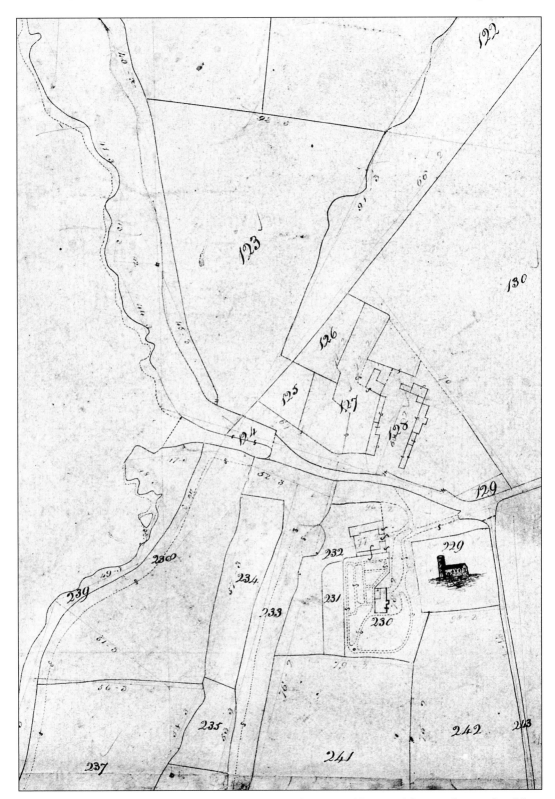

16 Burgh Castle, Suffolk, 1842. This map by Richard Barnes of Lowestoft is a good example of the most austere type of first-class map containing as it does little but construction lines, field boundaries, and the outlines of buildings. The pictorial church is exceptional ornamentation on a first-class map [PRO IR30 33/84]. Reproduced by permission of the Keeper of the Public Record Office.

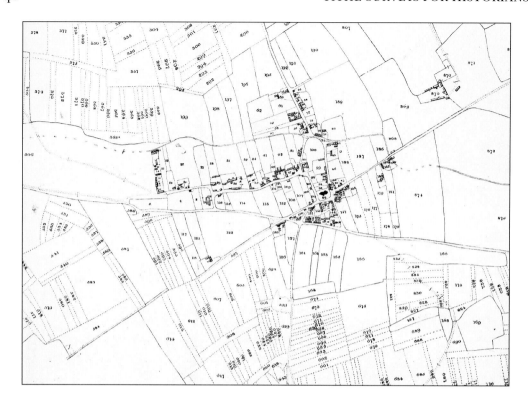

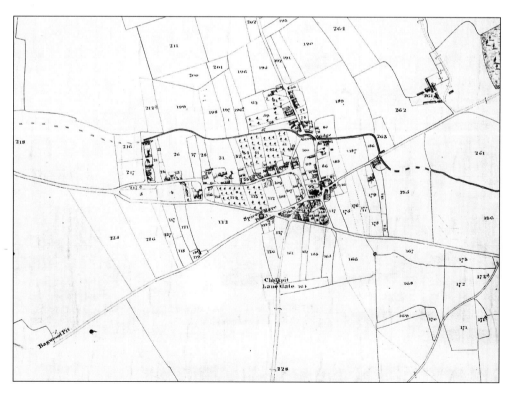

small part of a parish; events like whosesale enclosure causing such sweeping changes in parish cadasters were rare after about 1850.

As well as topographical detail, 66 per cent of maps provide at least some biographical information to help unravel their provenance (Fig. 19). Quite often they bear the name of the person who surveyed them and a date which may be the date of the survey or that of redrawing and amalgamation of some earlier surveys. Also an indication of the scale is usually shown in the form of a measured scale bar. First-class tithe maps are identified by the presence of the tithe commissioners' seal.

17 *(top left)* Part of the tithe map of Winterborne Kingston, Dorset, in 1844 showing the presence of open fields at this date [PRO IR30 10/251]. Photograph reproduced by permission of the Keeper, Public Record Office.

18 *(bottom left)* An extract from the altered apportionment map of the same part of Winterborne Kingston made in 1848 after enclosure [PRO IR30 10/251]. Photograph reproduced by permission of the Keeper, Public Record Office.

19 *(right)* Capel le Fern, Kent, 1840. This map has two unusual features: it carries a construction line diagram and it claims to be made for Poor Rate Assessment rather than for tithe purposes. It is likely that many other tithe maps served similar dual purposes [PRO IR30 17/70]. Reproduced by permission of the Keeper of the Public Record Office.

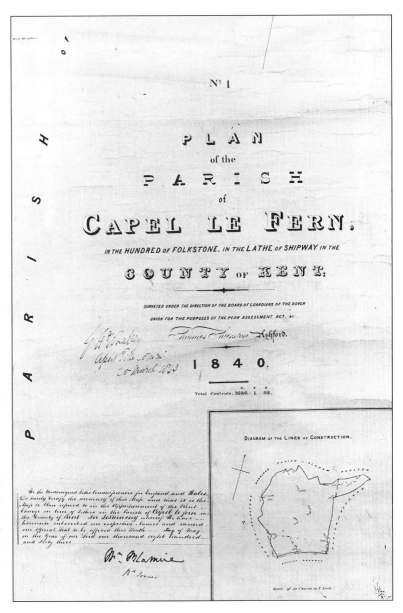

NEW SURVEYS AND MAPS BASED ON EXISTING SURVEYS

The one-eighth of all tithe maps sealed as first-class are almost all new surveys but it is impossible to ascertain how much copying of earlier work there is and how many new surveys there are, among the other 10,327 tithe maps. This distinction is rarely stated on the maps themselves (Fig. 20) which may mean that the map of Buslingthorpe, Lincolnshire copied from one of 1653, is not necessarily the 'oldest' tithe map of England and Wales. On the map of Great Hucklow, Derbyshire the surveyor says, 'Note – This Plan is made from the Township Plan, dated 1811 and from sundry Estate Plans upon various scales and degrees of accuracy and is adopted by the Landowners'. Those map-makers who consistently distinguished between copying and original work, such as Thomas Thurston of Ashford, Kent, are shining exceptions to the general rule. Even a statement 'surveyed by ...' in a map title does not necessarily indicate an entirely new tithe map as the survey referred to could have been made many years earlier. Compilation from enclosure maps may reasonably be suspected for those maps of very small areas of residual titheable land in districts where most tithes had been commuted earlier under the terms

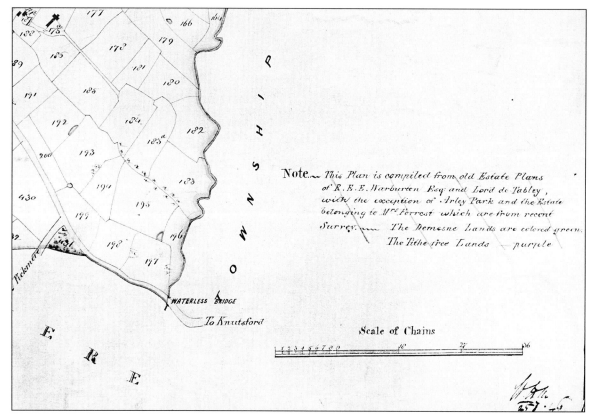

20 Aston, Cheshire, 1846. Notes as on this map which provide evidence of the provenance of the tithe map data are very much the exception rather than the rule [PRO IR30 5/25]. Reproduced by permission of the Keeper of the Public Record Office.

of an enclosure act. The inclusion of some tithe free land on a tithe map may also be an indication that the map is a copy but where tithe free land was scattered throughout a tithe district, it may well have been easier to survey the whole district and afterwards sort out which lands were titheable and which were not.

The presence of construction lines on a tithe map is not an infallible indicator of a new survey. In his instructions 'for the preparation of plans for the purpose of the Tithe Commutation Act', Dawson said that construction lines were necessary so that a map's accuracy could be tested. It would be perfectly feasible to re-use an old survey by replotting construction lines and measurements from the original field books, if still extant. Indeed, it is possible that a proportion of the 475 second-class maps with construction lines, were presumably submitted for first-class testing and failed for this reason. On the first-class map of Alkrington, Lancashire there is clear evidence of this as the surveyor notes, 'the trial lines were run in testing the accuracy of an existing plan and then formed the base lines of the new survey'. Equally, some 18 per cent of first-class tithe maps in the Public Record Office collection do not contain construction lines, though these must have been present on other copies of the maps for them to have been certified as first-class.

ORIGINAL AND STATUTORY COPIES OF TITHE MAPS

The Tithe Commutation Act required an original map and two statutory copies for each tithe district. The original map was intended to be retained by the Tithe Commission, one of the copies was destined for the relevant diocesan office, and the second copy was for the tithe district. Conventional wisdom has it that differences between an original tithe map and the two statutory copies reflect nothing more than the extent of variations in mid-19th-century clerical exactitude. Such a contention finds support in the provisions of the 1836 Tithe Commutation Act and furthermore, if the 1836 statute had been followed to the letter, it would now be the case that the Public Record Office tithe map collection, which represents the holdings of the Tithe Commission's London office, would comprise original and amended plans, whereas the maps held in county record offices, derived from diocesan and parish records, would represent statutory copies. Comparison of the original and copy maps of some 650 tithe districts which we have undertaken reveals an archival history both more complex and more interesting than the official blueprint sketched above. Not only do the tithe maps of different places differ in cartographic style and content, but there are also significant differences between extant examples of tithe maps for the same place.[40]

The assumption that the maps held in the Public Record Office represent the original or amended plans is confirmed by the data available in a majority of cases. It is not clear how some original maps escaped the bureaucratic net and found their way into local archives. All versions of the maps of every district should at one stage have been inspected in London, so the error could have been committed centrally in returning the wrong version to the diocese. Alternatively the original may have been either accidentally or deliberately retained by the landowners and copies sent to London.

The supposition that differences between the Public Record Office and diocesan maps are a result of poor copying is not entirely true. Many of the differences between the two sets are the outcome of a deliberate choice on the part of local landowners and surveyors to produce a map for local retention at a different scale and degree of detail from that submitted to the London office of the Tithe Commission. In most cases, the local copy is drawn at a smaller scale than the Public Record Office version, usually one inch to six chains in place of the three-chain scale. Differences in scale or the degree of accuracy of the local copy also produce discrepancies in the class awarded to maps of a given tithe district. At Clawton, Halwell, Morchard Bishop and Sampford Spiney in Devon, and Kimpton and Little Munden in Hertfordshire, the choice of a six-chain scale locally meant that diocesan copies were deemed second-class by the Tithe Commission whereas the original tithe maps for those parishes in the Public Record Office are first-class maps at a scale of three or four chains per inch.[41]

Other discrepancies arising from a deliberate choice on the part of the surveyors to produce two distinct versions for the diocese and the Tithe Commission include differences in the use of colour and decoration. Analysis of Devon tithe maps indicates that, although the majority of the maps exhibit no significant difference (82 per cent), 12 per cent of the tithe maps forming the Public Record Office set are more decorated than the corresponding county record office set and that 6 per cent of Devon's tithe maps are more decorative in the Devon Record Office (diocesan) version. In short, the assertion that discrepancies between original and copy tithe maps arise from transcription errors oversimplifies and understates the degree of difference. As a general indication of the extent of the variation, for more than 40 per cent of a sample 650 tithe districts analysed, there is some difference in map content between diocesan and Public Record Office maps. Furthermore, this analysis has been confined to diocesan versions of tithe maps held in county record offices. There is often a third version: the parish tithe map. Parish maps are likely to add a further dimension to the variations in tithe map content which have been discussed here.

A QUINTESSENTIAL TITHE MAP?

The general conclusion derived from inspection and analysis of every tithe map of England and Wales in the Public Record Office collection reported in Roger Kain's and Richard Oliver's *The tithe maps of England and Wales* is that it is quite illegitimate to speak of a 'typical' tithe map. The most likely single scale to be encountered is six chains to an inch (but 67 per cent are drawn at different scales); very many tithe maps were made in the three years 1839 to 1841 (but about a half are dated other than *circa* 1840); a 'typical' tithe map would be the work of a local surveyor (only a few hundred were produced by men working away from their immediate locality) (Fig. 21); and most tithe maps are second-class (only about one in eight are first-class). Beyond such basic facts it is unwise to predict from the characteristics of the corpus to the characteristics of an individual map. The area that an individual tithe map may cover varies from 74,918 acres at Elsdon,

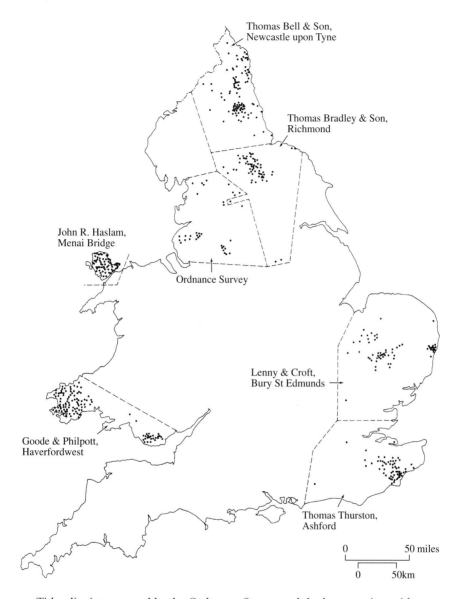

Thomas Bell & Son,
Newcastle upon Tyne

Thomas Bradley & Son,
Richmond

John R. Haslam,
Menai Bridge

Ordnance Survey

Lenny & Croft,
Bury St Edmunds

Goode & Philpott,
Haverfordwest

Thomas Thurston,
Ashford

0   50 miles

0   50km

21 Tithe districts mapped by the Ordnance Survey and the largest private tithe map-making practices. Compiled from data in R.J.P. Kain and R.R. Oliver, *The tithe maps of England and Wales: a cartographic analysis and county-by-county catalogue* (Cambridge, Cambridge University Press, 1995).

Northumberland to just 0.02 acres at West Wratting in Cambridgeshire (Fig. 22). The cartographic style and standard of execution of tithe maps also vary enormously, from the meticulous neatness of professional map-makers such as those of the Bell partnership (Fig. 23) to very crude sketches (Fig. 24) made by often anonymous surveyors. The presence or absence of particular items of topographic detail has little to do with the actual distribution of those features but rather reflects individual landowners' and map-

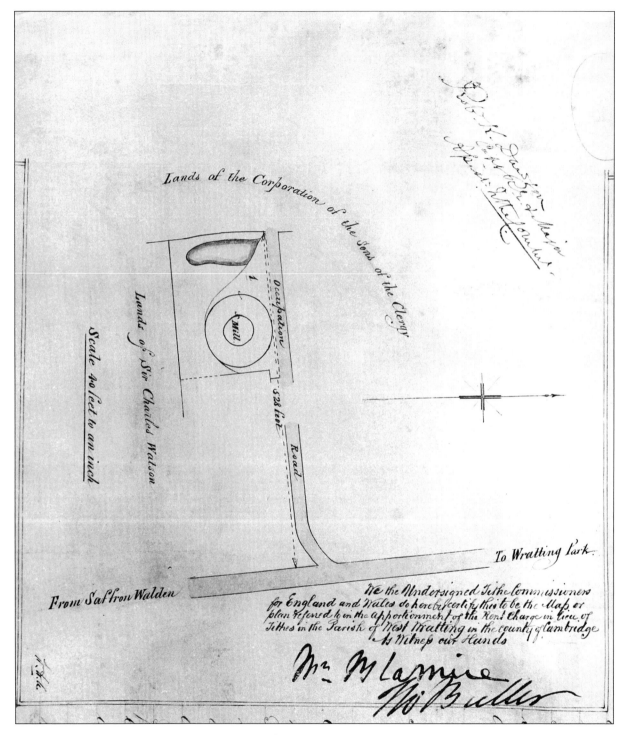

22 West Wratting, Cambridgeshire, *c.*1852. This is the smallest tithe district of all (0.02 acre) and the map is drawn on a page of the tithe apportionment [PRO IR29 4/93]. Reproduced by permission of the Keeper of the Public Record Office.

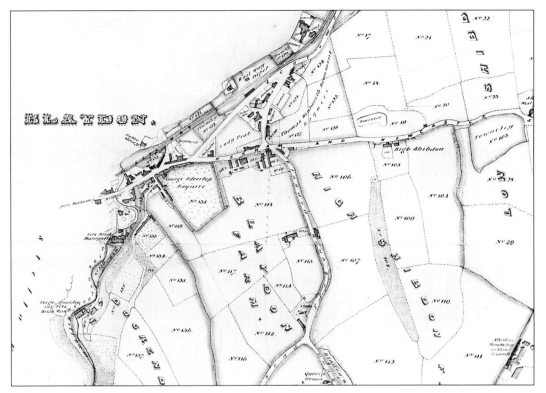

23 Winlaton, Durham, 1838. This is a good example of the carefully-executed cartographic style of the Bell family of Newcastle [PRO IR30 11/286]. Reproduced by permission of the Keeper of the Public Record Office.

24 Martindale, Westmorland, 'taken in September 1838'. This is one of the more crudely executed tithe maps [PRO IR30 37/53]. Reproduced by permission of the Keeper of the Public Record Office.

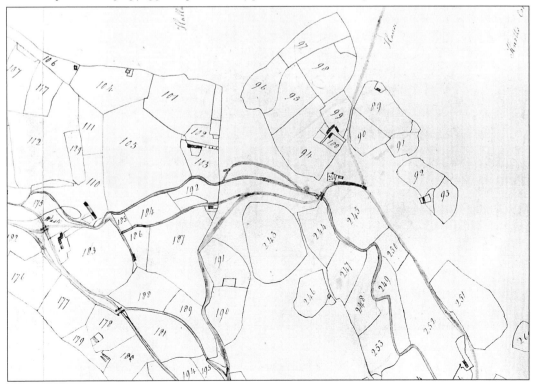

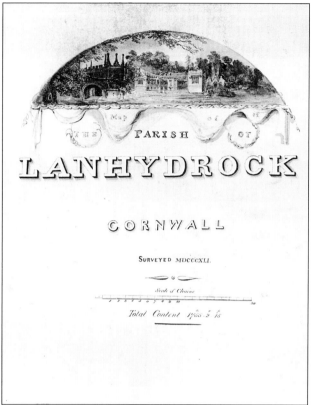

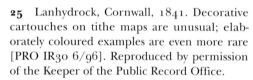

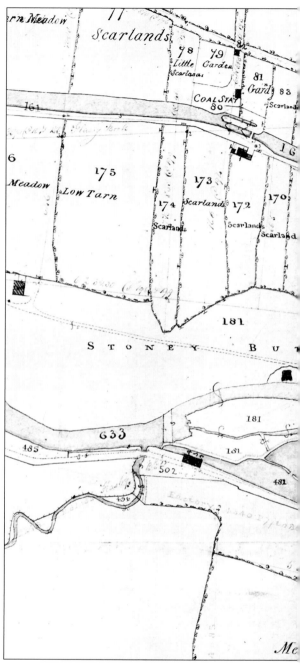

25 Lanhydrock, Cornwall, 1841. Decorative cartouches on tithe maps are unusual; elaborately coloured examples are even more rare [PRO IR30 6/96]. Reproduced by permission of the Keeper of the Public Record Office.

26 Gargrave, West Riding of Yorkshire, 1839. The name of Greenwood is usually associated with the brothers Christopher and John, the county map-makers, but John Greenwood also executed a number of very detailed first-class tithe maps. Had all tithe maps approached this standard, it is questionable whether the Ordnance Survey 1:2500 would ever have been made [PRO IR30 43/165]. Reproduced by permission of the Keeper of the Public Record Office.

makers' perceptions of what a tithe survey should contain and how it should be represented (Fig. 25). Local tradition of estate cartography was a powerful influence on the nature and content of tithe maps notwithstanding the fact that every tithe map stems from the national statutes which governed commutation in every parish and township in

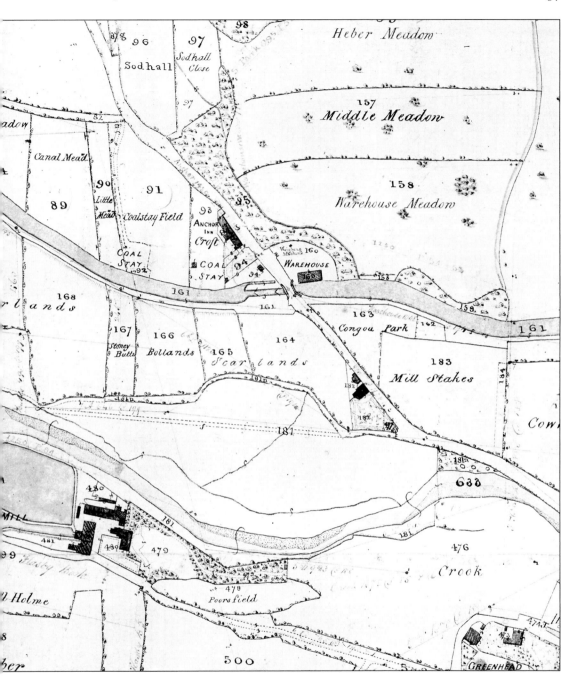

England and Wales where tithe was still payable. Tithe maps are heterogeneous. Each map was made by a private map-maker commissioned by local landowners. Though tithe surveys cover three-quarters of England and Wales, each map is unique. Tithe maps cannot be dubbed components of a 'national series' (Fig. 26).

TITHE APPORTIONMENTS

The apportionment is a roll of parchment sheets, 54 × 48cm. Blank *pro formas* with headings and ruled columns were printed by Shaw and Sons of Fetter Lane, London, and put on sale to valuers. The same forms were used regardless of whether rent-charge was apportioned by properties or by individual fields, and whether by valuation or by equal acreable charge. As a result the body of tithe apportionments is more uniform than the corpus of maps. Originally all apportionments were fixed to the maps but most have since been detached and are stored separately. The longest apportionment contains 399 pages, those of 100-200 pages are not uncommon, but the average is 23 pages. In total, the apportionments run to some 271,000 sheets of parchment.[42]

The first section of an apportionment contains a statement of the articles of agreement for commutation or a recital of the award, giving the names of the commissioners, assistant commissioner, surveyor or valuer and the owners of tithe. It also states the date of confirmation of the apportionment, the area of the tithe district, the area subject to tithes and an estimate of the area of arable, grass and other kinds of land subject to tithes. Comments on reasons for lands being exempt from tithes specify whether tithes had already been commuted, whether they were ancient monastic exemptions or whatever. Often, a list of tithe payers is attached.

The second and most important part of an apportionment roll is the schedule of tithe apportionment in which each tithe area, numbered on the accompanying plan, is listed under the name of its owner and occupier (Fig. 27). In a parish which still lay in open fields, as many as 3,000 separate tithe areas may be enumerated; in a majority there are several hundred. In some 744 districts (6 per cent) the rent-charge is apportioned by farms or estates, occasionally without a survey being made of each field; in a very few, no apportionment is made so that the whole titheable area of a district constitutes a single tithe area. Apportionment by holding is concentrated in north-east England and in parts of Wales and is related to the prevalence of modus payments and small rent-charges (Fig. 28). Where, as in the majority of schedules, a tithe area is a field, the field name is recorded; where it is not a field it is described, for example, as a 'house and garden', a 'piece of water', a 'chalk pit', or an 'ice house'. A few valuers, for example Charles Etheredge of Stanston in Norfolk, systematically omitted to record field names. The state of cultivation is entered for purposes of valuation according to local practice, almost all schedules distinguish arable, pasture and woodland and note orchards, market gardens and hop grounds which might carry an extraordinary rent-charge. There are some instances (195 in total) of actual crops being recorded, as at South Warnborough in Hampshire (Fig. 29). The practice is heavily concentrated in Cheshire and the surrounding counties of Denbighshire, Derbyshire, Flintshire, Lancashire and Staffordshire. It is clearly a regional phenomenon but also a personal one; most of the apportionments with cropping information in Derbyshire and Staffordshire, for example, are of districts valued by Joseph Bennett of Tutbury.[43]

In some areas the amount of detail in the state of cultivation column differs from district to district. In the Vale of Clwyd, for example, the state of cultivation columns

LANDOWNERS	OCCUPIERS	Numbers referring to the Plan	NAME AND DESCRIPTION OF LANDS AND PREMISES	STATE OF CULTIVATION	QUANTITIES IN STATUTE MEASURE			Amount of Rent-Charge apportioned upon the several Lands, and Payable to the Vicar			REMARKS
					A.	R.	P.	£	s.	d.	
Crompton Sir Samuel (Continued)	Francis Lees (Continued)		Brought forward	Meadow	6	0	21	...	12	9	
		44	Upper Lees	Meadow	2	0	10	...	13	3	
		45	Upper Lees adjoining Cottage	Meadow	2	0	16	...	13	7	vide IR29/32/127
		46	Cottage Garden and Stack Yard		...	...	24	...	2	3	
		47	Lane from River to Housons Gate		...	2	28	...	1	1	
					11	0	19	2	3	1	
	William Maulton	59	Cotton Field or New Field	Pasture	18	0	20	5	6	10	
		60	Great Meadow	Meadow	7	3	7	3	3	8	
		61	Top of Great Meadow	Pasture	4	2	12	1	8	0	
		62	Little Meadow	Meadow	3	0	23	1	6	4	
		63	Slade House with Outbuildings and Garden		...	1	32	...	3	9	
		64	Garden		...	1	32	...	3	9	
		65	Paddock	Pasture	...	2	5	...	4	10	
		66	New Meadow	Meadow	4	2	27	2	2	8	
		67	New Piece	Pasture	7	2	16	2	6	3	
		68	Hollow Pasture	Pasture	9	3	22	3	0	2	
		69	Corndale Meadow with Outbuildings	Meadow	5	2	18	2	11	4	
		70	Gorsy Close	Arable	7	2	36	2	14	10	
		71	Lane	Pasture	...	2	37	...	10	
		72	Little Gorsy Close	Arable	5	0	10	1	10	10	
		73	Lime Kiln Close	Pasture	11	1	24	3	9	5	
		74	Barn Meadow, Barn Cowhouses and Stack Yard	Meadow	8	0	0	3	5	0	
					95	0	31	32	18	6	
	Thomas Oakden	75	Cottage and Garden (Henry Oakden under tenant)		...	...	4	...	4		
		76	Rushley Farm House Outbuildings Orchard and Garden		...	2	0	...	4	3	
		77	Home Meadow	Meadow	1	0	4	...	10	7	
		78	Flax Croft	Meadow	...	3	4	...	8	4	
		79	Rushley near Redding	Pasture	21	1	36	9	4	8	
		80	Bridge Close	Pasture	6	0	30	1	15	3	
		81	Rushley Lea and Cow house	Meadow	8	0	14	4	12	9	
					38	0	12	16	16	6	

27 A page from the schedule of apportionment of rent-charge in Ilam, Staffordshire, where field-by-field apportionment was employed [PRO IR29 32/127]. Photograph reproduced by permission of the Keeper of the Public Record Office.

28 Llandefailog, Carmarthenshire, 1842. Tithe is apportioned on holdings and as a result the state of cultivation column is left blank [PRO IR29 47/28]. Reproduced by permission of the Keeper of the Public Record Office.

C.C.—London: Printed and Published (By Authority) by Shaw and Sons, 137 & 138, F

OCCUPIERS.	Numbers referring to the Plan.	NAME AND DESCRIPTION OF LANDS AND PREMISES.	STATE OF CULTIVATION.	QUANTITIES IN STATUTE MEASURE.			Amount of Rent-Charge apportioned upon the several Lands, and Payable to the Anthony Amiel Barker			REMARKS.
				A.	R.	P.	£	s.	d.	
		Pentre Cwn								
Harries Isaac	1562	Park Henry		7	2	2				
	1563	Cae Newydd Bach		4	.	10				
	1564	... Pant		6	2	32				
	1565	Park y dynen		6	1	10				
	1566	... y Pistill		6	1	2				
	1567	Cae pen y Close		8	2	1				
	1568	Upper Dingle		8	2	12				
	1569	Waun fach			2	10				
	1570	... Ganol		2	.	14				
	1571	Pentre cwn Homestead			2	.				
	1572	Park y Sedwen		6	2	13				
	1573	... y Banal		3	2	5				
	1574	... Cwm		4	2	10				
	1575	Waun dan ty		4	1	10				
	1576	Park lan dur		5	1	13				
	1577	Glandwr Cott Garden		1	.	5				
	1578	Marsh		3	.	13				
	1579	Lower Dingle		1	2	4				
				68	.	6	5	14	6	naa
		Ones y Coleg Lands								
Morgan John & others	1703	Slain Gain		2	1	34				
	1704			3	7					
	1705	House and Garden		2	8					
	1712	Llwynyceurys ucha		2	2	58				
	1706	House and Garden			22					

C.C.—London: Printed and Published (By Authority) by Shaw and Sons, 137 & 138, Fetter-lane.

29 A page from the schedule of apportionment of South Warnborough, Hampshire, in which the crops grown in each field are listed in the state of cultivation column [PRO IR29 31/232]. Photograph reproduced by permission of the Keeper of the Public Record Office.

some districts were left blank probably because rent-charge was apportioned on an acreable basis. In some Wealden parishes such as Penshurst, combinations of use, as for example 'meadow and arable', 'wood and pasture', are recorded. On the whole, such variants are quite rare; in a large majority of districts the basic distinction between arable and pasture is clearly made. Following the state of cultivation column, the statute acreage of each tithe area in acres, roods and perches is given together with the value of the rent-charge apportioned to it (in the usual form of entry where apportionment is parcel-by-parcel). A final column in the schedule of apportionment is left for 'remarks', which sometimes explain special valuations, such as those attached to mills or intakes from the waste. Most schedules are completed in manuscript, a very few (381 in all), like that of Deal in Kent (a part of a page of which is reproduced in Fig. 30), were printed. Most printed apportionments are of districts in Cornwall (103), Devon (80) and Suffolk (82).

The third section of the apportionment roll is a summary of the schedule of apportionment (Fig. 31). Here all landowners in the tithe district are listed alphabetically with names of the occupiers of their various holdings. The acreage of the holding and the total amount of rent-charge apportioned upon it are stated. At the end of the summary list these figures are totalled so that a global figure of the rent-charge for which

OCCUPIERS.	Nos. refer-ring to the Plan.	Name and Description of Lands and Premises.	State of Cultivation.	Quantities in Statute Measure.			REMARKS.
				A.	R.	P.	
		ARCHBISHOP'S LANDS (continued)		174	2	32	
Bedwell, John	394	Marsh	Arable	6	1	16	
Self	218	....	Arable	10	0	11	
	223	House, Garden, &c.		1	3	24	
	224	....	Arable	1	3	23	
Weston, Ambrose	228	....	Arable	6	0	32	
Smith, Jarvis	222	House and	Garden	3	3	13	
	248	Houses and	Gardens	0	1	3	
	249	,, ...	,,	0	1	0	
	250	,, ...	,,	3	2	26	
	251	,, ...	,,	0	2	18	Tithe Free
Dalhousie, Earl of	235	Coach House	Garden	1	2	12	
	516	Houses, &	Gardens	2	0	27	
	517	Path and	Garden	0	0	36	
	518	Naval Yard		4	1	8	
Themselves	519	Waste and	Garden	0	1	24	
	520	Beach & Waste to high water mark		2	0	10	
				220	1	36	
		TOWN OF DEAL, **BEACH AND ROADS, &c.**					
	523	Beach, &c. from high to low water mark		50	3	30	
	524	Beach and Road from Town to Sandown Castle		14	3	28	
		Houses and Streets in the Town of Deal		16	0	28	
		Ditto		42	1	32	
	525	Half of the Eastern Road, &c.		1	0	19	
	526	Half of S. W. Mill Road		0	2	30	
	527	Sandy End and Path		0	3	5	
	528	Mill Road from corner of Queen Street to Mill		2	1	21	
	529	Turnpike Road from Queen Street to Sholden Church		4	1	16	
	530	Turnpike Road, Prospect Place ..		1	0	20	
	531	Cottage Row and Path		0	1	18	
	532	Road through Upper Deal		0	3	38	
	533	Ditto		0	1	36	
	534	Pound Lane and Roads at back of Church		0	3	16	
	535	Road by Sholden Bank, &c.....		0	1	2	
	536	Road from Middle Deal to Upper Deal..................		2	0	36	
	537	Church Path		1	0	17	
	538	Gun Lane, &c.		0	1	37	
	539	Part of Western Road, &c.		1	0	27	
	540	Road to South Wall		0	2	2	
	541	Road from Sandhills to Middle Deal		3	1	38	
	542	North End of Lower Street, &c. ..		1	0	2	
	501	Houses, &c.................		0	1	24	
	502	Ditto		0	0	27	
	503	Ditto		0	0	15	
				148	2	14	

30 An extract from the printed schedule of apportionment of the parish of Deal in Kent [IR29 17/107]. Reproduced by permission of the Keeper of the Public Record Office.

SUMMARY.

D.D.—London: Printed and Published (By Authority,) by Shaw & Sons, 137 and 138, Fetter Lane.

LANDOWNERS.	OCCUPIERS.	Quantities in Statute Measure.			Rent Charge payable to Rector.		
		A.	R.	P.	£	s.	d.
John Cuming Bishop	In hand	170	"	22	18	6	"
Joshua Field as Trustee of Charity Estate	Thomas Hutton	18	1	37	20	10	.
Abraham Crowley	Henry Norris	"	1	2			
John Dicker	Himself	"	.	13			
Richard Dicker	Himself	"	.	10			
Charles Heath	Himself	1	1	35	.	11	.
George Hewett	Himself	"	.	3			
Thomas Laney (Lifeholder)	Himself	"	.	35			
Edward William Nash	Elizabeth Nash and others	2	1	24	.	17	.
Elizabeth Pearse	Thomas Pearse and another	43	2	12	11	11	6
John Seymour	Edward Silver and another	"	.	20			
William Sutley Sclater	Thomas Barton	9	"	15	2	8	.
John Jervis Tucker, Jedidiah Stephens Tucker, Thomas Spurhill Tucker and Benjamin Wadham Tucker	Richard Holding	218	1	19	68	2	.
Reverend Thomas Alston Warren	Himself and another	2	1	6	.	13	.
Thomas Moore Wayne Esquire	Himself	70	1	15	18	.	.
	William Shape	203	.	9	60	16	.
	Walter Dicker	331	.	29	105	12	.
	Reverend Thomas Alston Warren	13	.	28	4	18	.
	John Dicker Junior	7	"	34	2	10	.
	James Trodd	307	.	17	102	8	.
	George Lock	"	3	8	.	4	.
	John Sparshatt	558	.	33	174	.	.
	William Christmas	386	.	95	96	12	.
	Thomas Pearse	5	.	8	1	5	6
	Richard Holding	13	2	35	20	5	.
	Various Labourers	11	3	32	3	12	.
	Various Cottagers	2	"	34			
Reverend Thomas Alston Warren (Glebe)	Himself and another	41	3	.	12	"	.
	Roads &c	61	2	6			
		2569	.	2	732	"	.

(Signed)

Edward Hollis

31 The last page of the summary of the schedule of apportionment of South Warnborough parish in Hampshire [PRO IR29 21/232]. Reproduced by permission of the Keeper, Public Record Office.

tithes have been commuted in the district is stated. The acreage of roads, waste and other land exempt from tithe is usually stated, and finally the total amount of rent-charge agreed or awarded is stated.

The fourth and final section of the apportionment roll contains altered apportionments made after the original apportionment was confirmed. In a few parishes, parcels of land have passed undivided from generation to generation, but such places are exceptional. Over much of the country changes in ownership have been frequent, estates have been broken up and land has been put to new uses. In 1854 William Blamire stated that there were already 976 altered apportionments in the custody of the tithe office.[44] Altered apportionments record major changes in the shape, size and status of the original tithe areas resulting from severance or subdivision. The building of railways, construction of new roads, re-allocation of land under an enclosure award, and other public works all necessitated altered apportionments. When changes affected a large part of a parish a separate new apportionment might be made. Reference has already been made to an instance of this type at Winterborne Kingston in Dorset. New reference numbers given to altered tithe areas may be differentiated from the original numbers by the addition of a letter or sign—thus an original area 134 may be designated 134A, 134a, A134 or even A134aa.

TITHE FILES

A separate tithe file, kept for each tithe district, contains some additional information, not only on procedures adopted in commutation, but on farming practices in the locality. The tithe files were briefly described in an article written by the secretary of the Tithe Redemption Commission in 1957 but their modern use as a source of historical data dates from the years around 1960 when they were 'discovered' by a group of research students from the Geography Department, University College London. Two of these, Elwyn Cox and Brian Dittmer, have drawn attention to the value of tithe-file documents for agrarian historians in an important article in *Agricultural History Review*.[45] Although the files were heavily weeded before the First World War, surviving correspondence and miscellaneous notes throw light on the demeanour of the clergy, the interests of parishioners, property disputes, leases, the upkeep of roads, and the operation of local markets. In addition to these details are statements amplifying the terms of the agreement or award. The transfer of glebe lands, sale of tithe barns, conditions attached to compositions, arrangements for mergers and redemptions, reasons for exemptions and enquiries into the validity of settlements made at the time of enclosure may be recorded.

There are 14,829 tithe files in all and these can be classified into three broad groups on the basis of their contents. First, about 2,200 files relate to districts where tithe was no longer payable in 1836 or had been redeemed by merger in the land. Most of these contain little more than a brief statement by a representative of the Tithe Commission to confirm that all tithes had been extinguished.

A second group consists of some 6,000 files of districts where commutation was effected by compulsory award. Files for these places usually contain a draft award and minutes of meetings held in the presence of an assistant commissioner who called witnesses on behalf of various parties, cross-questioned them under oath, and recorded their statements either verbatim or as notes. It is difficult to generalise about information that might be recorded in these 'minutes'. Reasons for failing to reach an agreement varied considerably, but the more complex the problems, the more likely it is that extensive records were generated. Another variable is the attitude of different assistant commissioners, who differed in their interpretation of what they were expected to do. Furthermore, the weeding operation was carried out haphazardly, leaving some files almost empty whilst others were scarcely touched.

A third group of files are those of some 6,740 districts where tithe was commuted by agreement and where, therefore, an assistant tithe commissioner or local tithe agent was required to submit a written report on the agreement (see Chapter 2). To help the Tithe Commission's local representatives judge agreements and to organise and standardise their reports, they were issued (from November 1837) with forms on which a number of questions were printed with spaces for answers. These provide much information on local landscapes, farming practices and output of agriculture. Report forms have not usually been weeded out except where an agreement was replaced by a compulsory award. In some files a report is the only document which has survived.

Two basic types of printed report form were used (with minor changes in format over the years) and these have been described with the aid of specimen answers from an Essex and a north-west Wiltshire parish by Cox and Dittmer.[46] In any one county only one type of form was in general use. In mainly arable-farming counties of the country it was expected that agreed rent-charges would be checked by calculating a tenth of the gross produce of the crops, usually by multiplying estimated crop acreages by average yield. Grassland in these areas was valued according to the yield of hay and the agistment value of pasture. In mainly pastoral livestock-rearing counties of the west, an alternative much shorter form was used eliciting the value of grassland products, and calling for an estimate of the number of various sorts of stock kept. Figure 32 indicates that the 'arable' type of form was used in the east and south of the country and the 'pastoral' type in the west and in Wales. Some counties are in somewhat anomalous positions. Shropshire reports are of the 'arable' type, although in counties to the south and west, 'pastoral' forms were used. In view of the long tradition of dairy farming in Cheshire it might be expected that the 'pastoral' type of report would have been used there, but, for reasons that are not known, the 'arable' type was used throughout this county.

Both types of report contain a record of certain preliminaries: the dates and places of meetings, numbers of landowners and their interest, the quantity of glebe, amount of the rates, the value of tithes collected in kind or compounded during the years of average (1829-35), the relationship of this sum to that of neighbouring districts, whether the sum included amounts for personal, mineral or fish tithes, and whether the agreement reached was fair and could be confirmed. On 'arable' reports questions on these topics are printed and answered on the forms; with 'pastoral' reports this information is found in a supplementary hand-written report which the agent usually attached to his completed questionnaire. The critical questions were 'Is the agreement fair?' and 'Should the agreement be confirmed?' To help answer these, agents were asked to furnish some quantitative data on land use, crops and yields and add descriptive information on matters related to assessing a fair rent-charge.

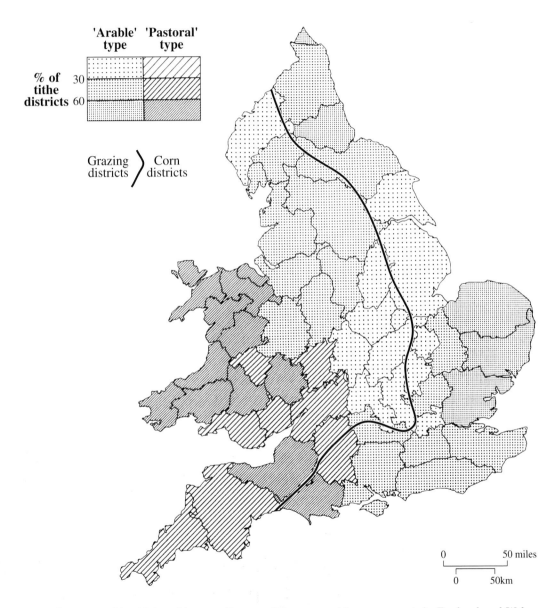

32 Coverage of 'arable' and 'pastoral' types of report on tithe agreements in England and Wales. Source: tithe files; the line dividing grazing and corn districts is from J. Caird, *English agriculture in 1850-51*, 2nd edition (London, Longman, Brown, Green and Longman, 1852), frontispiece.

QUANTITATIVE DATA ON FARMING IN TITHE FILE REPORTS ON AGREEMENTS

The 'arable' reports required local agents to provide either 'a rough valuation of the tithes of the parish' (on forms issued in 1837), or (from 1839 onwards) 'a description and rough estimate of the amount of the titheable produce' (Fig. 33). Under this heading a great deal of material useful to historians is provided. The valuations generally set out the titheable acreage of the district and the amounts of meadow and pasture, woodland, common and specialist land uses such as orchards, gardens and hops which, because of the high value per acre of their produce, were sometimes required to bear an extra-ordinary rent-charge. But of these land uses, only the arable and meadow and pasture categories are recorded over the whole country. Woodland is often not recorded because it was exempt from tithe, as in the Chilterns or in the Weald, and commons and unfarmed land were difficult to assess and, because of low titheable value, often did not merit careful measurement. 'Gardens' were sometimes narrowly defined as market gardens but more usually included cottage gardens where these were titheable. Hop acreages in areas where extraordinary charges did not apply were commonly subsumed in the arable acreage as were gardens when these were not separately identified. Orchards were either enumerated separately or included with pasture. In a separate table after the land-use data, the local agent or assistant commissioner set out acreages of crops grown on the arable, their yields and the prices which he used-to calculate the gross produce of the arable.

On the 'pastoral' type of report form, local agents were asked to estimate the acreage of arable defined as 'land actually ploughed in the present or last season, whether sown with corn, planted with roots or fallow, but excluding seeds'. They were also asked to state the number of acres of pasture including seeds. In the tithe apportionments, on the other hand, and also in 'arable' reports, the term 'arable' usually included land that had been ploughed within the years of average. For western counties, however, the 'pastoral' reports definition is a realistic interpretation of arable because seeds were usually pastured for at least three years and quite often for ten or more years before being ploughed up again. Further comments on land-use definitions are made in Chapter 4 below.

In 'pastoral' reports, the acreage of crops was not asked for but instead question 2 asked 'What is the course of Crops?' (Fig. 34). It is possible to derive estimates of the acreage of individual crops by dividing the acreage of arable by the number of courses (excluding the seeds courses) in the rotation. In fact, this is exactly the method by which most tithe agents produced their 'rough estimate of the amount of titheable produce' in eastern counties. However, for a number of reasons it is not possible to derive the acreages of all crops in all districts in this way. Firstly, more than one rotation might be stated without an indication of the proportion of the district to which each applied. Secondly, rotations were sometimes less than fully described: at Marham Church in Cornwall, William Glasson recorded a rotation of 'wheat, barley or oats—part potatoes and a small quantity of turnips'.[47] From such an imprecise description of the rotation it is not possible to derive crop acreages. Yield figures are not usually entered on the printed 'pastoral' forms but are to be found in manuscript reports which accompany them.

33 'Description and rough estimate of the titheable produce' at Coveney, Cambridgeshire [PRO IR 18/3728]. Reproduced by permission of the Keeper of the Public Record Office.

Parish of *Meavy*   County of *Devon.*

QUESTIONS.	ANSWERS
1.—How many Acres of Arable Land (including under that description the Land actually ploughed in the present or last season, whether sown with corn, planted with roots or fallow, but excluding seeds)?	500 $\frac{2}{3}$ of 750.
2.—What is the course of Crops?	Wheat, Barley, & grass out for 1 year
3.—What is the nature of the Soil?	gravelly
4.—What is the Sub-soil?	granite — slate.
5.—What description of Timber grown in the Hedge-rows, or otherwise; Oak, Elm, Ash or Beech?	Oak — Hazel — Ash & Willow
6.—What is the fair average rentable Value per acre of the Arable Land?	15/.
7.—What is the number of Acres of Pasture, including seeds?	750 M. & P. 500. / ⅓ of arable 250. / 750.

(o.1.)—58.

34 An extract from the report on the tithe agreement at Meavy, Devon[PRO IR 18/1396]. Reproduced by permission of the Keeper of the Public Record Office.

Local agents were not required to state the acreage of woodland on printed 'pastoral' forms; usually only coppice and underwood were titheable. Sometimes woodland amounts were written in at the end of a form or included in a covering manuscript report. This practice varied from agent to agent and from assistant commissioner to assistant commissioner as well as from county to county; woodland acreages were infrequently stated in Gloucestershire and Herefordshire, for example. Nor were acreages of market gardens or hops required for 'pastoral' forms which means that consistent data on hop cultivation in counties such as Worcestershire are not available.

In short, data on land use and crops in 'pastoral' reports are not as comprehensive or as consistently recorded as in 'arable' reports. On the credit side, assistant tithe commissioners and local agents were required to enter the number of cows, bullocks, horses and sheep kept in a tithe district in answer to question 12 of the 'pastoral' questionnaire. On 'arable' reports the produce of grassland was assessed by the agistment value of pasture and the yield of hay. Stock numbers were presented infrequently and incidentally in 'arable' reports or put, as in Lancashire, not in the form of numbers but rather expressed as the density of stock which the pasture could support.

DESCRIPTIONS OF PARISH FARMING IN TITHE FILE REPORTS ON AGREEMENTS

In 'arable' reports assistant commissioners were asked to 'Describe the parish and the quality of the lands, the system of farming, and whether the quality of the produce has been affected by any extraordinary instances of high or low farming.' On the relatively small number of report forms used in 1838, the same request was made but phrased as two separate questions. 'Pastoral' reports required 'Remarks, stating the peculiar circumstances of the parish which may affect the value of the tithe'. The difference in breadth of the questions is reflected in the value of the answers, though the predilections of a particular assistant commissioner could greatly influence what was written. Some made do with cryptic one- or two-sentence answers on 'arable' forms and others filled all available space on 'pastoral' reports and greatly exceeded their limited brief.

In any one county, one agent reported on a clear majority of districts. Therefore, the value of the descriptive material (as with the quantitative data) varies from one part of the country to another in line with the different approaches of particular commissioners. Over 80 per cent of the reports on agreements for Somerset districts were completed by R. Page who wrote much fuller answers than usual on 'pastoral' forms. On the other hand, John Farncombe who reported on 158 of the 188 agreements in Sussex wrote very brief, stereotyped accounts which depresses the value of the tithe files as a source in this county despite a good (58 per cent) coverage of reports on agreements. Some of the fullest descriptions were compiled by Henry Gunning who worked extensively in Norfolk, Suffolk and Cambridgeshire. His accounts usually occupy two full sides of closely written foolscap and discuss markets, the quality of different types of land, rotations, summer fallowing and the cultivation of root crops, meadows and pastures, types of stock, and the nature and extent of woodland and waste.[48] He was knowledgeable about high farming, frequently commenting on the types of manures and fertilisers employed, turnip culture, artificial feedstuffs and underdrainage. Gunning frequently spiced his factual accounts with anecdotes: at one parish he mentions the idleness and drinking habits of the population, at another he speaks of paupers having been recently shipped to North America. In several Denbighshire reports, John Fenton similarly found space to discuss local folklore. For instance, at Llanelian yn Rhos he wrote about the powers of the water well. By inscribing the name of a person on a stone and throwing it in the well, 'diverse disorders would fall upon them'. The malediction could only be removed by paying the keeper of the well to remove the stone. She reportedly enjoyed a thriving trade.[49]

Although most descriptive material in the tithe files relates to agriculture and local tithe practices, the files can throw light on many other topics such as church incomes, the condition of the clergy, attitudes of parishioners, relationships between labourers and farmers, and the general structure of the community and the way it organised and administered itself. This information is of great value to historians and historical geographers working on the 19th century. Much of it is unequalled in its wealth of detail at any other period. The problem is that information on a particular topic is probably scattered through many dozens or even hundreds of files so that most researchers have been unable to devote the time necessary to search through them. All the files have now been subject-indexed to enable material to be more easily retrieved.[50]

THE COVERAGE OF THE COUNTRY BY TITHE SURVEYS

The overall coverage of the 11,785 tithe surveys is 27.2 million acres or about 75 per cent of England and Wales. Many counties were almost entirely covered by the work of the tithe commissioners. The major exceptions, as Gilbert Slater demonstrated, were places which dealt with their tithes at the time of parliamentary enclosure (see frontispiece).[51] Tithe coverage is sparse in the extensively enclosed midland counties and much more complete in western districts and Wales. On the other hand, Westmorland, Lancashire and Gloucestershire are relatively scantily covered, while both Norfolk and the northern half of Yorkshire are rather more fully surveyed than might be expected from a map of enclosures. In detail, however, many parishes enclosed by act of parliament had not abolished their tithes. In Bedfordshire, Buckinghamshire, Northamptonshire, Leicestershire and Warwickshire, in particular, the incidence of enclosure and tithe surveys shows most imperfect correspondence.

Figure 32 indicates the coverage of England and Wales by the two types of printed reports on tithe agreements. There are marked variations in the availability of reports, county by county, reflecting both the general level of tithe commutation and the ratio of commutation by agreement and award. Highest percentages occur in Wales where much tithe remained and was commuted by agreement; Denbigh heads the list with 88 per cent and seven other Welsh counties exceed 70 per cent coverage. In East Anglian counties, a high proportion of tithe districts is covered by file report forms (Essex 71 per cent, Suffolk 68 per cent, Norfolk 66 per cent) as are districts in western counties (Somerset 66 per cent, Dorset 62 per cent, Hereford 61 per cent). The smallest numbers are to be found in midland counties where many districts had been exonerated from tithe payment at enclosure or where only small amounts remained payable and awaited compulsory award (Leicestershire 12 per cent, Middlesex 17 per cent, Bedfordshire, Northamptonshire and Nottinghamshire 18 per cent).

CUSTODY OF TITHE SURVEY DOCUMENTS

Most of the original tithe apportionments and maps and subsequent altered apportionments and maps are now in the custody of the Public Record Office at Ruskin Avenue, Kew, Surrey. Typescript catalogues of the documents are available in the search rooms at Kew and they have also been published in two volumes by the List and Index Society.[52] The catalogues have been prepared from the manuscript Tithe Redemption Office handlist and list in alphabetical order, county by county, those tithe districts with both a tithe map and apportionment. Though these remain the 'official' lists, they are now supplemented by the much fuller listings in Kain and Oliver, *The tithe maps of England and Wales.*

The Public Record Office has microfilm copies of all tithe apportionments and maps and microfiches of maps for counties from Bedfordshire alphabetically to Middlesex. Positive copies of these, or photographic prints from them, can be purchased.[53] It is fairly easy to use microfilm copies of tithe apportionments as the page size fits film format quite well. But most tithe maps are photographed on several frames of film which makes finding individual tithe areas a tiresome business.

Only one tithe file was kept for each district and that is now deposited with the Public Record Office. These are catalogued county-by-county with tithe districts arranged by alphabetical order of parishes within counties. This means that where tithe districts are coterminous with townships, for example, it is necessary to know both township and parish names to find the press mark of a tithe district. A list and index of all files is published.[54]

Two statutory copies of the tithe map and apportionment were produced at the time of commutation. One was deposited with the incumbent and churchwardens to be kept in the parish chest and another was deposited in the diocesan registry. These copies have sometimes been lost, damaged or transferred to a county record office. Most offices have fairly complete collections of statutory copy maps supplemented by modern copies on paper, microfilm or microfiche. The number of tithe surveys held by county record offices is increasing all the time by receipt of new depositions, usually from parish collections or documents which had strayed into private hands at some time in the past, and by acquisition of photocopies to fill gaps in collections. It is not only to county record offices that a student should turn for a locally held copy of a tithe survey, but to all ecclesiastical, municipal and university archives. For example, surveys of the diocese of Oxford are held in the Bodleian Library, those for the diocese of Ripon are in Leeds City Archives, for Gloucester in Gloucester City Library, for Cambridge in Cambridge University Library, while the Borthwick Institute of Historical Research holds some surveys of the diocese of York. A full list of diocesan repositories, together with addresses of county record offices, is to be found in the current edition of the HMSO publication, *Record repositories in Great Britain.*

4
THE ACCURACY OF THE TITHE SURVEYS

No one in the least familiar with the bitter struggles between tithe payers and tithe owners that endured without respite for centuries can have the slightest doubt that the parties brought together after 1836 to commute and apportion those precious objects of their strife would study every section of the tithe acts with minute attention, would haggle over their rights to take, or not to forgo, the smallest item of payment to which a claim might be made, and would follow closely behind the assistant commissioner or local tithe agent and the surveyor and valuer as they inspected the fields and drew their cadastral plan. So far as the interests of the parishioners were concerned, no survey, with the possible exception of an enclosure survey, was ever carried out under such close scrutiny. But are the records of the inquest truthful and how may their accuracy be tested?

An evaluation of accuracy is an essential step in the use of any historical data source but the level of accuracy which is acceptable should not be measured against some external absolute; the accuracy required will vary according to the questions being asked of the documents.[1] For the purposes of most historians and historical geographers, it is important to know to what extent a tithe district corresponded to a parish or township, to what extent a tithe area corresponded to a field, to what extent the state of cultivation corresponded with the actual land use at the time of the survey and to what extent estimates of crop acreages and yields reflected the actual produce of the land. To all these questions reasonably satisfactory answers can be given by examining the internal evidence of the documents themselves and subjecting them to comparison with independent sources. It would be incautious to disregard the strictures of the professional witnesses reviewed below, although their testimony may have been tainted with prejudice and was directed mainly towards planimetric inaccuracies in the tithe maps. In the final analysis, the surveys must be judged by their internal consistency and by their faithfulness to contemporary descriptions. As sources for reconstructing the salient features of mid-19th-century landscapes they pass all but the most stringent tests with considerable credit, if not flying colours.

THE LEGAL STATUS OF TITHE SURVEYS

Only tithe maps and apportionments have the status of legal documents. The tithe files contain, in addition to general correspondence, either a record of the way in which an agreement for commutation was reached or information which an assistant tithe commissioner used to impose a just award. None of this material has any legal status. On the other hand, the 1836 Act expressly directed the tithe commissioners to furnish maps that might be admitted as evidence in courts of law in deciding questions of title to land, general and public rights in a township, and the existence of common rights in an unenclosed parish. These requirements were relaxed by the Tithe Act Amendment Acts of 1837 and 1839 which released the commissioners from the duty of sealing maps that, in their opinion, did not warrant certification as true representations of exact quantities and boundaries.

The result of these government decisions, in the words of John Meadows White, solicitor to the Poor Law and tithe and enclosure commissioners, was that: 'five-sixths of the tithe maps are not only on too small a scale for ordinary practical purposes, but are perfectly useless for many of the public requirements, of the present day [1853]. Indeed, any professional man will bear testimony to the fact that if one of these secondary maps be produced to verify the parcels or boundaries of an estate, as part of the title, the fact of its not being a sealed map is at once notice that it is inaccurate and not to be relied on for legal testimony'.[2]

Only first-class maps were suitable for enclosure purposes under the 1845 General Enclosure Act. R.K. Dawson, appointed assistant commissioner under that act as well as the tithe acts, commented in evidence before the Select Committee on the Ordnance Survey of Scotland in 1856 that:

> no second-class map has been used for the purposes of enclosure; they must be first-class maps, because the Inclosure Commissioners are forced to certify that they have actually examined the maps and found them correct ... The second-class tithe maps are used only to a limited extent for the purpose of the Inclosure Act, when the landowners agree to accept them as the basis for settling their claims; but for the purpose of setting out the allotments, an accurate and perfect survey is invariably required.[3]

Courts of law have not always been consistent in their acceptance of tithe surveys as evidence, as P.W. Millard demonstrates in his review of tithe law. In the cases of Wilberforce v. Hearfield (1877) and Frost v. Richardson (1910) it was held that even a sealed map is not admissible as evidence of boundaries between two adjoining properties. But in Gifford v. Williams (1869) a tithe map was received in evidence on a question of title in a partition action. In Smith v. Lister (1895) a sealed tithe map was admitted in evidence on an issue of public right in part of a township while even a second-class tithe map was received in evidence of the non-existence of a public road in Attorney General v. Antrobus in 1905. In Stoney v. Eastbourne Rural District Council and the Duke of Devonshire (1927) an opposite judgement was made when it 'was held that a tithe map could not be accepted as evidence of the non-existence of a public right of way which might have been, but was not inserted in it and was not relevant to the purpose for which the map was made'.[4]

All tithe maps and apportionments, however, are still conclusive as evidence in disputes between tithe owners and tithe payers. They are good enough to have prevented frivolous litigation that might have resulted from the transfer of land with its attendant rent-charges as well as from changes in the state of cultivation, in the direction of roads, and in the removal of fences. Moreover, the maps have been considered sufficiently accurate to serve as the bases for other official enquiries. They were consulted, for example, by the Ordnance Survey (and sometimes found wanting) when drawing parish boundaries on the first 1:2500 plans.[5]

EXAMINATION AND TESTING OF MAPS BY THE TITHE COMMISSION

The linchpin of R.K. Dawson's scheme for obtaining accurate maps from unsupervised private surveyors which the tithe commissioners would be able to certify accurate, was the application of a system of rigorous checks to the completed work. This fundamental principle governed the detailed specification of the maps discussed above in Chapter 3, and was backed by the sanction of the commissioners who could refuse to accept a map unless it was corrected. They also had powers to require testing lines to be set out on the ground in residual cases of uncertainty or dispute. Professional land surveyors who, through their Land Surveyors' Club, had been vehemently opposed to the financial terms on which the then Tithe Bill had proposed to employ its members for tithe mapping, were also reluctant to submit their work to an official examination.[6] Many were particularly sensitive about their professional status and expertise and were quick to take offence when the accuracy of their maps was called into question. Surveyors did not, according to William Blamire, willingly submit maps for testing. Many an old country surveyor is reputed to have said, 'Neither our maps, nor our fathers', nor our grandfathers' were ever called into question qua accuracy, and we do not know why the Tithe Commissioners should now assume the power to test our maps, and we shall advise all parties who have confidence in us to refuse to permit our maps to be tested'.[7] The main object of the testing was to ensure that 'the system of triangulation adopted is perfect and complete *per se*, and next that the filling up of the triangles is accurate, and that the acreage given is fairly represented by the maps'.[8] Lieutenant Dawson, who was in charge of the department responsible for conducting the tests, explained the method used as follows:

> It is the duty of the examiner to see that the lines of construction, or measured lines, are systematically and properly disposed; and that the measurements recorded in the field-books are properly indicated on the map. Any discrepancy between the map and field notes leads to the rejection of the map; and when doubts arise as to the originality of the field notes, or from circumstances of a suspicious nature, such as apparent alteration in the field notes, or an unsystematic arrangement of lines of construction, recourse is had to testing upon the ground. The ground test consists of straight lines, measured by an independent surveyor, in the form of a triangle, with one or more interior proof-lines. The intersections of fences, and other detail determined by these lines, when laid down in position and compared with similar lines drawn upon the original plans constitute one of the severest tests that can be applied.[9]

When landowners desired a first-class map and had contracted for such with a surveyor, the completed map, preferably the plain, working plan, had to be sent with the field book to the Tithe Commission who returned its comments on specially printed forms with space for parish replies in explanation of examiners' remarks.

The work of testing maps must have been a prodigious effort. By 21 March 1844, the London office had tested 2,017 maps, the work of 405 surveyors, had approved 1,399, had rejected 521, and were still considering 97.[10] To expedite this operation, and presumably also to ensure consistency between examiners, these last were provided with printed examination papers which provided a 'check-list' of potential faults and a convenient schedule for organising their comments. Study of these examination papers is important as it reveals the range of tests which were applied and the particular aspects of accuracy with which the Tithe Commission was and was not concerned. All the checks were concerned with establishing the planimetric accuracy of a map and were not concerned at all with topographic content as regards buildings, types of roads, nature of boundaries, representation of land use by symbol, and other features often portrayed on a tithe map. The presentation of the latter information was incidental to commutation purposes and clearly the Tithe Commission was not concerned to verify it all, though landowners did have an opportunity to check such matters for themselves when the draft apportionment was lodged for their approval.

Lieutenant Dawson's office was certainly able to detect involuntary mistakes in maps. In one such map some 400 errors were pointed out and admitted and in that of Tonge in north Kent errors of up to 100 per cent were found (see above, Chapter 3).[11] By 1841 the tithe commissioners felt it necessary to warn that: 'maps are sometimes sent here containing errors of which the mappers are conscious, and the existence of which they attempt to conceal, by tampering with and making compensating errors in the field books, or original records of admeasurement which they are required to send with the maps. No examination in this office can enable us to detect here wilful and fraudulent errors of this description'.[12]

Landowners who were vigilant and exercised their rights could bring such frauds to light. A map was deposited in a parish for 21 days prior to confirmation of the apportionment. At the end of this period an assistant commissioner could be required to attend a meeting at which errors might be pointed out and it was his duty to see that the final map was corrected. But the tithe commissioners feared that landowners did not inspect maps carefully. The accuracy of a map could also be checked by setting out test lines on the ground and having them carefully measured. However, the Tithe Commission had no authority to defray the expense of such trials and no clear power to levy charges on responsible parties. It concluded in 1841: 'unquestionably we believe, that the maps to which we have attached our seal are very much more accurate than they would have been had they not gone through the ordeal of this office; but we think it prudent that the landowners should know what description of errors we can detect here, and what may escape detection'.[13]

R.K. Dawson, architect of the tithe survey, also had some reservations about the first-class maps considering that they:

> would have been better maps, certainly, if they had been founded upon a scientific basis of triangulation, as the maps of the Ordnance Survey are, and if they had been made under proper superintendence, supervision and control; but those maps were only first seen by the Tithe Commissioners when sent to them for the

purpose of examination, being then complete. The maps were made according to the instructions which the Commissioners had issued, but the Commissioners had no personal supervision of them during their construction, and therefore those maps, I dare say, will be less perfect than the finished maps of the Ordnance Survey.[14]

NINETEENTH-CENTURY MAP USERS' OPINIONS OF TITHE MAP ACCURACY

In making any assessment of 19th-century map users' opinions of tithe map accuracy it is important to distinguish between comments relating to first- and second-class maps. Second-class maps received almost universal condemnation as planimetrically untrustworthy. Most witnesses who appeared before various select committees on the Ordnance Survey and into matters such as town improvement, enclosure, and registration of title to land in the 1840s and 1850s would probably have agreed with Francis Marston of Hopesay near Ludlow, who was a practising farmer, a land agent with enclosure experience, and was employed as a tithe commutation surveyor and valuer. He dismissed second-class maps as 'not worth a straw'.[15] Indeed rather than use them he would prefer to 'go by my own eye; I could guess better than the measure stated in many second-class maps'.[16] Such opinions were probably formed without any 'scientific' sampling of this class of map and were doubtless coloured by the commentators' experiences or hearsay of one or two infamously inaccurate maps.

Of first-class maps opinion was more varied; they had their detractors, particularly within the Ordnance Survey, and their champions, amongst whom can be counted land agents and country solicitors who used tithe maps in day-to-day matters of rural land management. The sale and transfer of land from the mid-19th century was much facilitated by the availability of tithe surveys as William Blamire, copyhold and tithe commissioner, explained in evidence before a parliamentary commission in 1854: 'numbers of people come to the office daily to examine maps, and to get particulars of certain properties, and tracings of those properties which they attach to conveyances in place of or in elucidation of the old and original designation of the property ... and I observe in country papers when property is to be sold there are references to tithe maps. "Number so-and-so on the tithe map?" - Exactly'.[17]

Some support for the value of first-class tithe maps (and yet more castigation of the second class) came from other more unexpected quarters. The year 1845 has been described as 'the great railway year' which generated an increased demand for maps for plotting railway routes.[18] The published one-inch scale maps of the Ordnance Survey were not really suitable for this detailed work and engineers turned to the larger scale maps of the Tithe Commission. In April 1856 Lieutenant-Colonel Dawson said, 'numberless applications were made to the Tithe Commissioners for copies of their maps for setting out railways. Then was found the great inconvenience of the second-class maps. The first-class maps were found to be highly satisfactory; but the second-class maps to a very great extent were worthless'.[19] Yet engineer T. Hawksley had found some quite good second-class maps: 'their inaccuracy, such as it is, is mostly a minute thing ... we find when we come to put two or three triangles together, that they do not exactly meet at the points where they should meet, or they a little overlap or underlap each other, and then the surveyor compresses it or extends it a little to allow for that, and that results in a very small inaccuracy'.[20] On the other hand, Thomas Bauch, a railway engineer for more than twenty-five years who himself had prepared 'one or two' first-class tithe maps, also had 'occasion to use them in the preparation of railway plans where the Ordnance plans were not published, but I certainly have quite given them up'.[21] However, it appeared that it had been his practice to inspect hand copies rather than the original maps and that most of the errors he referred to arose in the copying operation. This should perhaps be taken as a warning by present-day students working with diocesan or parish copies of the tithe surveys.

Perhaps the most telling 19th-century assessment of the planimetric accuracy of the tithe surveys came not from the Tithe Commission, nor from land agents, engineers or solicitors familiar only with surveys of some local area, but from officers of the Ordnance Survey during discussion of a national cadastral survey in the 1850s. For a second time in the 19th century the government had to decide whether some if not all tithe maps could be incorporated into a cadastral survey of the kingdom. Lieutenant-Colonel Tucker of the Ordnance Survey boundary department, an officer of 29 years of varied experience on the duties of the Ordnance Survey in England, Ireland and Scotland, [whose] opinion deserves at least equal consideration to that of Lieutenant-Colonel Dawson, was directed by Lieutenant-Colonel Hall to examine the tithe maps.[22] His recommendation was that the second-class plans be rejected *in toto*. Similar conclusions were reached by another officer, Captain R.E. Gossett, who: 'carefully examined, and in many ways tested, a number of the picked best first-class tithe commission maps made by private surveyors; the result of my examination is the discovery that they are utterly worthless for incorporation into a general map of the United Kingdom. As to the second-class maps, the officials of the Tithe Office did not deem it worth my while to examine them, so inferior did they consider them'.[23]

On balance, 19th-century opinion on the planimetric accuracy of tithe maps, particularly of the second-class maps, was unfavourable. Much of this comment was, however, impressionistic; few commentators attempted to quantify the amount of error they encountered. The one or two much-publicised cases such as the Tonge map were eagerly seized upon by the anti-tithe survey lobby and used as ammunition for their condemnation of the whole body of tithe maps. Modern cartometric tests of tithe maps suggest that Marston and others were unfair in embracing all second-class maps with that judgement. A study of the planimetric accuracy of tithe maps carried out by J.M. Hooke and R.A. Perry suggests that maps like that submitted from Tonge were probably quite exceptional and that as a body second-class tithe maps are tolerably accurate.[24]

To the cartographic historian concerned with evaluating the work of country surveyors, perhaps in comparison with that of the Ordnance Survey, lapses in planimetric accuracy are evidence for a damning criticism of the tithe surveys. But, what is important in the assessment of tithe maps as sources of information for present-day historical studies is to set the assessment of accuracy into a context of questions being asked of the maps. What questions are historians asking that require the level of accuracy demanded by the

Ordnance Survey for a cadastral survey? The studies reviewed in Chapter 5 reveal few such questions. Rather the accurate transfer of elements of the mid-19th-century landscape from the tithe maps to modern base maps which is a fundamental use of tithe surveys, will depend for success as much, if not more, on the amount of landscape change since tithe times as on the accuracy with which lines were drawn on the original tithe maps.

CHECKING TITHE MAPS BEFORE EXTRACTING DATA

There are a number of simple checks which all users of tithe maps might consider before extracting data. For example, it is important to know what units the lines on a particular map are separating. Most, but not all, tithe maps mark the boundaries of unenclosed parcels of land by dotted lines and enclosed fields by solid lines. Dotted lines may represent property divisions, separating holdings in an open arable field or common meadow, or they may represent either permanent or temporary divisions between lands of different utilisation in a field belonging to a single farmer.[25] It is generally possible to confirm this distinction by referring to the apportionment but contemporary private estate maps may be of some help in reaching a decision. Private estate maps of this period are, however, of only limited value for general testing of tithe surveys, because most of them were either consulted by the tithe surveyors or are themselves copied from tithe maps. Some were drawn by the same surveyor. Estate maps and sales catalogues may be of most use in checking or amplifying data on the state of cultivation.

In many tithe districts map and apportionment were compiled at different dates, so that what appear to be inconsistencies are attributable to changes having taken place in the intervening period. Where apportionment was long delayed after approval of the map, perhaps because of disputes, land represented by woodland symbols on the map might have been cleared for grass or arable by the time it was described in the apportionment; similarly, tracts mapped as heath or marsh might be returned as improved land. In a few parishes changes were actually taking place at the time of the survey and these are occasionally noted in the 'remarks' column of the apportionment. References might be made here to felling and grubbing up of tree stumps, to enclosure of commons, or to tree planting. Where farm or estate boundaries are marked on a map, similar discrepancies may be noted. Again, they can often be ascribed to the use of an outdated map, but there is a further consideration that many holdings extend beyond parish boundaries and only small parts may be represented on one map.

In all studies using tithe surveys it is essential to proceed from a close study of the map to the apportionment and if this is done conscientiously there is very little room for doubt about the overall reliability of the record.

THE RELIABILITY OF SUMMARIES OF TITHE DISTRICT LAND USE IN APPORTIONMENTS AND FILES

The preamble to the tithe agreement or award usually states whether an entire parish is included in the survey or what portions are excluded, and these statements can be verified by reference to contemporary assessments for parish rates or for poor rates. The preamble is followed by a summary of the area of land (often only that which was titheable) given over to each of the states of cultivation recognised for commutation. Similar sets of data are often to be found in the tithe files. These summary statistics have been used in several studies as sources for land-use information but there is considerable doubt about their accuracy.[26]

In very many parishes these figures are derived from estimates, and inaccuracy can occur through misestimation. Some assistant tithe commissioners such as Charles Pym stated that they specifically viewed parishes to make their estimates, but others, including William Glasson who compiled a large proportion of Cornwall reports, accepted without question land-use data supplied by local landowners. Further, the summaries often refer to a time earlier than the date of agreement (though they are usually contemporary with that of an award). Although the date of confirmation of an agreement or award for commutation is inscribed upon the first page of the tithe apportionment, the date to which land-use summaries refer is rarely recorded in the apportionment. Occasionally it is stated in the tithe file. For example, the summary for Folkestone was taken from a survey made in 1830, while at Midley in Kent it was computed from the tithe map.[27] More commonly, the summaries are prefaced by statements such as, 'by recent survey', 'by actual survey', 'by new survey', or 'by admeasurement'.[28] Other statements suggest that some summaries are of much earlier date. At Bicknor near Sittingbourne in north Kent the summary was obtained 'from an old survey', while at Maidstone it had been computed 'from an old map'.[29] Tithe-free land, or land whose tithes had already been commuted, are not always described and included in the summaries.

Comments on the accuracy of the summary schedules have been made by a number of researchers who have used them. Elwyn Cox in his thesis on Essex agriculture says, 'the totals were more generally estimates, not calculated from the summation of the areas of each individual plot, and, therefore, their accuracy is suspect'.[30] Speaking more particularly of the Essex summaries he says, 'it seems likely that the proportions between the various categories of land were reasonably accurate, and that what errors there were cancelled each other out—there is certainly no evidence to suggest that the area of any one type of land was consistently over or under-estimated at the expense of others'.[31] In the Chilterns, F.D. Hartley found that some of the summary totals added up exactly to the total acreage of a parish, but others showed slight discrepancies.[32]

It is possible, also, to make some assessment of the accuracy of the summaries by comparing them with land-use data recorded in the schedules of apportionment, although allowance must be made for the fact that these may be some years apart in date, about two years on average, infrequently less than one year and rarely more than five. Schedules of apportionment describe the state of cultivation and list measured acreages of all parcels of land. By adding these up it is possible to obtain an accurate summary of the total acreage of various types of land in a parish. Such a comparison has been made for a sample of 41 Kent parishes containing 93,570 acres, or 9.4 per cent of the county area; it confirms Cox's conclusion that there is no systematic bias towards over- or under-estimation of acreages of particular categories of land use.

While for most tithe districts the two sets of data show a close correspondence, some differences could lead to an incorrect classification in very detailed choropleth mapping. With blocks of parishes, inaccuracies cancel each other out; for individual parishes errors may be very real. It would also be unwise to use the estimates to obtain a picture of land use unless the nature and extent of land exempt from tithe is known. Discrepancies are likely to be greatest in those parts of the country with large tracts of waste land, moorland, heath, and other types of land of low value which generated little titheable produce and were not carefully estimated or measured.

ENTRIES IN THE 'STATE OF CULTIVATION' COLUMN OF APPORTIONMENTS

Perhaps the most equivocal of all information contained in schedules of apportionment is that describing the state of cultivation of tithe areas. The exact criteria used for land-use classification are not immediately obvious. However, it is clear beyond doubt that the system of recording and mapping land use proposed by R.K. Dawson in 1836 was not widely followed once the Tithe Act was amended. This means that corroboration of the 'state of cultivation' is rarely found in the form of conventional symbols on the tithe map. Woods, gardens, hops and the like could be unequivocally identified in the field and are frequently shown by symbols on the maps. But the distinction between permanent grassland and rotation grasses was not always clear-cut. It is important to know how the tithe surveyors tackled this problem and so to be aware of how they classified land as 'arable' or 'pasture'.

Initially, the commissioners' interpretation of the Tithe Commutation Act itself serves as a guide. Land which was judged to have been ploughed within the previous three years for crops, rotation grasses, or fallow was to be regarded as arable. Lands 'which have not been under the plough within three years preceding Christmas 1836' were to be recorded as grass.[33] Even if these instructions were strictly followed, problems of interpretation remained in counties where convertible husbandry was widely practised in the mid-19th century.[34] Also different practices were adopted in compiling land-use data for schedules to agreements and for reports on agreements. In 'pastoral' reports on agreements, assistant tithe commissioners and local agents were asked to enter as arable 'land actually ploughed in the present or last season, whether sown with corn, planted with roots or fallow, but excluding seeds'. In 'arable' reports and all articles of agreements, on the other hand, arable land was usually any land ploughed in the previous three years (as defined by the Act) or perhaps in the previous seven years, the period over which the Act required tithe receipts to be averaged. Although what tithe valuers recorded as arable may not have been what modern surveyors would record as arable, we may be fairly sure that it was what local contemporaries would have understood by the term. A field survey was needed in order to apportion the tithe rent-charge equitably over various classes of land in a parish unless special arrangements for apportionment were agreed. Accuracy was essential. The value of tithes was frequently assessed at about one-fifth of the arable rent and at about one-eighth or one-ninth of the grassland rent. A difference in classification could cost tithe payers considerable sums of money, which in itself helped to ensure that unreasonable definitions would be challenged. As F.D. Hartley has neatly put it, 'on the one hand the parson and lay impropriator would claim their due; on the other hand the farmers and landowners would attempt to reduce the claim as much as possible. These two forces pulling against each other would surely produce a truthful record ... always the most important piece of evidence was that observed in the field'.[35]

In many tithe apportionments grassland is described simply as 'grass', but often a finer classification into pasture, downland, moorland, meadow, marsh and saltings is employed. Meadow is usually, but not always, defined as mown grassland, its produce being expressed in hundredweights per acre in the tithe files. 'Pasture' is land that was grazed and valued in shillings per acre or by the number of stock it supported. Marshland and moorland categories are probably the least satisfactory and accurate; often marshes were included in the pasture category. In some counties these inconsistencies may be partly explained by the fact that marsh and moor grassland was not liable to tithe on produce but was subject to a nominal modus. Therefore, it was unnecessary to distinguish between various types of grassland as the modus applied irrespective of quality, type, and gross produce.

In short, when any comparison is made on the basis of land-use data from tithe surveys it is imperative to ensure that like is compared with like. Arable land, as has been shown, meant different things to tithe agents in the west and east of England and even to compilers of the tithe apportionment and the tithe file of the same district in western counties.

CROP AND LIVESTOCK DATA IN THE TITHE FILES

Few of the crop acreages, yields and livestock numbers in reports on agreements in justification of an assistant commissioner's or local agent's assessment of a fair rent-charge have been taken from an actual survey. Frequently the arable acreage, itself often an estimate, was divided by the number of courses in the generally followed rotation. Nor were yields always those that had actually been obtained in the previous harvest. For the purposes of tithe commutation, a fair par rent-charge over the years of average, 1829-35, was required and to assess this, average acreages and average yields could be more appropriate and fairer than those relating to one particular season. It is important to remember that this generalising filter was applied by local agents at a stage when they were compiling data. For example, in districts of varied soils, farmers might practise two or three rotations but yields quoted would be a parish average for each crop. T.S. Woolley noted the implications of this mode of assessment when reporting on tithe districts in different parts of Kent. Of the calculations he made at Bromley he said, 'it is not to be supposed that the course of cropping on which I have founded my calculations is universally or even generally adopted in the Parish. Almost every occupier farms his land as circumstances may seem to require, without very rigid adherence to a particular rotation of crops'.[36] Other circumstances frustrated assistant commissioners in their quest for accuracy. Woolley thought three crops to a fallow a fair assessment in Beckenham but could not get more accurate details as all the farmers had gone to a ploughing match at Chislehurst and at Shipbourne he could make no valuation on his visit on 10 February 1845 as the land was covered with snow.[37] Sometimes local agents consciously depressed yields where they were convinced that unusually high farming with above-average investment was being practised. In 1837 at West Stow in Suffolk, T.S. Woolley wrote: 'in making my calculations I have taken an average of crops on the arable land, not taking the actual produce as now cultivated—but such as I think could be relied on with ordinary farms. The present produce would probably be much greater'.[38] In Warwickshire, on the other hand, the reverse happened where local agents found that yields were not as high as they ought to have been because of the local practice of close-cropping. The yields recorded in the valuations appear much higher than might be expected from local agents' frequent descriptions of low farming in their reports. Woodland yields quoted in the files are usually of little value as usually only underwood or coppice was titheable.

Because the data often include only the titheable portion of produce and because they were estimates of what might be produced on an average rather than what actually was obtained, it is to be expected that tithe file figures will differ from those recorded by other valuations made on a particular date. A.D.M. Phillips has compared tithe file crop data for two Staffordshire parishes with acreages of crops recorded in the state of cultivation columns of the apportionments. Both sets of data for Milwich parish date from 1838 and show some similarity for wheat, oats and fallow but little correspondence in acreages of seeds and clover. In Worston, where the report on agreement was made in 1838 but the apportionment was not confirmed until 1845, there is virtually no similarity. Phillips accepts that evidence from these two places is inconclusive but cautions: 'it is clear that variations existed between these crop estimates and those crop acreages recorded in the tithe schedules. At best, the crop estimates in the questionnaires should note broadly the main crops grown within a parish'.[39] A similar comparison with Nottinghamshire data has yielded more positive results. Here Phillips discovered three districts whose reports on agreements and schedules of apportionment listing crops were compiled in the same years. He concludes, 'although there is a high level of correlation between the tithe file and the tithe schedule crop data, the crop areas in the tithe files appear generalised, with crops occupying but a small acreage tending to be omitted'.[40]

Estimates of crop yields in the reports on agreements were just as subjective as estimates of acreage but were much less easily checked by the assistant commissioners. To a large extent the Commission's representatives were in the hands of the farmers but, of course, the tithe owner was present in the background poised to protest at any flagrant understatement of gross produce.

The cautionary comments discussed so far relate to counties where an 'arable' type of agreement report form was used. They must be applied with even greater force to that smaller number of counties where 'pastoral' type forms were employed. As noted in Chapter 3, actual acreages of crops are rarely stated in 'pastoral' reports; generally, the acreage of arable excluding seeds and then the usual crop rotation are given. From these data it is possible to derive estimates of the acreages of individual crops—dividing the arable acreage by the number of courses minus the number of seeds courses in the rotation. Where, as frequently occurs, more than one rotation is given, where the courses in a rotation are not numbered, or where two crops were grown in one course this method cannot be used. For example, at Marham Church in Cornwall, William Glasson recorded a rotation of 'wheat, barley or oats—part potatoes and a small quantity of turnips'.[41] With such an imprecise description of the rotation it is clearly not possible to derive crop acreages. Further problems arise where, as in many counties in the west of England and in Wales, leys were of considerable and variable length.

For a number of reasons, great caution must be taken in using tithe file livestock data. First, and in common with some of the land-use and crop data, stock numbers are very often generalised and rounded to the nearest 10 or 100. Sheep numbers in Devon appear to be rounded to the nearest 1,000. Some generalisation is to be expected in districts with extensive tracts of high, open moorland. Difficulties of estimating sheep numbers in such areas are frequently noted in North Riding files, but some commissioners, in Cornwall for example, took pains to count exact numbers. Secondly, the time of year when observations were made clearly influenced the number of animals available for counting, particularly in the case of sheep. If tithe data relate to the middle of winter, lambs and some first-year ewes might appear in the enumerations of lowland parishes, while if taken in June, as were the later, official Agricultural Statistics, this would be the time of maximum sheep numbers in upland parishes. In some places, particularly in Gloucestershire where it was the practice to buy in sheep according to the season, Charles Pym considered that numbers varied so much that he could not attempt to put a figure to them. In Monmouthshire, assistant commissioner John Johnes decided to circumvent this by making estimates of the numbers of stock he considered ought to be kept in a parish rather than recording the number he found at the time of his visit. Thirdly, a valuation of stock in a breeding parish was more difficult than in a grazing parish where simple counting of heads might suffice. As Frederick Leigh remarked at South Molton in Devon, to produce a realistic valuation of stock in a breeding parish, 'a knowledge of the business of rearing cattle, with its attendant casualties, varieties of seasons, and other risks of local character and fluctuations in prices, acquired by much observation and practice, is requisite'.[42] Fourthly, while references by assistant tithe commissioners and local agents to attempts consciously to deceive them about land use and crops are rare, they frequently felt that they were being intentionally misled by landowners about the number of stock kept on their farms. At Kings Caple, George Bolls said, 'but with regard to the quantity of stock, I will not vouch for its correctness as I find it almost impossible to ascertain the exact numbers of stock in Hereford'.[43] As with crop statistics, there was an element of recording what ought to have been, of what might have been expected on an average, rather than what actually was.

As far as the use of the cropping and livestock data from tithe files as a source for agricultural historians and historical geographers is concerned, the inexactitude of the statistics must be borne in mind when analysing them and it is unwise to place too much reliance on the precision of data for any one place. The contents of a single tithe file may yield only a small amount of information and that not always to be relied on, but all tithe data gain in strength when those for one parish are ranged alongside those of its neighbours and those for one region against those of another.

THE OWNERS AND OCCUPIERS OF LAND

When the commissioners enquiring into the registration of land reported in 1850, the bulk of the tithe survey was complete and the possibility was raised of using tithe apportionments and maps as the basis of a system of land registration. Conveyancing land at that time was a very expensive business as a result of the need of 'manifold, intricate, chargeable, tedious and uncertain' enquiries into the title of land.[44] A general register would have diminished such burdens and the commissioners recommended that it might be based on maps tested according to Dawson's procedure for examining tithe maps and that tithe apportionments should be the model for a land index. In evidence before the commissioners in 1857, William Blamire was of the opinion that for every parish for which there was a tithe survey there would not be the slightest difficulty in preparing an accurate statement of the owners of land and a map showing their respective lands for the purposes of land registration. It would also have been quite cheap. The tithe commissioners could have prepared a statement of the names of owners directly from the apportionments.[45]

For the purposes of the Tithe Act, an owner of land meant every person in actual possession or in receipt of rents and profits from a parcel of land. The owner of property so defined was the person who paid the incidental legal expenses of commutation and the individual was almost without exception the legal owner. Some mortgagees and tenants for life were, however, assumed as owners for tithe commutation, as R.E. Sandell has found in some Wiltshire parishes for which the pattern of landownership is known from other, independent sources.[46] In reply to a question about whether the Tithe Commission investigated the legal basis of an 'owner's' interest, William Blamire replied, perfunctorily, 'Oh dear, no'.[47]

An independent check on the names of occupiers of land listed in the schedule can be made by using parish rate books. A further check is provided by the census enumerators' books compiled for the censuses of 1841 and 1851. They record, house-by-house, the names of everyone living in a parish or enumeration district at the time of the census and in 1851 also record the acreages of farms. These names appear as occupiers in the tithe apportionments and the houses should be marked on the accompanying map. A number of studies reconstructing the demographic structure of parishes in the mid-19th century have combined tithe and census data and have commented on the accuracy with which the tithe apportionments record the names of land occupiers (see Chapter 5).

ALTERED TITHE APPORTIONMENTS

A few late altered apportionments may be compared directly with the first edition Ordnance Survey 1:2500 plans to test their accuracy. In a few exceptional instances, the land-use information in the Books of Reference compiled in connection with the 1:2500 plans published before 1880 and also the acreages of arable, grass and orchards in the Agricultural Statistics collected annually after 1866 may be compared with the tithe surveys. But no valid conclusions as to the accuracy of the original tithe surveys may be drawn from such comparisons because new apportionments for whole parishes were only required when field arrangements and land use were completely transformed by incidents such as enclosure. Moreover, some data recorded in the Ordnance Survey Books of Reference and in the Agricultural Statistics which appear to be equivalent are not strictly comparable with those in the tithe surveys.

5
TITHE SURVEYS AS A HISTORICAL SOURCE

The mid-19th-century tithe surveys are among the most frequently consulted classes of documents at the Public Record Office and in county and local archives. Large-scale tithe maps delineate parish boundaries and township boundaries, field boundaries, roads, waterbodies, buildings and other features. Accompanying apportionments provide statements of the total value of tithes, the method of apportioning the total sum by land parcels, schedules of areas and names of parcels, lists of names of landowners and occupiers and information on land use. Tithe files contain records of the process of commutation, reports on proceedings towards agreements and awards and calculations of tithe values. The files also contain descriptions of rural landscapes, and accounts of land management, improvements, rotations, crops, livestock husbandry and other activities.

Historians have used tithe surveys on their own and in conjunction with other sources. Tithe maps alone are the most important sources for tracing boundaries of parishes, townships and fields before major changes took place in the 19th century. Tithe maps also depict building plans and roads. Maps and schedules of apportionment need to be used together for reconstructing uses of land as woods, parks, marshes, heaths, moors, arable and pasture. Information on farming is drawn mostly from tithe files. Apportionments and maps are the principal sources for data on landowners and occupiers. In studying family histories, sources that may be used alongside tithe surveys include registers of births, marriages and deaths, census returns, lists of electors and rate assessments.

BOUNDARIES

Tithe maps are uniquely accurate, comprehensive records of boundaries of parishes, townships and fields on the eve of sweeping changes. Parish and township boundaries had remained largely unaltered since the 15th century. Field boundaries had been changing since the early 16th century: first, through encroachment into and reclamation of woods and wastes; secondly, by piecemeal enclosure of open fields; thirdly, by parliamentary enclosure of whole villages, exchanging and consolidating scattered strips and partitioning commons. In studies of early field systems and other relict landscape features, tithe surveys are of the greatest value where earlier sources of information are lacking and should be used only if drawbacks attending their recent date are respected.[1]

Parish and township boundaries
The tithe surveys provide the first nationwide delineation of parish, township, and hamlet (tithe district) boundaries and in many counties are the most complete record of their configuration before extensive changes were enacted in the last three decades of the

19th century. Both the Poor Law Commission and the Registrar General needed to know the extent of parishes for purposes of rating, registration and census enumeration. The Ordnance Survey was commissioned to engrave and publish tithe district boundaries on an edition of the one-inch Old Series maps known as the 'Index to Tithe Survey'.[2] Measured acreages of parishes and townships from tithe surveys are recorded in the abstract of the 1851 census.

The report on the 1851 census expresses dissatisfaction with the irregular shapes and sizes of parish boundaries: 'The old division of the country into parishes, townships, and counties, is open to many … objections … Parishes are, in many instances, almost inextricably intermingled; and they vary in population from single families to tens of thousands of families; in extent, from a few hundreds of acres to many thousands of acres.'[3] Over much of England, south and east of a line from the Humber to the Bristol Channel, most parishes were small in size, a majority under 3,000 acres. Parishes in the Weald, Fens and Wessex heathlands were larger than average for the southeast. In north-west England, large parishes, many above 12,000 acres in extent, were characteristic.[4] These large northern parishes were divided into townships and for purposes of administering poor laws, repairing highways, enumerating population and commuting tithes, townships were the smallest effective units of local government. Maps of tithe districts have been compiled from the Ordnance Survey 'Index to Tithe Survey', supplemented by examining some original tithe maps and Ordnance Survey 1:10,560 maps.[5]

Parish boundaries recorded in tithe surveys serve as a base-line from which later boundary changes may be traced. Notes made by assistant tithe commisioners explain the origins and later histories of some tithings, chapelries and extra-parochial places. Tithe files also contain minutes of evidence summarising inquiries and discussions concerning disputed parish boundaries, setting out reasons for decisions taken by assistant commis-sioners. These are of interest to ecclesiastical and political historians. By referring to tithe maps, some hitherto unconfirmed parish boundary markers have been identified. Markers were generally placed where a boundary crossed a highway, on a bridge spanning a stream where a boundary followed the middle of a channel, or over an open common lacking identifiable features. Some markers were depicted on tithe maps; others were recorded by the Ordnance Survey on their 1:2500 and 1:10,560 maps between 1841 and 1888.[6]

Tithe surveys were carried out at a time when population was increasing rapidly in some parishes, migration from many districts was accelerating and new employment opportunities were opening over much of England. In response to demographic, social, economic and political changes, functions and responsibilities of local government were reorganised. Parishes gradually lost all their powers. In 1836, ecclesiastical parishes were territories having their own churches and clergymen, generally receiving their own tithes. Before the institution of civil registration in July 1837, they were places where baptisms, marriages and burials were registered.

Parishes were subdivisions of counties. They were responsible for collecting rates and providing relief for the poor. The old, the sick, the demented, orphaned children, waifs, strays, foundlings and others in need of food, shelter and clothing were charges on the parish. In 1831, over one in ten of the population of England and Wales, probably about one and a half million individuals, received poor relief at one time or another during that year. Total expenditure, paid by parish ratepayers, amounted to £7,037,000 and parish poor rates were the heaviest burdens borne by rural ratepayers.[7] After the Poor Law Amendment Act was passed in 1834, new workhouses were established, governed by boards of guardians and financed by unions of parishes. In unions where boards of guardians required a new valuation, the Poor Law Commissioners might order 'a Survey, with or without a Map or Plan,' to be made. Copies of some maps prepared for poor rate assessments were submitted to the Tithe Commission for purposes of tithe commutation.[8] Many workhouses are depicted on these and other tithe maps.

One after another, during the period of tithe commutation, public services performed by parish officers were taken over by central government departments and newly constituted local boards employing full-time paid staff. Following the reform of the poor law, changes in the administration of local highways were enacted in 1835, policing was reformed in 1839 and in the 1840s, new laws were introduced to improve sanitation, health and public recreation. Other acts authorised public utility companies to supply clean water and street lighting. Police stations, peoples' parks, waterworks and gasworks appear on a few tithe maps. Sidney and Beatrice Webb describe the changing functions of parishes and W.E. Tate provides an authoritative guide to parish records.[9]

Field boundaries and field names

Most tithe maps show field (tithe area) boundaries and accompanying schedules of apportionment record names and areas of parcels. These are accurate and detailed, if late, evidence for studies of field systems and field names. Examination of tithe maps for many parts of England and Wales has brought to light numerous traces of unenclosed strips (Fig. 35). Tithe maps provide evidence for widespread cultivation in open fields in Worcester, Hereford, Shropshire and Cheshire.[10] In many districts in Wales, maps show arable open fields that were subdivided into strips or quillets. These arable fields covered a small proportion of the total area. Other fields in the same parishes were under grass: some were ploughed from time to time, some were managed as permanent meadows and some were kept as rough hill pastures. In the south-west peninsula of England, similar arrangements were recorded. Small, permanently cultivated fields were divided into unenclosed strips and tracts of grassland were occasionally ploughed and taken into temporary enclosures for cultivation. On light soils in the midlands, temporary intakes or breaks from heath and rough grazing were associated with small permanently cultivated open fields. Ideal forms of infield-outfield arrangement were represented in the Breckland and other sandy districts in the eastern counties (Fig. 36).

Tithe maps provide a wealth of information about shapes, sizes and forms of fields in the early nineteenth century. They indicate that unenclosed arable strips were widespread to the west of the Midland area defined by H.L. Gray, a pioneer in the use of tithe maps for reconstructing field systems. Infield-outfield arrangements have also been discovered in localities as far apart as Cornwall in the west, Suffolk in the east and Durham in the north of England. The maps do not indicate how these field arrangements functioned or whether they may be interpreted as relics of medieval systems. The depiction of open-field strips on tithe maps requires further evidence to show that such lands were subject to common field courses of cropping or communal grazing. The development of characteristic field systems in different regions is discussed by Alan Baker and Robin Butlin and a general theory of the formation of field systems is put forward by Robert Dodgshon.[11]

Field-name elements such as *furlong, flatt, shott, rigg, gore* and *butt* are medieval in origin. Some subdivided open fields are designated in apportionments as 'common fields' or 'town fields' and outfield parcels are named 'breaks' or 'intakes'. In some tithe files rights of grazing over commons and fallows are mentioned. The practice of regular fallowing may suggest a survival of an early system of farming. Sites of deserted medieval

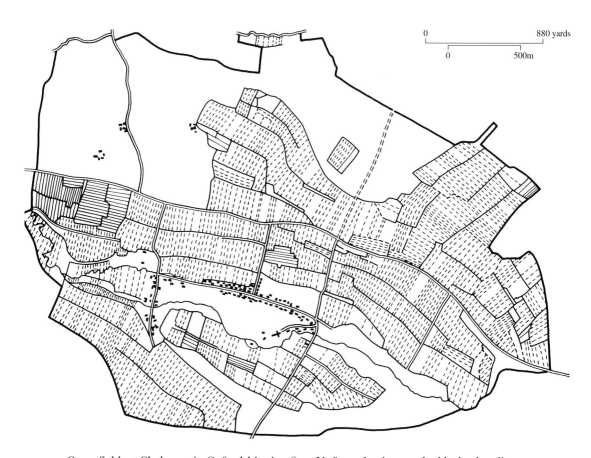

35   Open fields at Chalgrove in Oxfordshire in 1840. Unfenced strips, marked by broken lines, were ranged in arable open fields around a nucleated village. Ring-fenced farms lay on the northern and western edges of the parish. Source: H.L. Gray, *English field systems* (Cambridge, Mass., Harvard University Press 1915), 22.

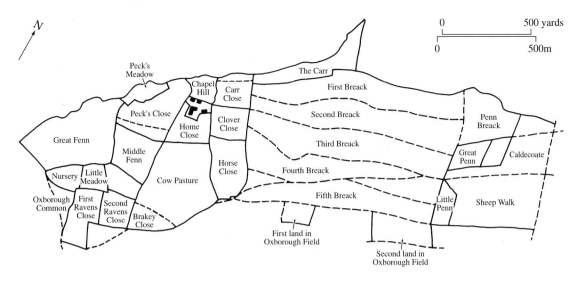

36 Infield-outfield at Caldecote, Norfolk, about 1851. In the west of the parish were low lying fen pastures. Meadows and arable closes were situated around the homestead. Stretching away to the east, on higher, drier ground, were five open brecks, broken (ploughed) and cultivated in turn for a few years. Beyond these lay unbroken sheep-walks. Source: J.E.G. Mosby, *Norfolk* (Land Utilisation Survey of Great Britain Report, Part 79, 1938), 131.

villages may be identified by names of farms or fields. By the time of the tithe surveys very few features apart from churches and ancient trackways can be confidently ascribed to pre-modern origins.

In old enclosed landscapes, changes in land use and farming practice may be inferred from discrepancies between field names and states of cultivation recorded in tithe apportionments. In east Suffolk, about a quarter of the area in fields named 'meadow' was used as arable in 1840.[12] Tithe maps are a useful source of evidence for dating hedgerows, confirming that particular boundaries existed at a specific date. Local historians have taken the initiative in recommending that field and minor names recorded in the tithe apportionments be adopted as names for new streets, housing estates, schools or hospitals. Most local authorities are pleased to preserve or revive historic names.

BUILDINGS AND ROADS

The tithe surveys provide an important datum line in the study of settlement patterns. Tithe maps accompanied by names and descriptions of premises provide a wealth of information about buildings and roads in the early 19th century. Most maps are drawn at scales large enough to represent building plans in detail and distinguish, by colour or shading, inhabited houses from uninhabited buildings. Public buildings, churches, chapels, important industrial and commercial establishments are frequently named on maps and names of inns, schools and manor houses are generally entered in apportionments under name and description of premises. Maps also differentiate between fenced and unfenced roads and paths. Some turnpike roads are identified but only a small proportion of other roads are named. Street names are often inscribed on maps of towns. During the century and a half since a tithe map was drawn the layout of a settlement may have changed very little or it may have been almost entirely transformed. The position of a church or other landmark will enable the present street plan to be compared with that represented in 1840.

Tithe maps provide detailed evidence for examining settlement morphology and analysing the spatial structure of built environments. To discover the people who inhabited those structures, historians have to retrieve names of owners and occupiers from tithe apportionments and match them with houses listed in census returns, rate books and other sources. Research into 'house repopulation' is discussed in a later section on rural society.

Settlement patterns

On mid-19th-century tithe maps, villages and hamlets are depicted at the end of their development as agrarian settlements, before the exodus of people to towns and before the advent of urban features such as railway stations to the countryside. Some tithe maps show the extent of village greens before enclosure encroached upon them or before rows of cottages tumbled into ruins. Some villages formed compact clusters around a church, a manor house, a village green, a bridge or a spring. Some were loosely strung out along a street, some had secondary settlements centred on a church, a chapel, mill, mine or two or three farms at the head of a valley. In some places, farmhouses and farm buildings were set alongside one another in a village street, in other places they were situated away from a village in the midst of their own fields. In some places, settlements were closely spaced along the line of a highway, in other places they were widely scattered. Christopher Taylor and Brian Roberts provide valuable introductions to the study of settlement layouts.[13] Some parishes were crowded with rows of cottages and alehouses, others had few inhabited houses. In some closed villages where a dominant landowner prevented families of labouring poor gaining settlement and entitlement to poor relief, some cottages shown on the tithe map were unoccupied. Dennis Mills has written a useful guide to open and closed villages, discussing problems of hiring farm labourers and paying for poor relief.[14]

In studies of urban areas, tithe surveys have been largely neglected. The usefulness of tithe maps and apportionments for identifying streets, buildings, land owners and occupiers of urban land has been noted by Brian Harley.[15] For tracing building plans and property boundaries in medieval towns, earlier and more detailed maps are preferred, but in the absence of reliable alternative sources, tithe surveys may be consulted. Terry Slater has measured dimensions of medieval burgage plots from tithe maps for towns in the west midlands.[16] Maurice Beresford has identified selions in fields of a 13th-century new town at Warkworth, Northumberland from blocks of parcels named on a tithe survey as 'The Tens' and 'New Town Butts'.[17] The tithe surveys present a pre-urban cadaster or ownership map for areas that were built over after 1840. David Ward has shown how streets in nineteenth-century Leeds were laid out within a framework of pre-existing property boundaries.[18] In planning building development, field boundaries might be ignored except where they were also boundaries of ownership. The pattern of streets was moulded by the shape of estates (Fig. 37). H.J. Dyos has recognised a similar relationship between property boundaries and shapes and sizes of building plots in the planning of Victorian Camberwell. Michael Jahn and others have demonstrated the survival of pre-urban features from tithe maps. In west London suburbs, traces of farm and field boundaries and village streets persisted after the coming of the railway.[19]

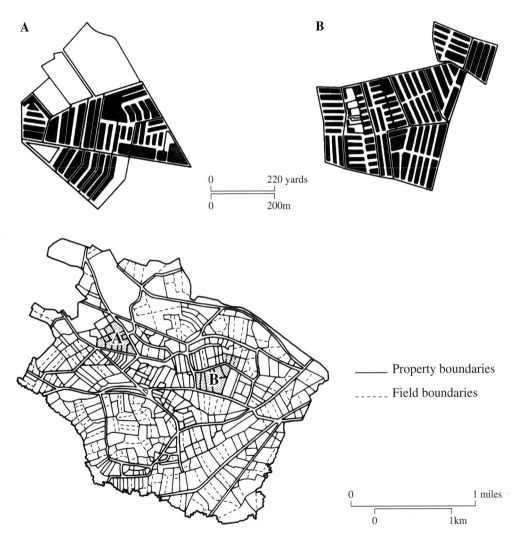

37 Pre-urban property boundaries and urban development in the Potternewton district of Leeds. The angular intersections of Victorian streets and terraces were planned to fit within property boundaries. Source: David Ward, 'The pre-urban cadaster and the urban pattern of Leeds', *Annals of the Association of American Geographers*, 52 (1962), 150-66.

Roads, tracks and paths

Tithe maps are of especial interest in recording roads, tracks and paths, and the surveys
have served as evidence for the defence and restitution of disputed rights of way.[20] Tithe
maps do not state directly whether roads were used or not and very few maps indicate
whether they were public or private. At Linstead in Suffolk, two roads are labelled 'public
right of way' and a map for Capel le Ferne in Kent names a 'right of road'. Some maps
represent all roads in colour but others represent only a part of the road network in
colour. Some maps identify roads by generic names such as 'occupation road', or 'foot
road'. Frequently, roads are noted as leading 'to' or 'from' a named settlement and, in
the absence of conflicting evidence, these have been presumed to be public roads, but it
is rarely possible to say from tithe maps whether they were carriageways, bridle ways or
footpaths (Fig. 38). Names of roads or streets inscribed on tithe maps throw light on
many different aspects of a locality's early history.[21]

For local historians, information about roads and paths is of value in showing how,
in the early 19th century, people were able to journey on foot and on horseback between
villages and towns and to outlying places in the same or in neighbouring parishes. Many
people in the country walked several miles each day to and from work. They went to
market once or twice a week. More than once a day they had to fetch pails of water from
a well and carry wood for their fires. Access to commons for grazing, fuel and rabbits was
important for some villagers. The network of roads and paths was denser than at present
but traffic moved much more slowly, mostly at walking pace, at the speed of the slowest
animal in a herd of cows, with frequent rests on uphill slopes and long waits for ferries at
river crossings. Local roads were unmetalled and apt to be dusty in summer and deeply
muddy in winter. Repairs consisted of scouring wayside ditches, filling potholes and miry
patches, cutting back hedges and lopping overhanging branches. Farm carts loaded with
hay and sheaves of corn could pass along most local roads only in dry weather in summer.
In tithe files, reports on local roads describe their condition as 'good' in 530 parishes in
England and Wales and 'poor' in 463 parishes. Unfavourable reports remark on the bad
state of roads in clay lowlands and hilly country, a fact which increased the cost of collecting
and marketing tithe in kind in these areas and affected assistant tithe commissioners'
judgements of what would be a fair monetary equivalent for tithe. Almost exactly the
same remarks had been made about the same places in county reports to the Board of
Agriculture written at the beginning of the 19th century.

The expansion of manufacturing and trade created an entirely new demand for
road improvements. Roads were expected to carry fast stage coaches and heavy wagons.
Wheeled traffic required hard, smooth surfaces to run on. Turnpike trusts were formed
by local initiative to provide suitable surfaces and charge tolls for maintaining them.
Turnpike roads are distinguished on 907 tithe maps, 8 per cent of the total. The highest
proportions were in Cheshire, Derbyshire, Durham, Herefordshire, Lancashire, Monmouthshire, Staffordshire, Worcestershire and West Yorkshire and were most numerous
in industrial districts in these counties. In 1838, about 22,000 miles of roads were turnpiked
and 104,770 miles of roads were still maintained by parishes.[22]

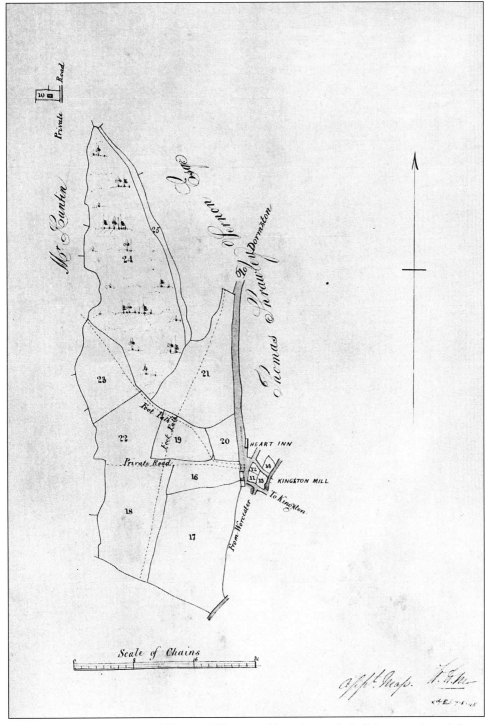

Private Road

10

To Praw to Dormston

Thomas Vernon Esqr

Mr Curtin

24

25

23

21

22   19   20   HEART INN

Foot Path

Foot Path

Private Road

16   KINGSTON MILL

18   From Worcester   To Kingston

17

Scale of Chains

Appt Maps

38 Rights of way in part of Kington, Worcestershire, about 1848. Private roads and foot-paths are indicated and the roads 'to Dormston', 'to Kington' and 'from Worcester' are named. The numbering of tithe areas is discontinuous and this map may derive from the enclosure map of *c*.1782 of which no surviving copy is known [PRO IR 30 39/77]. Reproduced by permission of the Keeper of the Public Record Office.

LAND USE

The tithe surveys are the fullest and most reliable source of information on land use around 1840. Most tithe maps represent by conventional signs or by colour, woods, coppices, plantations and parks. In some areas they also depict heaths, marshes, orchards, hop grounds, gardens and exposures of rocks. On a few maps arable and grass are differentiated by tinting. In the 1930s, the first nation-wide exploitation of the wealth of information from tithe surveys led to the compilation of maps of land use for comparison with those being prepared by the first Land Utilisation Survey of Great Britain. L. Dudley Stamp, the director of the survey, recognised that tithe surveys provided 'an invaluable source of information' for constructing 'a Land Utilisation map of approximately a century ago'.[23] Since the Second World War, particularly since 1960, great advances have been made in mapping land use data. Broad regional contrasts in 19th-century England and Wales are now clear and the distribution of arable land has been mapped on a field-by-field basis and from parish summaries for much of East Anglia, the Home Counties and southern England. Northern England and the west country await detailed study and further research remains to be done on non-agricultural land.

Woods, plantations and parks

In many parts of 19th-century England, the cutting of ancient woods slowed down as consumption of wood and charcoal for domestic fires declined. Coke was substituted for charcoal in iron smelting and glass making; iron was substituted for timber in building mills and factories; imported softwoods were substituted for native hardwoods in house building and furniture making. Districts that had been stripped almost bare of trees by the end of the Napoleonic wars began to recover a wooded appearance. In addition to self-sown seedlings filling gaps in old woodlands, many timber trees were planted at intervals in quickset hedges. Some tithe maps show the character of hedges in great detail. New plantations were formed within and around edges of parks and landscape gardens. Names and descriptions in tithe apportionments indicate changes in the location of woods. Many parcels of land bearing names of old woods and clearings are recorded in state of cultivation columns as arable or grass. Conversely, some parcels described as fields are recorded as being used for plantations, coppices or woods. Comparisons between descriptions of woods at different dates reflect changes in composition such as from wood to coppice or from oak-wood to beech plantation. Occasionally, tree symbols on maps imply a change from hardwoods to conifers. Tithe surveys provide incomplete coverage of woodland because in many districts woods were exempt from payments of tithes.

Features of parks are often copied from private estate maps and may represent landscapes at an earlier date than that of the tithe award. The depiction of parkland is uneven. It is represented on more than half the maps for Hertfordshire, on 22 per cent of Bedfordshire maps, on 17 per cent of Buckinghamshire maps, but on only 11 per cent of maps in neighbouring Oxfordshire. Some parks are shown in great detail (Fig. 39). Different species of trees are mapped at Madeley in Shropshire but ornamental features at Blenheim, Chatsworth, Woburn and other celebrated landscape gardens are not depicted.

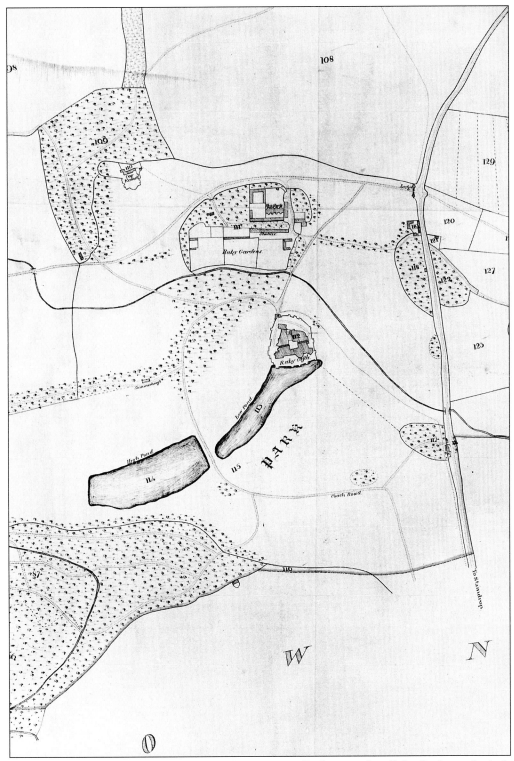

39 Parkland on the tithe map of Raby and Keverstone, Durham, *c*.1839. Raby Castle overlooked a low pond. Raby gardens, stables and dog kennels are shown in separate enclosures. Lodges and a coach road are also labelled [PRO IR 30 11/213]. Reproduced by permission of the Keeper of the Public Record Office.

Marshes, heaths and moors

By 1840 tracts of undrained meres and marshes in Shropshire, Cheshire, Lancashire, Nottinghamshire, Yorkshire, Lincolnshire, Cambridgeshire, Norfolk and along the Thames estuary were being drained with new deep ditches. Steam pumps are mentioned in tithe files for five places in Cambridgeshire, one place in Norfolk, one in Nottinghamshire and one in Somerset. In clayland districts, soil drainage was improved by various methods of underdrainage and tile drains had recently been introduced in different parts of the country. Tile drainage is mentioned in tithe files at nine places in Norfolk, at eight places in Shropshire, at four places in Suffolk, at two places in Cheshire, at two in Nottinghamshire, at two in Staffordshire, and at one place each in Cambridgeshire, Durham, Kent, Northumberland and Oxfordshire.

Tracts of heath and sheepwalk on light sandy soils in southern England continued to be broken up and brought into cultivation. A comparison between tithe estimates dating from 1837 to 1846 and areas of heath represented on relevant portions of late 18th-century county maps suggests that about one-fifth of the former area of Breckland heaths disappeared in a span of little more than half a century.[24] On light soils in south Lincolnshire, tithe estimates of cultivated land indicate that a peak of heath reclamation occurred in the mid-19th century, not earlier.[25]

The last great advance on the margin of cultivation in England was at the expense of moors. In many upland districts, newly enclosed land was not brought into regular cereal production but was sown with mixtures of grass seeds to produce crops of hay and to improve the quality of grazing. In parts of Wales, in west Cornwall, in Cumberland, in north Lancashire and on the east moor of Derbyshire, arable cultivation reached its highest limits at the time of the tithe surveys. In mid-Ribblesdale, however, some fields named 'barley croft' and 'wheat field' were recorded in the state of cultivation column as meadow and pasture, implying that former cropland had been laid down to grass.[26] The most searching and comprehensive studies of the changing position of the moorland edge have been conducted by John Chapman on the North York Moors and in Monmouthshire (Fig. 40). In north Yorkshire tithe surveys mark the uppermost limit of cultivation but in Monmouthshire the highest point was reached before the Napoleonic wars and there appears to have been more reversion to waste than intaking in the uplands in the periods from 1780 to 1800 and from 1815 to 1835.[27]

Arable land

Arable cultivation attained its maximum extent between 1840 and 1870. A comparison of acreages of arable recorded in the tithe surveys with arable acreages reported in the agricultural statistics for 1872 and those recorded in the area books for the first edition 1:2500 Ordnance Survey plans *c.*1875 indicate that tithe surveys were completed a few years before the maximum. Some differences in area resulted from different methods of collecting and compiling data but most reflected changes in agriculture (Table 1). From 1873, when wheat imports first exceeded home production, and 1879, when the price of wheat fell below 45 shillings per quarter, the area of land in crops continued to fall to

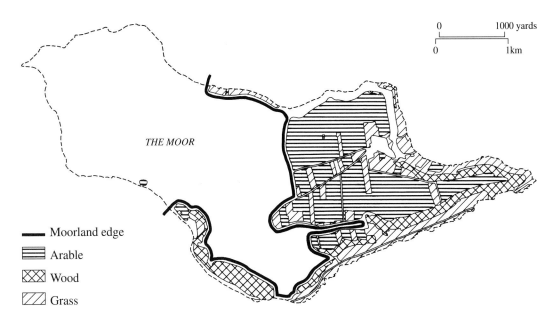

0   1000 yards

0   1km

THE MOOR

▬▬ Moorland edge

▤ Arable

▨ Wood

▧ Grass

40 Land use and the moorland edge at Levisham, North Yorkshire, in 1847. The position of the moor wall formed a continuous limit to cultivation at this period. Source: J. Chapman, 'Changing agriculture and the moorland edge in the North York Moors, 1750-1960', University of London M.A. thesis (1961).

reach a minimum in the 1930s. The Land Utilisation Survey of Great Britain, directed by L. Dudley Stamp, recorded the state of cultivation at the depth of the depression and many county reports draw comparisons between the distribution of arable land mapped in the 1930s and at the time of the tithe surveys.

The first study of changes in land use from 1840 to 1932 was conducted by E.C. Willatts, secretary of the Land Utilisation Survey.[28] Willatts had long known of the existence of the tithe surveys because the apportionment for his native parish of Wraysbury in Buckinghamshire had been reproduced in a local history published in 1862. A copy of the accompanying map, mounted and heavily varnished, hung in the office of an estate agent in Windsor. This survey and others for neighbouring parishes had been carried out by the same firm and Willatts was invited to make tracings. At about the same time, the secretary of the tithe commissioners offered to show Stamp and Willatts the contents of the tithe archives. Following this introduction, members of the Land Utilisation Survey were granted permission to pursue their searches among the records free of the usual charges. Willatts' method was to study land use in sample parishes, mapping the distribution of arable, grass, woods, heaths, houses and gardens in the 1930s and around 1840 (Fig. 41). In many places in the London basin, the arable area had declined in the face of invasion by both the area under grass and the built-up area. Areas of woods and heaths decreased very slightly.

At the time Willatts was exploring the Tithe Commission records, H.C.K. Henderson was independently inspecting tithe surveys in parish chests in mid-Sussex. Henderson

Table 1

Area of arable, meadow and pasture and cultivated land in England and Wales 1770-1872

Date	Source	Arable land (acres)	Meadow and Pasture (acres)	Cultivated Area (acres)	Ratio of arable:grass
1770	Arthur Young	10,300,000	16,700,000	27,000,000	0.67
1801a	B.P. Capper	11,350,501	16,796,458	28,146,959	0.68
1801b	Crop return	7,860,000	-	-	-
1808	W.T. Comber	11,575,000	17,495,000	29,070,000	0.66
1827	W. Couling	11,143,370	17,605,630	28,749,000	0.63
1840	Tithe files	15,092,555	16,363,409	31,455,964	0.92
1851	James Caird	13,667,000	13,332,000	26,999,000	1.02
1854	Agricultural Statistics	15,261,842	12,392,137	27,653,979	1.23
1872	Agricultural Statistics	18,136,369	11,522,712	29,659,081	1.57

Sources:

1770 – Arthur Young, *The farmer's tour through the East of England* (London, 1771), vol. IV, 256-61, 455-92

1801a – B.P. Capper, *A statistical account of the population and cultivation, produce and consumption of England and Wales* (London, 1801)

1801b – M. Turner, 'Arable in England and Wales: estimates from the 1801 crop return', *Journal of Historical Geography*, 7 (1981), 291-302 (excluding fallow etc.)

1808 – W.T. Comber, *An inquiry into the state of national subsistence* (London, 1808); on Capper and Comber see also H.C. Prince, 'England *c.* 1800', in H.C. Darby (ed.), *A new historical geography of England* (Cambridge, 1973), 403

1827 – W. Couling, 'Evidence to House of Commons Select Committee on emigration from the United Kingdom, 1827', cited in G.R. Porter, *The progress of the nation*, 2nd edition (London, 1847), 155-8

1840 – Estimates of land use in the tithe files. Only those data covering more than 90 per cent of the tithe district are included; county figures have been obtained by multiplying the sum of the available tithe file acreages by weighting factors equivalent to total county area : area of county with tithe-file data; county figures were then aggregated to produce national figures (excluding seeds in western counties; includes some 'rough grazings')

1851 – Caird, *English agriculture in 1850-51* (London, 1852), 522

1854 – BPP (HC) LIII, 495, Agricultural statistics (England), 1854. General summary of returns. (The arable acreage includes clover and seeds)

1872 – L.D. Stamp, *The land of Britain, its use and misuse*, 3rd edition (London 1962), appendix 8

was interested in the changing extent of arable land over a long period, comparing areas shown on large-scale county maps of the 18th century, tithe surveys, Ordnance Survey Books of Reference for the 1870s and Land Utilisation Survey maps. His method was to map a large block of country, relating changes to different soils and economic conditions. The maximum extent of arable on heavy soils in this area of southern England is represented on the tithe surveys (Fig. 42). Henderson also examined changes in a band of country stretching across Derbyshire from the crest of the Pennines to the eastern border. He supervised research on tithe surveys by a number of graduate students at Birkbeck College London but the project was discontinued at the outbreak of the Second World War.[29]

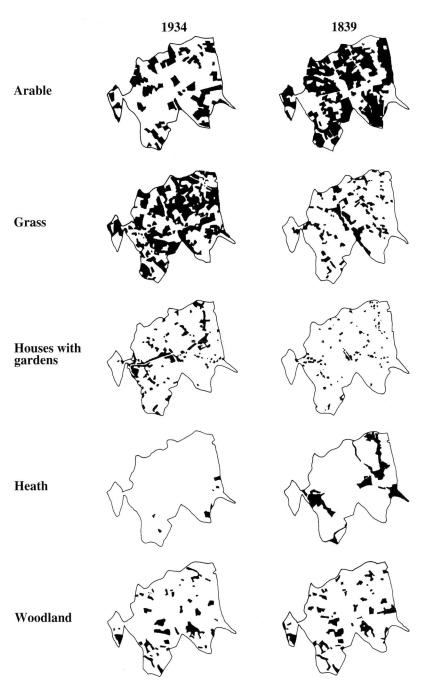

41 Changing land use in a Chiltern parish: Great Missenden, Buckinghamshire, in 1934 and 1839. The area of land in grass and houses with gardens increased whilst arable land and heath decreased. Source: E.C. Willatts, *Middlesex and the London region* (Land Utilisation Survey of Great Britain Report, Part 79, 1937).

42 Arable land in the Adur basin, Sussex. The area covers about 300 square miles, about half of which was under the plough about 1845. Source: H.C.K. Henderson, 'Our changing agriculture: the distribution of arable land in the Adur basin, Sussex from 1780 to 1931', *Journal of the Ministry of Agriculture*, 43 (1936), 625-33.

The largest and most complex study of arable from the tithe surveys, carried out in connection with the Land Utilisation Survey, was published in J.E.G. Mosby's report on Norfolk.[30] Mosby's study covers an area of about a thousand square miles in west Norfolk and relates cultivation not only to soil and changing economic conditions but also to differences in land tenure and farming practices. The account deals with field arrangements, fold courses (a local practice of folding sheep over common arable fields) and crop rotations. A few local histories written before 1939 refer to tithe surveys in discussions of land use and farming. Post-war volumes of the *Victoria County History* draw upon tithe surveys for areas in different land use categories, comparing these measurements with data for other periods.

After 1950, work on the tithe surveys was resumed under the direction of H.C. Darby at University College London. Darby was interested in the tithe records as a statistical source to be compared with Domesday Book of 1086. From tithe map and apportionment data, maps of different land use categories have been compiled for large blocks of country. The first comprehensive study of land use in the Chilterns, a tract of 1,300 square miles, was carried out by David Hartley.[31] Hartley's work broke new ground in relating agricultural practices to soils, prices, sizes of farms and estates and interrelations between different types of land use. He also devised an efficient method of abstracting data from the tithe surveys and plotting them on modern base maps. His method can be summarised as follows.

Transferring information from a tithe apportionment and tithe map to a modern base map

To facilitate the task of abstracting items of information from a tithe apportionment and map and plotting them on a modern base map, it is recommended that a new abstraction form be compiled. On a sheet of ruled paper the lines should be numbered consecutively from 1 to the highest number listed in the tithe apportionment. The numbers are those of tithe areas, parcels of land for which tithes were separately apportioned, referring to numbers on the tithe map. Most tithe schedules list tithe areas in alphabetical order of landowners and their tenants. Where landholdings were spatially fragmented or intermixed with properties of other owners, it is difficult to find corresponding numbers on the tithe map. The search for tithe area numbers is simplified by looking for them in strictly numerical order. On the new abstraction form, information from the state of cultivation column may be abstracted as a letter-coded land use category, such as A for arable, M for meadow, H for heath, W for wood or G for garden. Names of landowners and occupiers may be abbreviated to the first four letters of a surname and two initials. Thus James St George Dormer may be abbreviated as DORMJS, the earl of Leicester as LEIC, omitting his title, and the Eastern Counties Railway as ECR. It is convenient to transfer the coded information to a modern base map, referring to the tithe map to locate tithe area numbers. An Ordnance Survey 1:25,000 map is ideal for an enclosed parish; a 1:10,000 map is more suitable where tithe areas are unenclosed strips. With coloured pencils a land use map can be drawn directly from information on the new form. This procedure not only saves time in cross-referencing between an unwieldy tithe apportionment and a very large map, but it is also automatically self-checking. Failure to abstract information from the apportionment is revealed by gaps on the abstraction form, whilst failure to transfer all information to the base map is revealed by gaps on the coloured land-use map.

Michael Naish, another of Darby's students at University College London, took land use studies a step further in his research on the changing agricultural landscape of the Hampshire chalklands.[32] Naish looked closely at varied combinations of agricultural land uses, showing how farms contained different proportions of arable, downland pasture, water meadow, dry meadow, pasture, heath, common and woodland. He was among the first geographers to discover that tithe files contain questionnaires estimating crop acreages and describing farming practices. This opened the way to fuller studies of crop and animal husbandry. A study of agricultural changes in north-west Wiltshire by Brian Dittmer, another University College student, examined relationships between arable, meadow, pasture, commons and woodland.[33] By the time of the tithe surveys, over 70 per cent of heavy soils in that western region were recorded as being under grass. A fellow student, Elwyn Cox, completed a county-wide survey of Essex, whose one million acres represent the largest tract of land for which field-by-field distribution maps of all categories of land use have been compiled.[34] This was a great feat of organisation. The study also makes important advances in refining measurements of different types of land use and ratios between arable and grass.

In midland shires, where tithes had been abolished for whole parishes or parts of parishes under enclosure awards, coverage of tithe surveys is patchy and it is not possible to reconstruct land use maps for large continuous blocks of land. Attempts have been made, with varying degrees of caution and confidence, to evaluate and interpret parish estimates of arable and grass acreages in the apportionments. Within territories of county size, the estimates may be used to assess broadly the magnitude of contrasts between farming regions and draw comparisons with earlier and later evidence. The estimates may show a bias towards meadow and pasture in parishes where acreages refer to land remaining subject to tithes after arable open fields had been enclosed and rendered tithe-free. In other parishes, estimates cover all land, including areas exempt from tithes. In some midland parishes, enclosure was followed by laying down arable to grass but, in many districts, the arable area remained unchanged. Studies in east Yorkshire and east Worcestershire have used evidence from apportionments selectively.[35] More recent studies, carried out by Tony Phillips at the University of Keele, have used information from tithe files for Staffordshire, Nottinghamshire and Herefordshire to supplement or substitute for estimates from tithe apportionments.[36]

Acreages of arable land recorded in tithe surveys for south-west England include land occasionally ploughed but sown with grass seeds and kept under grass for three or more years, in some places up to ten years. Tithe survey parish estimates do not distinguish between these long leys and regularly cropped land. In Cornwall, tithe estimates give a false impression that arable land covered between 50 per cent and 70 per cent of most parishes and that meadow and pasture occupied less than 10 per cent of the surface. The area of grass is greatly understated.[37] In southern and eastern England, more reliable figures from parish and township estimates in tithe files have been used to calculate proportions occupied by different categories of land use.[38]

Market gardens, orchards, hops, reeds and osiers
Most studies of land use have focused on areas under grass and arable and the relation between the two categories but intensive types of use merit special consideration. The tithe surveys offer reliable information on orchards, hops, reeds and osiers because these

types of use either bore extraordinary rent-charges or were allowed some relief from assessed values if the use of the land changed. No special supplement was charged for market gardens but valuations were higher than for other arable land because productivity was higher. Around London and other cities, areas of market gardens are identified in tithe apportionments and are remarked upon in tithe files. A few tithe files include notes on the quality of market gardens, rating some more highly than others.

Small orchards were present in every part of England and were particularly numerous in the west country, in Devonshire, Somerset, Gloucestershire, Herefordshire, Worcestershire and Shropshire. They were also numerous in the south and east, in Suffolk, Sussex and, above all, in Kent, the leading fruit-growing county. Commercial orchards were generally valued more highly than small plantations producing fruit for family consumption. David Harvey considers the mid-19th century a formative period in the emergence of commercial fruit production in Kent. He relates expansion in acreage and changes in varieties of fruit cultivated to increasing national demand and changes in consumer preferences, using data from tithe surveys and other sources. The coming of the railway was essential for rapid transportation of perishable consignments from west Kent.[39]

Hops were grown in many different localities. They are mentioned in tithe files for 66 parishes in Herefordshire, 30 in Sussex, 22 in Worcestershire, 11 in Essex, 10 in Surrey, 10 in Hampshire, 10 in Nottinghamshire and at 2 places each in Shropshire, Somerset and Suffolk. Hop growing was reported in tithe files for 66 parishes in Kent. Hop grounds are listed in 62 per cent of Kent's apportionments but are represented on only 21 per cent of its tithe maps.

Reeds and osiers are mentioned in tithe files for 10 parishes in Norfolk, 7 in Berkshire, 5 in Staffordshire, 3 in Middlesex, 2 each in Derbyshire, Devon, Dorset, Essex, Nottinghamshire, Suffolk, Surrey, Wiltshire, Worcestershire and at 1 place in Buckinghamshire, Cornwall, Kent, Lancashire, Northamptonshire, Oxfordshire, Rutland and Somerset.

FARMING

In the 1830s and 1840s, remnants of regional peasant farming, ancient customs and social cohesion were being crushed relentlessly by parliamentary legislation and cumulative pressures exerted by capital investment and free competition, checked only by the corn laws. Agricultural land was becoming concentrated in the hands of fewer large estates and the area let to farmers on short-term leases was expanding. By 1850, tenants occupied about 85 per cent of all farmland in England and Wales. Smallholders and farm workers were ceasing to earn money from part-time employment. Domestic crafts and trades such as spinning, handloom weaving, knitting, lacemaking, cobbling, tailoring, nailmaking, blacksmithing, carpentry, bricklaying and thatching were in decline. An increasing proportion of farm labourers was employed as wage-earners working exclusively for one farmer. Farm servants who boarded with their employers were fast disappearing. Wages were forced down by farmers who spent increasing sums of money on labour-saving machinery, including seed drills and threshing machines. Some farmers bought materials to increase productivity of crops and livestock. Improved seeds, improved breeds of cattle and sheep, imported oil cake, imported guano and bone meal raised production costs but secured higher yields.

Capital investment in modernisation was the basis of high farming, a system that was maintained precariously by high prices as well as high output. Contemporary reports in the *Journal of the Royal Agricultural Society of England* and articles written for *The Times* by James Caird applauded these innovations and welcomed their contribution to agricultural progress.[40] William Cobbett was one of the few writers who blamed agricultural 'improvers', together with fundholders, stock-jobbers and 'placemen' for destroying a close-knit, paternalistic rural society. He decried the loss of independent small farmers and lamented the disappearance of cottagers and rural craftsmen, the decline of farm servants and the pauperisation of farm labourers.[41] Among recent accounts of agricultural changes, viewing the period of the tithe surveys from a historical perspective, are volume VI of *The Agrarian History of England and Wales* and Mark Overton's reappraisal of the concept of agricultural revolution.[42]

Local historians are interested in national trends as a background to specific aspects of farming in their own localities. Tithe files offer a wealth of detailed information on local landscapes and rural economies. Roger Kain's indexes list and describe the main contents of each file under a number of standardised headings. Some 200,000 entries direct historians to files providing information on particular topics and furnish local historians with inventories of information relating to particular places.[43] The files record enormous variations in standards of husbandry, in crop yields, in labour relations and in village welfare. Some villages and some farms survived as archaic relics from earlier times; other farms applied the latest scientific discoveries and practised methods in advance of their contemporaries.

In assessing the value of tithes, assistant commissioners considered effects of efficient or slack management. In arable districts, they asked whether quantities of produce were affected by extraordinary instances of high or low farming. They collected evidence for tithe-payers avoiding liability to higher tithe charges that would be incurred if waste lands were reclaimed for cultivation. Witnesses before a House of Commons select committee inquiring into the state of agriculture in 1836, stated that tithes were 'a chill to improvement', because farmers were charged with perpetual tithes out of landlords' investments and tenants' good husbandry. A Sussex farmer concluded that any improvement producing a return of 10 per cent would be nullified by tithe payments and a Gloucestershire farmer estimated that tithes 'taken at the gross tenth, might have been in some cases more than the rent'.[44] In some districts, tithe files noted a lack of expenditure on underdrainage, fertilizers, implements, accommodation for livestock, and repairs to buildings, roads and fences. Assistant commissioners did not venture opinions on whether such investments would earn adequate returns. They did not question the wisdom of agricultural improvement.

Crops and livestock

By far the most important information contained in tithe files relates to crop acreages, yields and livestock numbers. Acreages and yields of crops had been recorded in tithing surveys made in the 18th and 19th centuries before the Tithe Commutation Act of 1836. These data were used by historians in the 1920s.[45] A small number of schedules of apportionment compiled after 1836, for 195 tithe districts, list crops in the state of cultivation column and a few tithe maps are coloured and labelled to indicate crops growing in fields.[46] Information obtained from tithe maps and schedules of apportionment pales to insignificance alongside the vast quantities of data available from the tithe files. Many files contain questionnaires, those for eastern districts designed for investigating arable farming, for western districts addressed to pastoral farming. At the University of Leeds, Glanville Jones, and at University College London, a group of graduate students including Michael Naish, Elizabeth Burrell, David Gramolt, Malcolm Postgate, John Chapman, Alan Baker, Wynn Edwards, Elwyn Cox and Brian Dittmer began to exploit the immense riches of tithe files in the late 1950s and early 1960s.[47] Early investigations of measurements of crop acreages in tithe files for Hampshire and Suffolk disclosed inaccuracies but descriptions of soils and observations on crop rotations, yields, manures and livestock husbandry are accurate and authoritative.

Historians and geographers face two main problems in dealing with tithe file data: first, how to treat statistical material of uneven quality; second, how to make the best use of valuable qualitative statements about farming practice. By abstracting data for large numbers of parishes and by grouping wide ranges of measurements into categories, errors and omissions which impair the use of data at a scale of individual parishes may be subsumed in broader measures at a regional level. In 1963, in a study of the mid-19th-century agricultural geography of Essex, Elwyn Cox first mapped qualitative, contemporary descriptions of soils contained in tithe files. He then related appraisals drawn from the files on the management of grassland to quantitative data from maps and apportionments, comparing estimates of acreages of grass mown for hay from file questionnaires with acreages under grass recorded in apportionment summaries. A survey of livestock farming is supported by information from files on livestock numbers and animal products. In analysing regional variations in crop husbandry, tithe files yield basic data for answering two crucial questions: they indicate where different crops were grown and what rotations were followed in different districts. From information abstracted from 296 files for the whole county of Essex, Cox maps distributions of crops and fallows, yields and rotations. His map of barley as a percentage of arable highlights the contrast between agriculture on lighter soils in north and east Essex and that on southern claylands, a distinction that cannot be inferred from distributions of land use categories (Fig. 43). A survey of farming regions is based on observations by assistant commissioners on such diverse topics as markets, transport, leases, buildings, draining, embanking, manuring, marling and liming.

For north-west Wiltshire, tithe files contain a 'pastoral' type of printed form for reporting estimated acreages in different land use categories, crop rotations and livestock

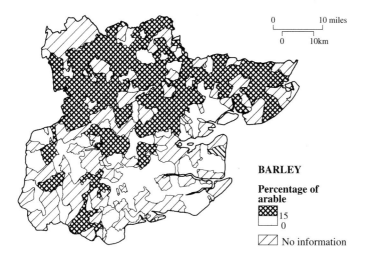

BARLEY

Percentage of arable

15
0

No information

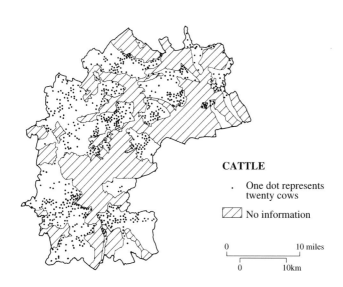

CATTLE

.   One dot represents
    twenty cows

No information

43 Barley as a percentage of arable in Essex and herds of cattle in north-west Wiltshire. Barley was widely grown on light loams and chalky boulder clay soils in north Essex. In north-west Wiltshire, cattle were concentrated on valley meadows. Source: E.A. Cox and B.R. Dittmer, 'The tithe files of the mid-nineteenth century', *Agricultural History Review*, 13 (1965), 1-16.

numbers. Brian Dittmer uses these statistics to depict significant regional concentrations in livestock enterprises. By calculating a stocking density, a ratio of acres of meadow and pasture to one head of livestock and plotting such values on a map, he assesses differences in the quality of grazing between different localities. Maps of average annual rentable values indicate contrasts between arable and pasture land, confirming the superiority of productivity in the clay vales compared with the Cotswold region. Cox and Dittmer's most original contributions to tithe studies are to demonstrate the value of mapping crop and livestock distributions over areas large enough to conceal imperfections in data for individual parishes. In 1965, they published jointly the first and still one of the most valuable introductions to tithe files as a source for reconstructing the agricultural geography of mid-19th-century England and Wales. Their article describes the contents of the files, critically assesses the accuracy of the evidence and shows, with reference to Essex and north-west Wiltshire, how the evidence may be interpreted. They conclude that 'any work that uses the tithe maps and apportionments would be incomplete without reference to the tithe files and the unofficial, supplementary tithe documents in the county record offices'.[48]

Farming on light and heavy soils

Many observers of English agriculture in the mid-19th century, including James Caird, held an opinion that high farming was more advanced on light soils than on heavy soils and that farming on claylands was generally backward and depressed. Examination of tithe files for north-west Wiltshire, where farmland in clay vales commanded higher rents than in the Cotswolds, casts a shadow of doubt on the validity of this view. In the 1970s, Tony Phillips set out to draw a fuller comparison of levels of productivity on light and heavy soils to test Caird's hypothesis. For Staffordshire, Nottinghamshire and Hereford-shire, he mapped assistant commissioners' classifications of soils, plotted arable and grass as proportions of total acreages covered by apportionment summaries, plotted wheat, barley, oats, turnips, beans and peas, clover and seeds, and fallow as percentages of arable recorded in file questionnaires, and mapped crop yields and distribution of livestock enterprises from file reports (Fig. 44).[49] He concluded that farming practised on light soils about 1840 was clearly different from that on heavy soils: 'Light-land farming systems were more flexible and structurally better balanced. Mixed-farming practices had been widely adopted, giving farmers the choice of both cereals and livestock as saleable products. Heavy-land farming revealed many of the features attributed to it in this period: wheat was the main cash crop, while fallows persisted and were areally significant'.[50] A study of tithe evidence for Suffolk not only draws a contrast between agricultural systems on light and heavy land but differentiates farming on claylands in southern Suffolk from that on other heavy land in the county. Proportions of bare fallows, pulse crops, roots and clover and yields of wheat in this southern clayland area are closer to those prevailing on light soils than on other heavy soils.[51] A statistical analysis of tithe rent-charges for parishes in Dorset demonstrates a general relationship between tithe rent-charge, farm rent, land use and soil.[52] Light lands appear to have been most highly valued. Tithe file data have been used to characterise Essex agriculture in its 'golden age'.[53]

Regina Porter has used data on crops listed in the state of cultivation column of apportionments for 44 districts in Cheshire to describe in detail relations between soils and cropping. Because crops are located in particular fields, it is possible to analyse small site variations in soils, slopes, drainage conditions and micro-climates. Underdraining on heavy soils was neglected until the second half of the 19th century.[54] A broader picture of farming in Cheshire about 1840 is based on an analysis of valuers' estimates of crops recorded in tithe files.[55] Over much of the county the standard of farming was below what valuers expected but on some tracts of sand and loams the adoption of four-course rotations was raising productivity. Tithe files report that the extension of coal mining into east Durham, beginning in the 1820s had, within twenty years, stimulated agricultural improvements by

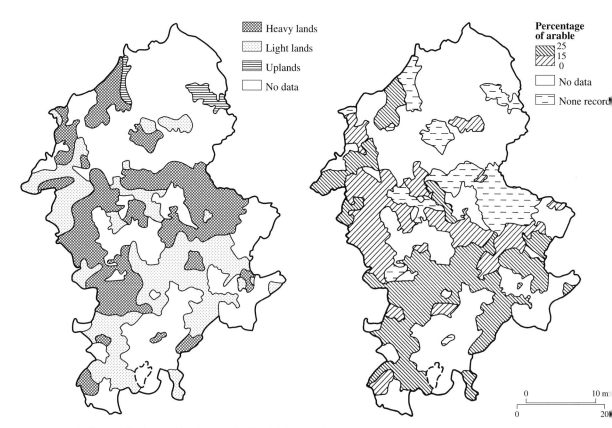

44 Soils and barley cultivation in Staffordshire. Evidence from tithe files indicates that barley was more frequently grown on light soils than on heavy soils. Source: A.D.M. Phillips, 'A study of farming practices in Staffordshire around 1840', *North Staffordshire Journal of Field Studies*, 13 (1973), 27-52.

increasing demand for hay, milk and potatoes and supplying manure in return. In 1838 at Hetton, an assistant commissioner remarked: 'some good land but a considerable quantity of thin cold stiff soil which but for the propinquity of the collieries and the consequent facility for procuring additional manure would make but a poor return to the cultivator'.[56] In most parts of England heavy soils were poorly farmed at the time of the tithe surveys, awaiting underdrainage and improvements in grassland management.

A national atlas of agriculture

In 1978, Roger Kain and a group of co-workers at the University of Exeter began to compile a computer atlas of agriculture in England. The project indexed and analysed some 200,000 entries from nearly 15,000 tithe files and produced over 1,000 maps, from which 582 have been selected for publication.[57] The maps plot key crops, yields and livestock distributions for 31 counties having tithe file data for more than 20 per cent of their parishes or townships. Maps drawn for single counties and for England and Wales as a whole are presented here as examples. In Norfolk, the four-course rotation had been adopted in most parishes by 1840 (Fig. 45). Turnips were grown wherever possible

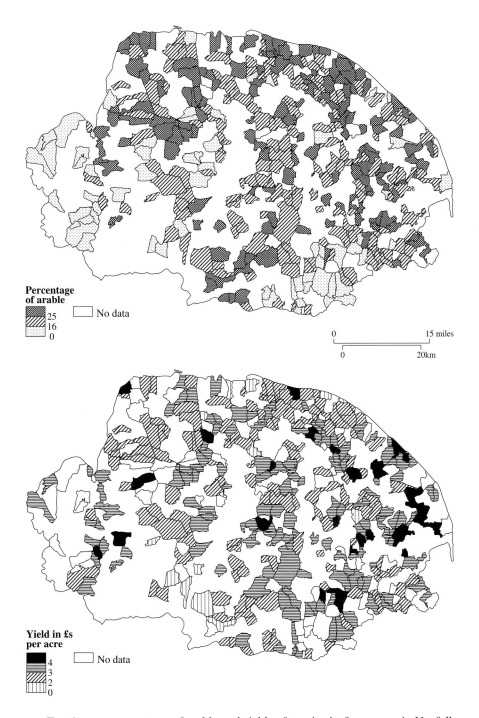

**Percentage
of arable**

25
16
0

No data

0   15 miles

0   20km

**Yield in £s
per acre**

4
3
2
0

No data

45 Turnips as a percentage of arable and yields of turnips in £s per acre in Norfolk.
Turnips were grown in every part of Norfolk in 1840 but they occupied a higher
proportion of arable in the Good Sand region and yields were highest in the Norwich
loam region. Source: Roger J.P. Kain, *An atlas and index of the tithe files of mid-nineteenth-
century England and Wales* (Cambridge, Cambridge University Press, 1986), 78, 82.

and, where they were not successful, winter tares were sown. At Buckenham, on stiff soils in south Norfolk, an assistant commissioner noted: 'winter tares also are sown in some considerable quantity and are fed off by sheep early in the spring; this is practised upon these lands which are too heavy for turnips or other roots. This is a system of husbandry which seems on the increase, rendered almost necessary by the increase in the number of sheep kept; and is superseding the somewhat disheartening system of long summer fallows as a preparation for barley'.[58]

The final maps in the *Atlas and Index* summarise the gross output of the principal grain crops in England in the mid-1830s (Fig. 46). The country is divided into five regions of nearly equal size to enable gross quantities of output to be compared. Wheat output in East Anglia was more than twice that in the south west and twice that in the north east. The contrast between barley output in southern regions and the north was more pronounced and East Anglia was far ahead in production. Oats, on the other hand, was widely grown in northern England. When all grains are added together, differences between north and south are narrowed but East Anglia holds a clear lead. A third of all English grain was produced in six eastern counties, just about the same as the total for the two western regions.[59] In Table 2 crop acreages and yields for tithe districts are aggregated by counties. Acreages are expressed as percentages of total arable land and mean yields are calculated for the sum of tithe district data. These values may be compared with statistics from other sources collected in *The Agrarian History of England and Wales*.[60]

LANDOWNERS AND OCCUPIERS

Through much of the 19th century large estates grew larger. At the apex of the social pyramid were a few aristocratic landed families who continued to add to their vast holdings by marriage, inheritance and judicious purchases. The dukes of Westminster, Bedford, Devonshire, Northumberland, Portland, Buccleuch, Sutherland, marquesses of Bute, Anglesey, Londonderry, Hertford, earls of Derby, Fitzwilliam, Dudley and Ancaster enjoyed great incomes from rents from agricultural land that increased even during lean years of depression from 1815 to 1835. They also received increasing incomes from urban properties, royalties on mineral workings, revenue from plantations overseas and interest from investments in industry, canals, turnpikes and government stock. Great landowners dominated national and local politics. The Reform Act of 1832 and the repeal of the corn laws in 1846 did not disturb their supremacy. Speaking in the debate on the corn laws in 1845, Richard Cobden told the House of Commons: 'The landlords have absolute power in the country'.[61] Big business amassed great wealth and some bankers, brewers, ironmasters and other manufacturers acquired large landed estates by buying land from small landowners. The creation of these new estates added to the total area of land held in estates of more than 3,000 acres and increased the total number of large landowners. A significant amount of land was held by the church, universities, schools, hospitals, city livery companies and other charitable foundations whose land management policies were cautious and conservative. The amount of land in middling-sized and small estates was

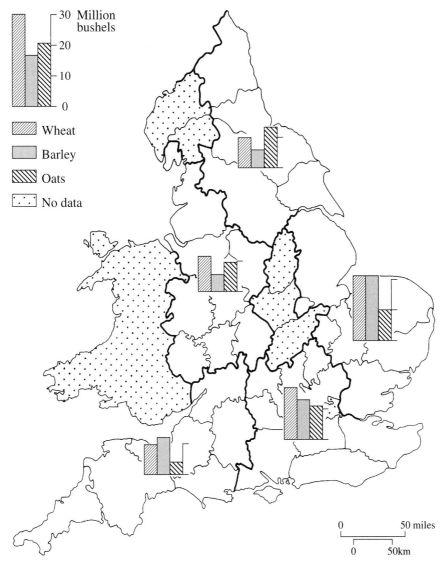

46 Output of wheat, barley and oats in million bushels, in five English regions. Wheat and barley were equally dominant in eastern England; wheat production was ahead of barley in southern England; barley was ahead of wheat in south-west England; wheat was ahead of oats in the West Midlands; oats was ahead of wheat in the north-east. Source: as for Fig. **45**, 467.

declining and at the bottom of the scale were tens of thousands of smallholders owning less than 30 acres, some of whom were struggling to maintain their independence.

Large landowners spent part of their income advancing political ambitions, rebuilding and enlarging country houses, extending parks and plantations and improving facilities for hunting, shooting and fishing. They employed increasing numbers of indoor and outdoor servants. In 1841, about 8,000 were recorded in the census as gamekeepers.[62] Investment in agricultural improvements was uneven. Some landowners built commodious

Table 2

Crop acreages as percentages of county arable acreages and crop yields,
as recorded by assistant commissioners and local agents in their reports on tithe agreements

County	Estimated arable acres	Wheat a	Wheat b	Barley a	Barley b	Oats a	Oats b	Pulses a	Pulses b	Turnips a	Turnips b	Seeds a	Seeds b	Bare Fallow
England														
Bedfordshire	177,557	22.8	22.7	13.2	31.4	7.4	36.9	13.6	21.8	11.4	3.5	16.5	21.0	16.0
Berkshire	263,956	24.0	24.2	15.6	34.7	8.4	40.3	5.7	29.4	17.7	2.7	23.3	22.7	5.0
Buckinghamshire	260,405	23.3	21.0	14.8	28.4	10.0	34.7	7.2	25.5	13.8	3.6	20.5	19.1	6.9
Cambridgeshire	367,370	23.1	22.4	10.8	30.0	13.6	39.6	5.5	23.9	5.0	3.4	28.2	21.5	10.8
Cheshire	180,344	31.4	20.6	3.6	29.4	32.1	26.2	-	-	2.5	2.7	-	-	16.4
Cornwall	206,096	32.7	17.9	29.5	28.2	10.2	31.0	-	-	-	-	-	-	-
Cumberland	-	-	-	-	-	-	-	-	-	-	-	-	-	-
Derbyshire	166,426	24.4	22.3	6.4	29.4	24.2	30.6	2.3	27.6	6.7	3.2	21.1	24.6	14.3
Devonshire	373,120	34.2	15.6	23.8	25.9	12.4	28.3	-	-	-	-	-	-	-
Dorset	135,599	34.0	20.4	25.1	29.7	11.0	32.8	-	-	-	-	-	-	-
Durham	341,828	22.4	17.1	4.6	27.3	22.3	26.7	2.5	20.4	5.1	3.1	21.8	19.0	20.8
Essex	768,156	25.6	24.6	18.5	34.5	6.2	41.1	8.8	25.8	7.3	3.2	17.9	22.8	15.5
Gloucestershire	257,805	31.6	19.6	20.5	27.1	1.2	27.5	6.4	23.2	-	-	-	-	-
Hampshire	688,576	20.6	21.5	15.2	27.9	5.7	35.0	2.2	24.3	16.4	2.5	33.8	17.6	4.4
Herefordshire	212,456	33.8	-	15.7	-	1.1	-	8.0	-	-	-	-	-	-
Hertfordshire	260,638	23.4	21.6	20.1	29.4	6.7	33.6	5.3	22.2	13.1	2.5	19.6	21.0	11.9
Huntingdonshire	114,986	23.7	22.0	16.6	31.4	6.0	35.1	11.3	22.8	2.7	2.6	15.8	22.5	21.1
Kent	505,030	27.6	25.6	13.3	33.7	10.6	39.1	11.0	26.2	12.0	3.0	19.2	22.1	5.7
Lancashire	330,290	26.8	22.9	2.2	28.3	27.5	30.7	2.6	24.0	-	-	-	-	-
Leicestershire	-	-	-	-	-	-	-	-	-	-	-	-	-	-
Lincolnshire	865,678	24.9	22.9	10.3	31.1	13.8	38.0	5.6	22.7	12.1	2.5	24.2	22.5	7.7
Middlesex	106,217	-	-	-	-	-	-	-	-	-	-	-	-	-
Monmouthshire	-	-	-	-	-	-	-	-	-	-	-	-	-	-
Norfolk	864,264	23.5	23.3	22.3	31.5	2.8	35.7	1.9	26.5	24.2	2.8	24.9	23.1	2.1
Northamptonshire	-	-	-	-	-	-	-	-	-	-	-	-	-	-
Northumberland	580,264	19.3	19.5	4.9	30.7	22.6	31.7	1.6	26.4	6.4	3.1	26.3	-	16.9
Nottinghamshire	-	-	-	-	-	-	-	-	-	-	-	-	-	-
Oxfordshire	264,041	24.0	22.9	17.2	33.3	6.6	38.7	7.0	30.0	13.9	2.5	23.9	21.3	7.1
Rutland	36,610	19.5	23.5	19.2	33.6	6.0	40.0	10.7	22.0	13.0	2.5	23.1	23.8	8.3
Shropshire	388,386	23.6	19.5	9.9	26.4	14.7	25.7	0.8	21.1	9.7	2.6	24.1	20.8	14.4

County	Estimated arable acreage	1	2	3	4	5	6	7	8	9	10	11	12	13
Somerset	255,943	34.1	21.0	17.3	31.3	2.7	30.8	6.2	29.6	12.1	2.6	27.7	21.9	9.9
Staffordshire	326,252	21.9	21.3	12.7	28.8	13.0	27.9	1.3	23.3	14.0	2.7	19.4	21.9	9.8
Suffolk	665,716	23.9	23.2	23.3	32.4	1.6	36.9	5.9	25.1	9.3	2.8	25.2	20.7	12.7
Surrey	233,401	23.2	20.9	9.2	31.6	14.3	35.6	5.0	22.9	7.4	2.8	24.8	–	13.5
Sussex	409,633	22.6	25.6	6.1	34.4	18.7	35.6	1.8	26.0	7.7	2.6	26.6	22.8	12.8
Warwickshire	268,049	22.4	23.1	12.0	32.6	10.3	37.4	7.4	24.3	–	3.0	–	–	–
Westmorland	–	–	–	–	–	–	–	–	–	–	–	–	–	–
Wiltshire	303,833	34.5	22.0	28.1	30.2	5.0	28.9	2.5	28.7	–	–	28.7	–	–
Worcestershire	201,722	36.2	22.5	9.5	34.0	1.7	32.0	14.8	19.0	–	–	19.0	–	–
York City & Ainsty	1,247	–	–	–	–	–	–	–	–	–	–	–	–	–
Yorkshire, E. Riding	503,821	22.0	18.6	10.4	28.0	16.6	32.5	5.5	19.6	10.3	2.7	21.2	20.9	13.6
Yorkshire, N. Riding	434,768	23.6	19.4	7.5	30.4	17.0	29.4	4.8	18.6	9.1	2.9	19.0	23.6	16.9
Yorkshire, W. Riding	512,276	22.6	21.0	13.6	30.5	12.1	33.2	2.9	22.3	12.5	2.9	22.2	21.1	11.5
Wales														
Anglesey	66,978	9.4	–	19.7	–	43.8	–	–	–	–	–	–	–	–
Brecon	84,007	–	–	–	–	–	–	–	–	–	–	–	–	–
Caernarvonshire	51,724	–	–	–	–	–	–	–	–	–	–	–	–	–
Cardiganshire	126,772	–	–	–	–	–	–	–	–	–	–	–	–	–
Carmarthenshire	157,725	–	–	–	–	–	–	–	–	–	–	–	–	–
Denbighshire	92,167	24.5	16.0	24.9	20.0	31.5	32.0	0.8	14.0	–	–	–	–	–
Flintshire	56,550	32.0	–	18.9	–	28.2	–	1.3	–	–	–	–	–	–
Glamorgan	150,393	–	–	–	–	–	–	–	–	–	–	–	–	–
Merionethshire	24,832	13.9	–	18.4	–	47.0	–	–	–	–	–	–	–	–
Montgomeryshire	71,379	26.1	–	20.9	–	33.0	–	1.3	–	–	–	–	–	–
Pembrokeshire	101,170	–	–	–	–	–	–	–	–	–	–	–	–	–
Radnorshire	38,021	–	–	–	–	–	–	–	–	–	–	–	–	–

(i)   Columns 'a' are the mean percentages of the sample sown with each crop or left in bare fallow in the years of average, 1829-35. Sample sizes vary for each crop; samples smaller than 10 per cent of districts are omitted.

(ii)   Columns 'b' are the mean yields for each crop. For wheat, barley, oats and pulses these are in bushels/acre; for turnips the figure is an expression of the titheable value in £/acre; for seeds in cwts/acre.

(iii)   County units are those employed by the Tithe Commission.

(iv)   Estimated arable acreage in each county is obtained by multiplying the total acreage enumerated in tithe file reports on agreements by a weighting factor equivalent to the ratio of county area : sample area. County areas are those calculated from tithe maps under the direction of R.K. Dawson and recorded in the 1851 census of population.

(v)   In all Welsh counties and in Cornwall, Devonshire, Dorset, Gloucestershire, Herefordshire, Monmouthshire, Somerset and Worcestershire, arable land excludes seed crops.

(vi)   The symbol '-' is used where data are unavailable, where individual crops cannot be distinguished, and where data relate to very small samples (fewer than 10 per cent of tithe districts).

farmhouses with spacious outbuildings for their tenants; some invested in underdrainage; a few estates owned their own limekilns, brickworks and joineries. A few landowners built cottages for farmworkers but many were opposed to tied cottages. Some landowners resisted the building of chapels and the opening of schools, expressing fears that these places would disseminate subversive ideas and foment discontent. A few landowners attempted to restrict the sale of liquor.

In the early 19th century farmers constituted the largest single occupational group in England and Wales but their numbers were decreasing. In 1851, fewer than a quarter of a million were enumerated as farmers.[63] A majority were tenants and the size of tenant farms was increasing. On light soils in eastern England, many farms were over 300 acres and a few were more than 1,000 acres in extent. In pastoral districts in the west of England, farms were commonly 100 to 150 acres in size but many were smaller. In the 1840s many occupied farms as tenants-at-will. Long leases were not being renewed and family succession was declining. Many farms were changing hands; new occupiers were moving from distant places; some occupiers were renting land from more than one proprietor or buying land to add to their holdings. Farmers were becoming more mobile and more versatile. Their success depended more on their ability to raise capital and manage businesses efficiently than on soil quality or the labour of large numbers of hired hands.

Landed estates and their owners

Advances have been made in studies of landed estates and the structure of landowning society using data from tithe surveys. Tithe surveys are among a small number of sources that record measurements of landed property. Domesday Book of 1086 lists names of King William's tenants-in-chief and the number of hides they held. The tithe surveys, the *Return of Owners of Land*, 1873, Lloyd George's inquiry into the ownership and value of land, 1910-14, and the National Farm Survey of 1941 record owners' names and the size of their estates. The tithe surveys are equalled in coverage, in scale and in precision of locating estate boundaries only by the large-scale surveys carried out from 1910 onwards. Tithe surveys provide fairly comprehensive land inventories for 11,875 parishes and townships about 1840.

Tithe surveys provide single pieces of information essential for genealogists in tracing the descent of manors. They record precisely how many acres were owned by individuals whose changing fortunes are investigated by family historians. Studies for which one or two pieces of information are drawn from tithe surveys, include Russell Howes' biography of Joseph Pitt, a Gloucestershire landowner; J.D. Marshall's history of the Cavendish family in Furness; Sue Farrant's accounts of changing landownership in the lower Ouse valley in Sussex; Wyn Ford's search for the succession of owners of Boltro Farm, Cuckfield, from 1663 to 1966; L.W. Lloyd's tracing of the descent of Corsygedol, the principal estate of Ardudwys in Merioneth; and a history of the development of Coleshill, a model farm in Oxfordshire, compiled by Architects in Agriculture Group.[64]

The simplest method of transcribing holdings of named landowners from schedules of apportionment to a modern base map is to identify and mark individual parcels, then

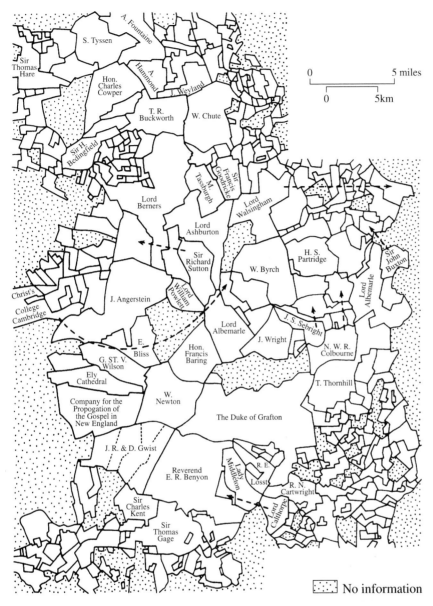

47 Landed estates in the Suffolk and Norfolk Breckland. The largest estates were situated on the lightest sands. Source: M.R. Postgate, 'Historical geography of the Breckland, 1600-1850', University of London, M.A. thesis (1961).

[∴∴] No information

draw lines around boundaries of estates. Studies in agrarian history follow this procedure for single parishes, groups of parishes or blocks of territory.[65] Aileen Carpenter has reviewed the value of such maps and the utility of tithe surveys as a source for reconstructing estate boundaries.[66] One of the largest areas for which landed estates have been plotted is the Breckland (Fig. 47). In a study of this region, Malcolm Postgate uses tithe apportionments to analyse the composition and management of estates of different sizes.[67]

A map of estate boundaries is both laborious to construct and limited in its usefulness. There is little justification in producing maps of boundaries for this date simply because tithe surveys make it possible. Regional variations in sizes of landed estates can be shown more easily and more precisely by plotting apportionment data at a parish scale. One of the simplest ways of showing variations is to divide the number of owners of land in a parish into the total acreage of the parish and then to plot the results by a choropleth technique. This technique is used by Dennis Mills to produce a map of the density of owners (number of owners divided by the area of the parish) for the whole of Leicestershire, identifying 'open' and 'closed' parishes on the basis of their landownership structure.[68] As tithe survey coverage for Leicestershire is incomplete, Mills also obtains numbers of owners from land tax assessments. From these analyses he derives a four-fold classification: squire's township, absentee landlord township, freehold *morcellement* and divided township.

Methods of analysis have since been refined. James Yelling has produced a map of estate structure in east Worcestershire by mapping the proportion of the cultivated acreage of parishes held in estates exceeding 150 acres.[69] This analysis shows that the largest estates occur where parishes themselves are largest. Although it does not completely describe the estate structure of a region, it provides a check on regional contrasts. For example, a strong relationship exists in one part of the study area, where large estates were concentrated in 1840, between large owners and the incidence of non-parliamentary enclosure. Other studies of regional patterns of landownership in the middle years of the 19th century include those by J.S. Ingleson in central Durham, Heather Fuller in Lincolnshire and Brian Short in south Devon, where he compared landownership in the mid-19th century with that revealed by Lloyd George's inquiry.[70] Alastair Pearson and Peter Collier have applied a geographical information system (GIS) to data from the tithe survey to analyse landownership as a factor in agricultural productivity at Newport, Pembrokeshire.[71] In this study, GIS analysis does not yield conclusive results but it offers a new and potentially valuable approach to historical research.

In Essex, a count of owners of land at the time of the tithe surveys and from the *Return of Owners of Land, 1873*, has been made by F.M.L. Thompson and reported in *English landed society in the nineteenth century*.[72] Thompson finds 20 owners in the group of 'greater gentry' in Essex at both dates and in the group of 'squires' 111 at the time of the tithe surveys and 115 in 1873. A comparison of their names reveals that this appearance of stability is deceptive because among the 'greater gentry' four families represented in the 1840s owned no land by 1873 and three families listed in 1873 had not owned land in Essex in the 1840s. Markedly different degrees of mobility are observed when changes amongst lesser landowners are taken into account. The rising price of land and restricted availability of property made it easier for mercantile and industrial entrepreneurs to buy themselves into these groups. In 1873, no fewer than 38 per cent of owners of 'lesser yeoman' sized estates and 23 per cent of 'greater yeomen' were newcomers since the 1840s. Comparison of the names of landowners in the tithe surveys with those in the 1873 return shows that only 60 per cent of owners in the two yeoman groups survived as landowners through the thirty-year period. Throughout the spectrum, a continuous contraction and expansion of estates occurred, with the result that in Essex the proportion of the surface area owned in estates of over 1,000 acres increased only very slightly.

Table 3

Landownership in Kent in 1840 and percentage changes in number of owners and acreage of estates 1840-73

Categories of owner	Size class (acres)	Number of owners 1840	Percentage change in number of owners 1840-73	Acreage owned 1840	Percentage of total area 1840	Percentage change in acreage 1840-73	Average acreage 1840
Small proprietors	1-100	7,376	-14	132,314	14	-13	18
Lesser yeomen	101-300	1,009	+3	171,417	19	-13	170
Greater yeomen	301-1,000	441	-9	225,903	25	-9	512
Squires	1,001-3,000	107	+1	171,758	19	+8	1,605
Greater gentry	3,001-10,000	32	+53	165,309	18	+47	5,165
Nobility	Over 10,000	4	0	49,817	5	+8	12,454
Totals		8,969	-11	916,518	100	0	102

Sources: Tithe apportionments *c.* 1840; R.J.P. Kain, 'The land of Kent in the middle of the ninteteenth century', unpublished University of London PhD thesis (1973), 368; W.E. Baxter's edition of the 1873 Return of Owners of Land published as *The Domesday Book for the County of Kent*, Lewes, 1877.

In Kent, similar changes in the structure of landownership occurred in the generation between the tithe surveys and the 1873 return. Table 3 is compiled by entering on a computer file names of landowners and acreages of their estates from summaries in schedules of tithe apportionments for all parishes in 1840 and names and acreages of estates listed for the whole county in the 1873 return. By 1873, the total number of owners had decreased by 11 per cent from 1840. The redistribution of land is reflected in both upward and downward movements within the spectrum of estate sizes. The percentage of the total area held in estates of under 1,000 acres decreased by 12 per cent while the percentage of the total area held in large estates increased by the same amount. Within the range of large estates, those between 3,000 and 10,000 acres gained most; their numbers increased by 53 per cent and the area they held expanded by 47 per cent. Not only were fewer small properties recorded in 1873 but there was greater turnover among small owners; many former owners departed and some newcomers joined their ranks before 1873. Owners of large estates stayed put and some increased their holdings, while mercantile and industrial entrepreneurs bought extensive tracts and attained the status of landed gentry. The acreage of land held by corporate institutions scarcely changed. In Kent, the proportion of the area owned by estates over 1,000 acres increased from 42 per cent in about 1840 to 50 per cent in 1873.

Tithe surveys and land tax assessments
The decline of small landowners at the height of the enclosure movement in the late 18th and early 19th centuries has been a matter of deep concern to the public at large and continues to be reexamined and discussed by historians at the present time. Identification of small owners rests largely on unreliable evidence from parish land tax assessments. More reliable data from tithe surveys have been relatively little used because they relate to a late date in the course of decline and are absent from many districts where tithes were abolished at the time of an enclosure award.

David Grigg was among the first to study landownership changes by combining land tax and tithe data. For 12 parishes in the Holland division of Lincolnshire he compares the percentage of total parish areas owned by owner-occupiers in the tithe apportionments with earlier land tax data.[73] In four parishes no change occurred, in seven the importance of owner-occupation declined, while in one it increased. The tithe apportionments show that owner-occupiers still held an important place in fenland farming in the mid-19th century. Furthermore, he suggests that the proportion of land held by owner-occupiers is related to the date of enclosure; old enclosed parishes had smaller numbers of owner-occupiers. W.M. Williams' study of Ashworthy extends forward in time from the tithe survey.[74] He compares the ownership structure at the time of the tithe survey with that in 1873, 1922 and 1960, and finds that as estates broke up the number of owner-occupied farms increased.

In using names from schedules of tithe apportionments, it is dangerous to infer from repetition of a landowner's name in the occupier's column that that person was an owner-occupying farmer. Some farms might be temporarily 'in hand'. In mid-19th-century

Kent, for example, tithe surveys record some 32 per cent of land in the occupation of its owners. This figure includes not only owner-occupied farms, but farms 'in hand' and also woods, parks and pleasure grounds. Conversely, it is unsafe to presume that all occupiers named in tithe apportionments as holding land owned by another person were tenant farmers. Colin Thomas would be correct in concluding, with a cautionary note about the ambiguity of name evidence, 'that the tenant farm dominated the landscape and was the keystone of social relationships in all Merioneth parishes at this time'.[75]

Land tax returns present even more serious problems of interpretation than tithe surveys. It is difficult, if not impossible, to derive 'acreage equivalents' from monetary payments made by landowners. Reassessments, voluntary redemptions, rating of 'non-land' property and variations in rent per acre within parishes upset simple ratios of tax paid to acres owned. Tithe surveys provide a check on the extent of errors in 'acreage equivalents'. The most exhaustive comparative test of land tax acreage equivalents against tithe survey acreages is that conducted by Sarah Banks. For 89 west Norfolk parishes she compares the percentage of land owned by the largest landowner, the four largest owners, the average size of estate and the total number of landowners as calculated from the 1831 tax assessment and the tithe surveys. The overall structure of landownership drawn from each source is quite similar. For estate-size categories represented by few holdings and especially for individual holdings, land tax assessments are unreliable. In west Norfolk, the most reliable comparisons are for parishes containing large numbers of similar-sized estates.[76]

Landowners and urban development

Tithe surveys have not been widely used in studies of urban expansion, partly because other large-scale plans are available and partly because few tithe surveys depict towns at moments of rapid development. In recording patterns of landownership, tithe surveys are exceptionally valuable. Studies by David Ward, H.J. Dyos and Michael Jahn show that 19th-century building development fitted closely the shapes of landed estates. Michael Thompson tabulates landowners' holdings in Hampstead by size-categories and examines the character, location and timing of building development for different sizes of estates.[77] Martin Daunton uses tithe apportionment data for 27 towns to examine relationships between proportions of land held by the three largest landowners in each town, their tenurial systems and housing conditions. Results of the analysis indicate little more than 'a tenuous connection between concentrated ownership and short leasehold, and between fragmented ownership and feeehold'.[78] Neither quality of housing nor levels of rent were related closely to sizes of estates. In addition to mapping boundaries of properties and limits of building from the tithe survey for Wakefield, Keith Cowlard also links names of owners from the apportionment with the 1841 poll book to investigate political affiliations. Landowners were equally divided in their allegiance to the Tory candidate and his opponent.[79]

In his book on the impact of railways on Victorian cities, J.R. Kellett emphasises the 'importance of comprehensive knowledge of property titles as a sound basis for all urban history'. In Birmingham, his analysis of ownership patterns, based partly on tithe surveys, demonstrates the influence of landowners on routes taken by railways through urban and suburban districts.[80] P.S. Richards is fortunate in having an altered apportionment, made in the 1880s, for Wolverton, a railway town in north Buckinghamshire.[81] Reapportionment was usually occasioned by an event which radically altered the existing pattern of tithe areas, such as the cutting of a railway line through fields and across roads or the subdivision of tithe areas into building plots. Comparisons of original and altered tithe apportionments and Ordnance Survey large-scale town plans can provide valuable pictures of 19th-century urban development.

Farm size and tenure

Acreages of land occupied by individuals are listed in summaries to schedules of apportionment. Acreages may be grouped into size-categories for single parishes, series of parishes or whole counties, providing the coverage of tithe surveys is fairly complete. For Kent, nearly 900,000 acres enumerated in tithe surveys were occupied by 6,100 farms or other holdings over 10 acres in size (Table 4). The average size of farms was just under 150 acres and about 49 per cent of the county was occupied by farms in the 101 to 500-acre size-class. In tithe files, assistant commissioners commented that few farms were over 350 acres and only one farm in Kent was over 3,500 acres. At Rainham in Kent, about 80 per cent of the land was occupied by 13 substantial yeomen whose farms were over 100 acres but none was more than 450 acres.[82] Many other local studies, including parish histories in recent volumes of the *Victoria County History*, analyse farm sizes for single parishes. R.E. Sandell's transcript of names and acreages of all occupiers of more than 50 acres is exceptional in covering tithe apportionments for an entire county.[83] More frequently, historians have compared data from tithe surveys with earlier, fragmentary information. Among pioneer studies tracing changing farm sizes is Victor Skipp's analysis of a west midlands parish.[84] Comparisons between sizes of farms occupied by tenants and owner-occupiers and comparisons of proportions of farms in different size-classes occupied

Table 4
The size of farms in Kent c.1840

Size class (acres)	Number of farms	Total acreage	Percentage of total acreage	Average size in acres
10-50	2,670	64,102	7.1	24
51-100	1,072	77,994	8.7	72
101-500	2,016	440,587	49.0	218
501-1,000	250	169,959	18.8	679
1,001-2,000	75	103,077	11.5	1,374
Over 2,000	17	43,917	4.9	2,583
Totals	6,100	899,636	100	147

Source: R.J.P. Kain, 'The land of Kent in the middle of the nineteenth century', unpublished University of London PhD thesis (1973), 389.

by tenants and owner-occupiers at different dates may be based on tithe data. No study of farm size, consolidation or tenure can now ignore evidence from tithe surveys.

The layout of farms

By locating all tithe areas, usually fields, listed under the name of each occupier in an apportionment, it is possible to reconstruct boundaries of farms about 1840. This is a laborious task and most researchers have selected a few farms for sample studies. Contrasting forms of layout are illustrated in Fig. 48. A highly fragmented farm is exemplified by William Hussey's 63-acre holding, consisting of 77 scattered strips in the open fields of Winterborne Kingston, Dorset. At an opposite extreme is a compact, ring-fence farm of Reach Court at Cliffe, Kent. Intermediate states of fragmentation are represented by Oxenhoath and East Court farms, both in Kent.

Studies of changes in farm and field boundaries have used tithe surveys as a source for plans about 1840. John Mosby examines the relation between land use and changing layout in Norfolk.[85] Others have traced boundaries of farms characteristic of 'types of farming' regions, have examined farms whose summer pastures lie at a distance from their homesteads, have described changes following enclosure and consolidation of holdings, and have investigated 19th-century farm enlargement.[86] In Kent and other old enclosed regions, compact farms are associated with arable cultivation, whereas fragmented farms are associated with sheep husbandry, with woodland-pasture enterprises and other types of mixed farming. The relation of farm shape to proportions of arable and grass may be measured statistically.[87] Tithe surveys are the fullest and most accurate source of information for reconstructing farm boundaries in the 19th century and provide a reliable base for comparison with earlier and later surveys.

Mining and manufacturing

Tithe surveys are valuable in locating sites of mining and manufacturing about 1840. Extensive use has been made of tithe maps in a survey of quarries and brickworks in Staffordshire. Names of 'brick kiln', 'stone quarry' and other features are inscribed on maps. Plans of workings, associated buildings and ponds are linked with names of their owners and occupiers who, in turn, are identified in 1851 census enumerators' books. Brickmakers and their families are traced from census to census.[88] A study of coal-mining in Somerset and south-west Lancashire uses tithe surveys in conjunction with rate assessment surveys and estate, mineral, canal and railway plans for locating working and disused collieries and tracing extension of transport links to pits.[89] Tithe surveys are useful in reconstructing sites and environs of mills and factories, whose size and labour force are indicated by census data, descriptions in trade directories and local rate books.[90] Tithe maps have been examined closely in studies of early industrial sites for which they 'provide valuable detail'.[91] Tithe surveys make a small but important contribution to studies in industrial history. They are especially valuable in depicting early layouts or use and ownership of sites before mines were opened or factories built.

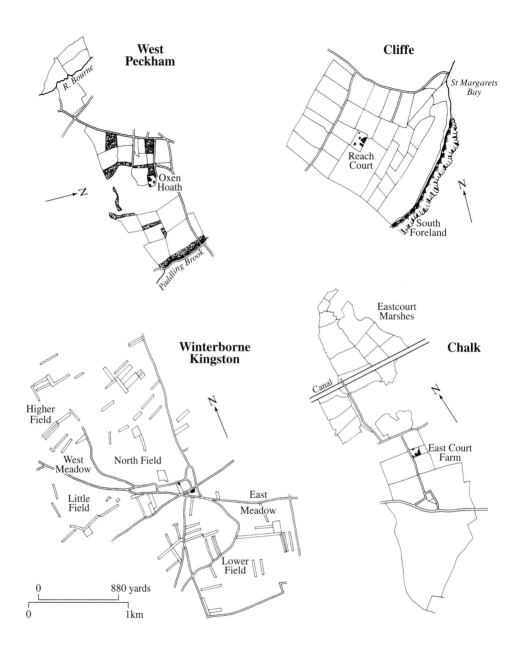

48 Farm layouts about 1840. Oxen Hoath Farm, West Peckham, in the Weald of Kent, consisted of three separate parts. Reach Court, Cliffe, in east Kent, where the English Channel cuts across the North Downs, was a compact ring-fenced farm. East Court Farm, Chalk, near Gravesend, held a portion of north Kent marshland and a portion of upland. A farm at Winterborne Kingston in Dorset consisted of many scattered strips in arable open fields. Source: Roger J.P. Kain and Hugh C. Prince, *The tithe surveys of England and Wales* (Cambridge, Cambridge University Press 1985), 231.

RURAL SOCIETY

Local history is centrally concerned with peoples' own localities: where they live now
and places from which their families came. Present-day residents are interested to know
who occupied the land on which their houses are built, how 19th-century occupiers
earned their living, who their neighbours were and how they related to each other. If a
house stood on the site of the present house, how did its plan differ from the present
and what functions did its outbuildings serve? Were households in the early 19th century
larger or smaller? Did they include servants and lodgers as well as family members and
did families include grandparents as well as parents and children? Did 19th-century
residents work on the premises or away from home? Information on sizes of households,
names and relationships of family members, their ages, sexes, occupations and birthplaces
are recorded in the 1841 and 1851 census enumerators' returns.

House repopulation

In 1962, in the first of a series of articles on 19th-century social structure in parts of
Wales, Spencer Thomas initiated a particularly fruitful line of inquiry with tithe surveys,
linking tithe-survey personal names and acreages with occupational groups and other
data from the 1841 and 1851 census enumerators' returns.[92] He considers that problems
of defining farms from occupiers' holdings in tithe surveys can be resolved by cross-
checking with the census and that the accuracy with which the latter records the occupation
'farmer' can be ascertained by reference to tithe apportionments. From differences found
between the census and tithe apportionment for Llansantffraid, a parish which he has
studied closely, he concludes that no standard criterion for defining the occupation of
'farmer' was applied in the 1841 census. More recently he has tested data on farmers
from the 1851 census for a group of south-west Carmarthenshire parishes against tithe
surveys and parish rate books and finds that the census data are much more reliable than
tithe surveys in respect of occupational classification. He concludes that: 'occupation in
the Tithe Apportionment did not necessarily mean that the people named lived there.
Neither did it guarantee that the occupiers worked the farm as tenants because they
might well have been agricultural labourers in the employ of another tenant working
more than one farm'.[93] Other studies of Welsh villages—such as those by G.J. Lewis of
Bow Street, north of Aberystwyth, and Colin Thomas's work with communities in the
lower Teifi valley—also note discrepancies between tithe and census data with respect to
occupation structure.[94] In some east Yorkshire parishes, June Sheppard has found only
very small discrepancies between names of occupiers in tithe apportionments and farmers
listed in enumerators' books.[95]

In 1971, Adrian Henstock of Nottinghamshire Record Office published the first
results of work that he and an adult-education class carried out with tithe surveys and the
census.[96] He has coined the phrase 'house repopulation' to describe this work which
links households enumerated in the census with actual buildings on the tithe map.
'Depending on circumstances it may be found that no more than one in four or even six

households can be placed with certainty at first, but, having once established these "hooks", the remainder can be pinned up in between.'[97] For the Wiltshire town of Bradford in 1841, house repopulation has been pursued to the fullest extent that complementary evidence from census enumerators' books, *Pigot's Directory* and local newspapers will permit. Gee Langdon has drawn from the tithe map and other sources a faithful picture of a rural market town.[98] Not only are innkeepers, shopkeepers, craftsmen, schoolmasters and clergymen named and members of their families counted but those born in Scotland, Ireland and foreign countries are identified. A curious feature recorded both in the tithe surveys and in census reports is a large number of empty houses. Some were under construction, some were falling derelict and some were simply vacant, awaiting purchasers or tenants.

Dennis Mills has refined and extended the technique of house repopulation to embrace 'community reconstruction' which provides one of the tools for his penetrating studies of social structure in the village of Melbourn in Cambridgeshire in the 19th century. In an exploratory article describing work in progress he says: 'while the Tithe Award presents a considerable amount of evidence of social solidarity, the data within it cannot be fully utilised without recourse to the other major documents available for the period. Kinship links between owners and occupiers will become much more certain when the Tithe Award data are fully integrated with those from the Family Reconstruction forms. The linchpin in this exercise will be the Census Enumeration Schedules of 1841, which give a static picture of each household at that date, while the Tithe Award makes it possible to place the households both spatially and within the socio-tenurial networks within the village.'[99] He presents some house repopulation results in a map of the central part of Melbourn and a schedule, listing people resident in each tenement, their occupations, and some references to the 20th century illustrated by photographs of the High Street in the 1930s and 1977.[100] Fig. 49 is a map of Buriton, Hampshire, in 1841 compiled using similar techniques by E. M. Yates.[101] It is based on the tithe map and the 1841 census and identifies heads of households, their residences and employment. Once houses have been repopulated, the residential pattern can be analysed. For Melbourn, Dennis Mills has examined kinship networks by measuring the residential propinquity of kin as a contribution to understanding mobility and segregation in 19th-century society.[102]

People at home and on the move

Many landscapes depicted from tithe surveys are without people. People named as owners and occupiers in schedules of apportionment account for a minority of the total population. A majority of women, children, soldiers, sailors, students, lunatics, paupers, landless workers, itinerant traders and vagrants are excluded. Gangs of agricultural workers hoeing and singling turnips, lifting potatoes, cutting and laying hedges and digging ditches, teams of seasonal haymakers, harvesters, sheep shearers, fruit pickers and threshing machine contractors are unlikely to be recorded in apportionments. Encampments of navvies digging canals, tunnelling and building bridges for railways are not recorded.

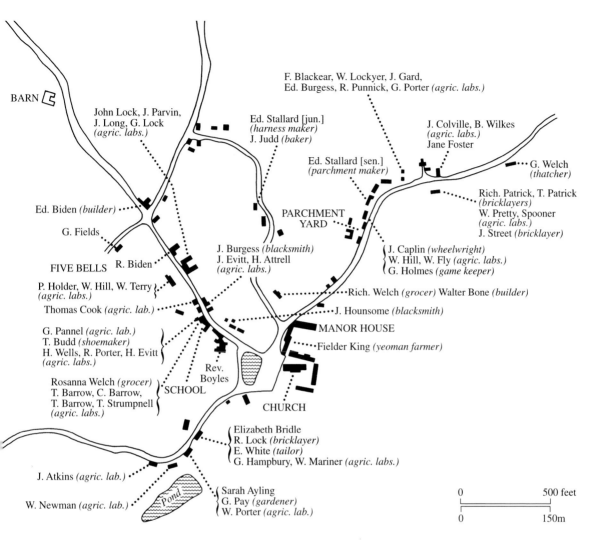

BARN

F. Blackear, W. Lockyer, J. Gard,
Ed. Burgess, R. Punnick, G. Porter *(agric. labs.)*

John Lock, J. Parvin,
J. Long, G. Lock
(agric. labs.)

Ed. Stallard [jun.]
(harness maker)
J. Judd *(baker)*

J. Colville, B. Wilkes
(agric. labs.)
Jane Foster

Ed. Stallard [sen.]
(parchment maker)

G. Welch
(thatcher)

Ed. Biden *(builder)*

PARCHMENT
YARD

Rich. Patrick, T. Patrick
(bricklayers)
W. Pretty, Spooner
(agric. labs.)
J. Street *(bricklayer)*

G. Fields

J. Burgess *(blacksmith)*
J. Evitt, H. Attrell
(agric. labs.)

J. Caplin *(wheelwright)*
W. Hill, W. Fly *(agric. labs.)*
G. Holmes *(game keeper)*

FIVE BELLS R. Biden

P. Holder, W. Hill, W. Terry
(agric. labs.)

Rich. Welch *(grocer)* Walter Bone *(builder)*

Thomas Cook *(agric. lab.)*

J. Hounsome *(blacksmith)*

G. Pannel *(agric. lab.)*
T. Budd *(shoemaker)*
H. Wells, R. Porter, H. Evitt
(agric. labs.)

MANOR HOUSE

Fielder King *(yeoman farmer)*

Rev.
Boyles

Rosanna Welch *(grocer)*
T. Barrow, C. Barrow,
T. Barrow, T. Strumpnell
(agric. labs.)

SCHOOL

CHURCH

Elizabeth Bridle
R. Lock *(bricklayer)*
E. White *(tailor)*
G. Hampbury, W. Mariner *(agric. labs.)*

J. Atkins *(agric. lab.)*

W. Newman *(agric. lab.)*

Pond

Sarah Ayling
G. Pay *(gardener)*
W. Porter *(agric. lab.)*

0   500 feet

0   150m

49 House repopulation of Buriton, Hampshire. Heads of households and their occupations listed in the 1841 census are located on the tithe map of 1840. Source: E.M. Yates, 'The evolution of an English village', *Geographical Journal*, 148 (1982), 182-206.

There were also many unnamed shepherds, drovers, tinkers, carters, inland waterboatmen and gypsies who wandered across parish boundaries. In woods and coppices, there were hurdle makers and charcoal burners; in marshes, reed cutters, moss gatherers, eel trappers and duck hunters who moved unnoticed from place to place. A new age of mobility was first recorded in the 1841 census, when 5,016 persons were enumerated as passengers in railway trains. These may have included a few people located in the tithe surveys: landowners travelling from country estates to town houses or farmers visiting relatives in distant places.

People named in tithe surveys need to be identified in other records and linked to other members of their families. E.A. Wrigley describes some of the methods used in nominal record linkage and sets out some of the rules to be observed in checking personal identifications.[103] A question about place of residence concerns what is a 'house'. In the censuses of 1841 and 1851, a house is defined as 'all the space within the external party walls of a building', which corresponds to a house plan on a tithe map. In the *Report on the sanitary condition of the labouring population of Great Britain* in 1842, Edwin Chadwick defines a house as 'each separate occupation under the same roof', which counts each flat, tenement or chamber as a separate dwelling place.[104] The census simply records many apartment dwellers as 'lodgers'. Other sources listing peoples' addresses in the mid-19th century include rateable valuations, rate books, electoral registers and directories. A general characteristic of data abstracted from these sources is that they indicate frequent changes in the names of occupants of houses. Large households with resident servants or lodgers have higher rates of turnover in names than small households consisting of nuclear families. Changeover among younger people is indicative of in and out migration occasioned by marriage or by moves to towns or neighbouring villages in search of employment. Among older age groups death accounts for increasing numbers of losses. Females were generally more mobile than males, rich people were more migratory than poor and farmers moved more frequently than labourers.[105] Tithe surveys provide a static setting for the comings and goings of many people, most of whom are not recorded in the schedules. Historians and geographers may begin to restore throngs of ordinary people to the largely empty landscapes represented in tithe surveys.

GUIDE TO FURTHER READING

R.J.P. Kain and H.C Prince, *The tithe surveys of England and Wales* (Cambridge, Cambridge University Press, 1985). The chapters on the nature of tithes, the Tithe Commutation Act of 1836, and tithe maps, apportionments and files are largely superseded by this present book. Chapters on field systems, land use, farming, landowners and rural social structure provide a comprehensive review of secondary works using tithe surveys as a source to about 1984.

E.J. Evans, *The contentious tithe: the tithe problem and English agriculture 1750-1850* (London, Routledge and Kegan Paul, 1976). This is still by far the best study of the impact of tithe on rural communities in England and Wales and of the administrative history of tithe commutation.

R.J.P. Kain and Elizabeth Baigent, *The cadastral map in the service of the state: a history of property mapping* (Chicago and London, University of Chicago Press, 1992). A comparative review of the tithe surveys of England and Wales with mapped cadastral surveys in other European countries and the New World.

Catherine Delano-Smith and R.J.P. Kain, *English maps: a history* (London, British Library Publications, 1999). This book sets the tithe surveys into the context of the cartographical history of England.

J.V. Beckett and J.E. Heath, *Derbyshire tithe files, 1836-50* (Chesterfield, Derbyshire Record Society, Vol. 22, 1995). An edited transcript of the contents of all the tithe files of Derbyshire parishes with a substantial introduction that sets the Derbyshire material firmly into its national context.

R.J.P. Kain, *An atlas and index of the tithe files of mid-nineteenth-century England and Wales* (Cambridge, Cambridge University Press, 1985). A cartographical reconstruction of the agricultural geography of England and Wales, county-by-county, based on quantitative information in the tithe files. The book also discusses the tithe files of each county, their compilation and their contents. There are extensive indexes to the main categories of papers found in each tithe file, the contents of which are also indexed under 182 subject categories. Consultation of the indexes should enable a student to determine whether inspection of the original tithe file in the Public Record Office is worthwhile for their needs.

R.J.P. Kain, *A socio-economic survey of land use and the agricultural economy: the 1836 national tithe files database on CD ROM* (Marlborough, Adam Matthew Publications, 1995). The database contains all the quantitative data on agriculture from assistant tithe commissioners' and local tithe agents' reports on tithe agreements. There is also the full set of records from which the published index in Kain, *An atlas and index of the tithe files* was derived. The database is provided with powerful search mechanisms, calculative functions, and a graphing capability. The complete dataset, or users' search results can be freely exported into other software.

R.J.P. Kain and R.R. Oliver, *The tithe maps of England and Wales: a cartographic analysis and county-by-county catalogue* (Cambridge, Cambridge University Press, 1995). This is a comprehensive survey of all the tithe maps held in the Public Record Office. In addition to the cartographic analysis, there is a comprehensive catalogue which provides information on the dates, scales, surveyors, cartographical characteristics, and topographical content of each tithe map.

Robert Davies, *The tithe maps of Wales: a guide to the tithe maps and apportionments of Wales in the National Library of Wales* (Aberystwyth, National Library of Wales, 1999). The National Library of Wales holds the diocesan copies of Welsh tithe surveys. This guide book is a complete inventory of the collection and says much that is new about tithe commutation, particularly on the role of valuers and the costs of commutation.

E.J. Evans and A.G. Crosby, *Tithes. Maps, apportionments and the 1836 Act: a guide for local historians* (Salisbury, British Association for Local History, 1997). This is the third edition of a guide first published in 1978 by the Standing Conference for Local History as one of a series which explored 'national statutes and the local community'. Eric Evans' authoritative discussion of the Tithe Commutation Act has been reproduced unchanged through the various editions. For this latest edition, Alan Crosby has added a brief survey of the 'practical value' of tithe maps and apportionments for local historians.

William Foot, *Maps for family history: a guide to the records of the tithe, valuation office, and national farm surveys of England and Wales, 1836-1943* (London, PRO Publications, 1994). This guidebook is focused on the particular needs of genealogists and is valuable also for the brief descriptions of those Public Record Office classes which contain papers related to tithe commutation on matters such as boundary awards and chancel repairs.

W.E. Tate, *The parish chest: a study of the records of parochial administration in England*, 3rd edition (Cambridge, Cambridge University Press, 1969). An invaluable guide to parish records, few of which are now kept in parish chests. Most are deposited in county record offices.

A.R.H. Baker and R.A. Butlin (eds.), *Studies of field systems in the British Isles* (Cambridge, Cambridge University Press, 1973). A detailed account of the origins and regional distinctiveness of British field systems.

L.D. Stamp, *The land of Britain, its use and misuse*, 3rd edition (London, Longmans Green, 1962). Lists and summarises reports of the Land Utilisation Survey of the 1930s, commenting on the value of tithe surveys for reconstructing land use maps for the 1840s.

G.E. Mingay (ed.), *The agrarian history of England and Wales*, Vol. 6, 1750-1850 (Cambridge, Cambridge University Press, 1989). An authoritative survey of agrarian history in the period leading up to the tithe surveys.

James Caird, *English agriculture in 1850-51*, 2nd edition (London, Longman, Brown, Green and Longman, 1852). A series of contemporary reports on the state of agriculture in different counties in England by the agriculture correspondent of *The Times* and advocate of 'high farming'.

F.M.L. Thompson, *English landed society in the nineteenth century* (London, Routledge and Kegan Paul, 1963). An assessment of the role of landowners in a period of rapid political, economic and social change.

Dennis R. Mills, *Lord and peasant in nineteenth-century Britain* (London, Croom Helm, 1980). An analysis of changing social relationships in the countryside using a variety of statistical sources and literary evidence.

NOTES

Introduction

[1] J.H. Andrews, *A paper landscape. The Ordnance Survey in nineteenth-century Ireland* (Oxford, Clarendon Press, 1975); H.D. Clout and K. Sutton, 'The cadastre as a source for French rural studies', *Agricultural History*, 43 (1969), 215-23; R.J.P. Kain and E. Baigent, *The cadastral map in the service of the state: a history of property mapping* (Chicago and London, University of Chicago Press, 1992)

[2] E.J. Hobsbawm and G.F.E. Rudé, *Captain Swing* (Lawrence and Wishart, 1969); J.P.D. Dunbabin, *Rural Discontent in nineteenth-century Britain* (London, Faber, 1974); A. Charlesworth, *Social protest in a rural society: the spatial diffusion of the Captain Swing disturbances 1830-1831*, Historical Geography Research Series No.1 (Norwich, Geobooks, 1979); A. Charlesworth (ed.), *An Atlas of Rural Britain, 1548-1900* (London, Croom Helm, 1983)

[3] E.J. Evans, *The contentious tithe: the tithe problem and English agriculture, 1750-1850* (London, Routledge and Kegan Paul, 1976); E.J. Evans and A.G. Crosby, *Tithes: maps, apportionments and the 1836 act: a guide for local historians* (Salisbury, British Association for Local History, 1997)

[4] R. Dymond, 'Devonshire fields and hedges', *Journal of the Bath and West of England Society*, 4 (1856), 132-48.

[5] 1986 and 1995 respectively; both are published by Cambridge University Press.

Chapter 1: The Nature of Tithes, pp.1-12

[1] J.A. Venn, *The foundations of agricultural economics*, 2nd edn (Cambridge, Cambridge University Press, 1933), 150-82; R.E. Prothero (Lord Ernle), *English farming past and present*, 6th edn (London, Heinemann and Frank Cass, 1961), 332-48.

[2] A. Young quoted in J.D. Chambers and G.E. Mingay, *The agricultural revolution, 1750-1880* (London, Batsford, 1966), 45.

[3] P.W. Millard, *The law relating to tithes and payments in lieu thereof*, 3rd edn (London, Butterworth, 1938).

[4] E. Kerridge, *The agricultural revolution* (London, Allen and Unwin, 1967), 272.

[5] Venn, *Agricultural economics* (see note 1), 158.

[6] A.G. Little, 'Personal tithes', *English Historical Review*, 60 (1945), 67-88.

[7] E.J. Evans, *The contentious tithe. The tithe problem and English agriculture, 1750-1850* (London, Routledge and Kegan Paul, 1976), 17-18; C. Hill, *Economic problems of the Church, from Archbishop Whitgift to the Long Parliament* (Oxford, Clarendon Press, 1956), 86.

[8] Evans, *Contentious tithe* (see note 7), 7; Hill, *Economic problems of the Church* (see note 7), 78.

[9] E.J. Evans, 'Tithing customs and disputes: the evidence of glebe terriers, 1698- 1850', *Agricultural History Review*, 18 (1970), 17-35.

[10] R.J.P. Kain, *An atlas and index of the tithe files of mid-nineteenth-century England and Wales* (Cambridge, Cambridge University Press, 1986).

[11] Evans, *Contentious tithe* (see note 7), 42-93; references to local studies are given in R.J.P Kain and H.C. Prince, *The tithe surveys of England and Wales* (Cambridge, Cambridge University Press, 1985), 10, 259 (note 11).

[12] Laura Brace, *The idea of property in seventeenth-century England: tithes and the individual* (Manchester, Manchester University Press, 1998), 86-111.

[13] H. Grove, *Alienated tithes ...* (London, privately printed, 1896); Evans, *Contentious tithe* (see note 7), 8.

[14] Hill, *Economic problems of the Church* (see note 7), 132-46.

[15] Hill, *Economic problems of the Church* (see note 7), 95.

[16] Evans, *Contentious tithe* (see note 7), 21-2; Prothero, *English farming past and present* (see note 1), 341.

[17] Evans, *Contentious tithe* (see note 7), 21.

[18] W.R. Ward, 'The tithe question in England in the early nineteenth century', *Journal of Ecclesiastical*

History, 16 (1965), 67-81.

[19]   Quoted in Evans, *Contentious tithe* (see note 7), 18.

[20]   PRO IR 18/13853.

[21]   E.J. Evans, 'A nineteenth-century tithe dispute and its significance: the case of Kendal', *Transactions of the Cumberland and Westmorland Antiquarian and Archaeological Society*, new series, 74 (1974), 159-85.

[22]   Venn, *Agricultural economics* (see note 1), 154-62; Evans, 'Tithing customs and disputes' (see note 9), 17-35 and 'A nineteenth-century tithe dispute' (see note 21), 159-83; E. J. Evans, 'Some reasons for the growth of English rural anti-clericalism', *c.*1750-*c.*1830', *Past and Present*, 66 (1975), 84-109; further references to local studies are given in Kain and Prince, *Tithe surveys of England and Wales* (see note 11), 16, 260 (note 24).

[23]   Hill, *Economic problems of the Church* (see note 7), 81-2.

[24]   Cited in Venn, *Agricultural economics* (see note 1), 151-2.

[25]   A. Young, *Travels during the years 1787, 1788, and 1789 ... with a view of ascertaining the cultivation ... of the kingdom of France* (Bury St Edmunds, Rackham, 1792).

[26]   Best, *Temporal pillars* (see note 11), 66.

[27]   Evans, *Contentious tithe* (see note 7), 44.

[28]   Evans, 'Some reasons for the growth of English rural anti-clericalism' (see note 22); 'A nineteenth-century tithe dispute and its significance' (see note 21); *Contentious tithe* (see note 7), 42-66.

[29]   A valuable account of the part played by opponents to tithes in the English Revolution is Margaret James, 'The political importance of the tithes controversy in the English Revolution, 1640-60', *History*, 26 (1941) 1-18. The objections of tithes by Quakers are discussed in B. Reay, 'Quaker opposition to tithes 1652-1660', *Past and Present*, 86 (1980); 98-120: A.D. Gilbert, *Religion and society in industrial England, church, chapel and social change, 1740-1914* (London, Longman, 1976); Evans, *Contentious tithe* (see note 7), 58-62.

[30]   A.B. Anderson, 'A study in the sociology of religious persecution: the first Quakers', *Journal of Religious History*, 9 (1977), 247-62.

[31]   N.C. Hunt, *Two early political associations. The Quakers and the Dissenting Deputies in the age of Sir Robert Walpole* (Oxford, Clarendon Press, 1961), 62-112; E.J. Evans, 'A history of the tithe system in England, 1690-1850, with special reference to Staffordshire', unpublished University of Warwick Ph.D. thesis (1970), 178-239.

[32]   F.M.L. Thompson, *Chartered surveyors: the growth of a profession* (London, Routledge and Kegan Paul, 1968), 100-3; tithe payment is also regarded as unimportant in J.D. Chambers and G.E. Mingay, *The agricultural revolution* (London, Batsford, 1966), 45-6; H.C. Prince, 'The changing rural landscape 1750-1850' in G.E. Mingay (ed.), *The agrarian history of England and Wales*, Vol. 6, 1750-1850 (Cambridge, Cambridge University Press, 1989), 30-6.

[33]   J. Billingsley, *General view of the agriculture of the county of Somerset* (Bath, R. Cruttwell, 1797), 35; N. Kent, *General view of the agriculture of the county of Norfolk* (Norwich, Norfolk Press, 1796), 153-5.

[34]   Thomas Rudge, *General view of the agriculture of the county of Gloucester* (London, Richard Phillips, 1807), p.60.

[35]   J. Boys, *General view of the agriculture of the county of Kent* (London, Sherwood, Neely and Jones, 1813), 43.

[36]   D. Walker, *General view of the agriculture of the county of Hertford* (London, W. Bulmer, 1795), 24, 74, 78.

[37]   J. Baker, 'Tithe rent-charge and the measurement of agricultural production in mid-nineteenth-century England and Wales', *Agricultural History Review*, 41 (1993), 169-75.

[38]   PRO IR 18/12734.

[39]   PRO IR 18/12865.

[40]   PRO IR 18/11142.

[41]   PRO IR 18/2050.

[42]   R.J.P. Kain, 'Contemporary opinion concerning the possible conversion of pasture to arable after tithe commutation', *Cantium*, 6 (1974), 77-9.

[43]   R.J.P. Kain, 'The land of Kent in the middle of the nineteenth century', unpublished University of London Ph.D. thesis (1973), 323-8.

[44]   Evans, *Contentious tithe* (see note 7), 69.

[45]   E.L. Jones, 'The changing basis of English agricultural prosperity, 1853-73', *Agricultural History Review*, 10 (1962), 102-19.

[46]   Evans, *Contentious tithe* (see note 7), 163. See also G.E. Mingay, *Rural life in Victorian England* (London, Heinemann, 1977) and his *The agricultural revolution. Changes in agriculture, 1650-1880* (London, Black, 1977); Prince, 'Changing rural landscape 1750-1850' (see note 32).

[47]   R.C. Russell, *The enclosure of Barton-upon-Humber, 1793-1796* (Barton-upon- Humber, Workers'

Educational Association, 1968); R.C. Russell, *The enclosures of East Halton, 1801-1804 and North Kelsey, 1813-1840* (North Lindsey Branch of Workers' Educational Association, 1974); T.W. Beastall, *The agricultural revolution in Lincolnshire* (Lincoln, History of Lincolnshire Committee, 1978), 35-41.

48 Evans, *Contentious tithe* (see note 7), 94.

49 V. Lavrovsky, 'Tithe commutation as a factor in the gradual decrease of landownership by the English peasantry', *Economic History Review*, 4 (1933), 73-89. See also G.E. Mingay, *Enclosure and the small farmer in the age of the industrial revolution* (London, Macmillan, 1968), 22, 24.

50 Ward, 'The tithe question' (see note 18), 72.

51 E.C.K. Gonner, *Common land and enclosure* (London, Macmillan, 1912), 16-18. See also W.H.R. Curtler, *The enclosure and redistribution of our land* (Oxford, Clarendon Press, 1920), 162, 200.

52 British Parliamentary Papers [BPP] House of Commons (HC), 1836, XLIV, 'A Return from the Inclosure and other Private Acts in which provisions are included for the Commutation of Tithes, of the Proportion in Land, Yearly Money Payment, or Corn Rent, allotted in Lieu of Tithe', 344 pp.

53 Ward, 'The tithe question' (see note 18), 71.

54 Millard, *Law relating to tithes* (see note 3), 12. Ward also cites these figures in 'The tithe question in England' (see note 18), 70; Evans' calculations from the 1836 'Return from the Inclosure and other Private Acts' puts the proportion of acts which dealt with tithes at a lower figure of about 60 per cent of all 3,700 acts. See *Contentious tithe* (see note 7), 111.

55 Millard, *Law relating to tithes* (see note 3), 12, 16, 18, cites as examples of these: Brinklow Inclosure Act, 1741, 14 Geo. 11, Cap. 14; Vicar's Rate in Halifax Act, 1830, 10 Geo. IV, Cap. 14; Kendal Corn Rent Act, 1834, 4 & 5, Will. IV, Cap. 16.

56 William Cobbett, *Rural rides* (London, Everyman edition, Dent, 1912), Vol. 2, 124.

57 G.F.E. Rudé, 'English rural and urban disturbances on the eve of the First Reform Bill, 1830-1', *Past and Present*, 37 (1967), 87-102; E.J. Hobsbawm and G.F.E. Rudé, *Captain Swing* (London, Lawrence and Wishart, 1969); Dunbabin, *Rural discontent in nineteenth-century Britain*; Charlesworth, *Social protest in a rural society*; J. Stevenson, *Popular disturbances in England, 1700-1870* (London, Longman, 1979); R.A.E. Wells, 'The development of the English rural proletariat and social protest, 1700-1850', *Journal of Peasant Studies*, 6 (1979), 115-39.

Chapter 2: The Tithe Commutation Act of 1836, pp.13-30

1 J.A. Symon, *Scottish farming past and present* (Edinburgh, Oliver and Boyd, 1959), 81-3; Christabel S. Orwin and Edith H. Whetham, *History of British agriculture 1846-1914* (London, Longman, 1964), 183-6; R.C. Simington, 'The tithe composition applotment books', *Analectica Hibernica*, 10 (1941), 295-8; J.H. Johnson, 'The Irish tithe composition applotment books as a geographical source', *Irish Geography*, 3 (1958), 254-62.

2 W.R. Ward, 'The tithe question in England in the early nineteenth century', *Journal of Ecclesiastical History*, 16 (1965), 67-81.

3 E.J. Evans, *The Contentious tithe: the tithe problem and English agriculture, 1750-1850* (London, Routledge and Kegan Paul, 1976), 116.

4 Evans, *Contentious tithe* (see note 3), 119.

5 Evans, *Contentious tithe* (see note 3), 121.

6 Hansard's Parliamentary Debates [Hansard], 3rd series, XXXI, 185-6.

7 Hansard, 3rd series, XXXI, 721.

8 P.O'Donoghue, 'Opposition to tithe payments in 1832-3', *Studia Hibernica*, 12 (1972), 77-108.

9 E. J. Evans, *Tithes and the Tithe Commutation Act 1836* (London, Bedford Square Press, 1978), 13-14. A second edition of this work was published by Phillimore, Chichester for the British Association for Local History in 1993 and an extended edition by E.J. Evans and A.G. Crosby as *Tithes: maps, apportionments and the 1836 Act: a guide for local historians* (Salisbury, British Association for Local History, 1997).

10 6 and 7 Will. IV, cap. 71; W. Eagle, *The acts for the commutation of tithes in England and Wales*, 3rd edition (London, Saunders and Benning, 1840).

11 W. Vamplew, 'Tithes and agriculture: some comments on commutation', *Economic History Review*, 2nd series, 34 (1981), 115-19.

12 The administrative model of the new Poor Law is discussed in A.E. Davies, 'The New Poor Law in a rural area, 1834-1850', *Ceredigion*, 8 (1978), 246-90, and R.N. Thompson, 'The working of the Poor Law Amendment Act in Cumbria, 1836-1871', *Northern History*, 15 (1979), 117-37. On the relationship between the Poor Law Amendment Act and the Tithe Commutation Act see R.R. Oliver and R.J.P. Kain, 'Maps and the assessment of parish rates in nineteenth-century England and Wales',

Imago Mundi, 50 (1998), 156-73.

13 M.C., 'William Blamire (1790-1862), tithe commissioner, M P', *Dictionary of National Biography*, 2 (Oxford, Oxford University Press, 1973), 654-6; D. Spring, *The English landed estate in the nineteenth century: its administration* (Baltimore, Johns Hopkins, 1963), 166; Evans, *Contentious tithe* (see note 3), 136.

14 Spring, *The English landed estate* (see note 13), 167.

15 E.C.K.G., 'Richard Jones (1790-1855), political economist', *Dictionary of National Biography*, 11 (Oxford, Oxford University Press, 1973), 1045; Richard Jones, *Literary remains, consisting of lectures and tracts on political economy, edited with a prefatory notice by Rev. William Whewell* (London, John Murray, 1859).

16 Richard Jones, *A few remarks on the proposed commutation of tithes* (London, John Murray, 1833); Jones, *Remarks on the government bill for the commutation of tithes* (London, John Murray, 1836).

17 Evans, *Contentious tithe* (see note 3), 137.

18 Evans, *Contentious tithe* (see note 3), 137.

19 H.M. Chichester, 'Robert Kearsley Dawson', *Dictionary of National Biography*, XIV (London, Smith Elder, 1888), 228; J.E. Portlock, *Memoir of the life of Major-General Colby* (London, Seeley, Jackson and Halliday, 1869); J.H. Andrews, 'The Ordnance Survey in nineteenth-century Ireland', unpublished Trinity College Dublin M.Litt. thesis (1971), 190-1, and 258-9; Rosemary L. Harris, 'The Ordnance Survey Memoirs', *Ulster Folklife*, 1 (1955), 43-52.

20 W. Porter, *History of the Corps of the Royal Engineers* (London, Longman Green, 1889), Vol. 2, 243.

21 R.J.P. Kain and E. Baigent, *The cadastral map in the service of the state: a history of property mapping* (Chicago and London, University of Chicago Press, 1992), 265-330.

22 Harriet M.E. Holt, 'Assistant commissioners and local agents: their role in tithe commutation, 1836-1854', *Agricultural History Review*, 32 (1984), 189-200.

23 Evans, *Tithe Commutation Act* (see note 3), 15.

24 Buckinghamshire Record Office, Townsend Mss D85; A.H. Plaisted, *The manor and parish records of Medmenham* (London, Longmans Green, 1925) provides an account of the family and estate.

25 R.J.P. Kain, *An atlas and index of the tithe files of mid-nineteenth-century England and Wales* (Cambridge, Cambridge University Press, 1986), 11-15.

26 R.J.P. Kain, 'The tithe files of mid-nineteenth century England and Wales', in M.A. Reed (ed.), *Discovering past landscapes* (London, Croom Helm, 1984), 56-84.

27 A. Clapham, *A short history of the surveyor's profession* (London, Royal Institution of Chartered Surveyors, 1949).

28 G.H. Whalley, *The Tithe Act, and the Tithe Amendment Act ...* (London, Shaw and Sons, 1838), 304-6.

29 Whalley, *The Tithe Act* (see note 28), 201-4. Extant tithe boundary awards are held in the Public Record Office (class TITH 1); see William Foot, *Maps for family history: a guide to the records of the tithe, valuation office, and national farm surveys of England and Wales, 1836-1943* (London, PRO Publications, 1994), 19.

30 Transcripts of these are printed in Whalley, *The Tithe Act* (see note 28). Similar examples are occasionally found in tithe files and more frequently among the papers of solicitors who acted for tithe owners and tithe payers. See, for example, the papers of Thomas Salt, solicitor, in the Shropshire Record Office, and Burrow and Co., solicitors of Cullompton, in the Devon Record Office. We are grateful to Harriet M. E. Holt for drawing our attention to these collections.

31 Evans, *Contentious tithe* (see note 3), 129.

32 Our enquiries at the Public Record Office, the Tithe Redemption Commission, the Board of Inland Revenue and other government departments have failed to discover the unpublished papers of the Tithe Commission for England and Wales for the period between the passing of the Tithe Commutation Act and the late 1850s when the business of commutation was virtually complete. Their discovery would be a matter of the first importance for understanding further the organisation of commutation, much of which at present must be inferred from the one side of correspondence preserved in parochial files. See J.V. Beckett, 'Tithe commutation in Nottinghamshire in the 1830s and 1840s', *Transactions of the Thoroton Society*, 96 (1992), 146-65 and J.V. Beckett and J.E. Heath (eds), *Derbyshire tithe files 1836-50* (Derbyshire Record Society, Vol. 22, 1995).

33 Evidence from Kain, *Atlas and index of tithe files* (see note 25) and Holt, 'Assistant commissioners and local agents' (see note 22).

34 Evans, *Contentious tithe* (see note 3), 145.

35 Evans, *Contentious tithe* (see note 3), 141.

36 Shropshire Record Office 3651/T/1, Tithe commutation papers, records of proceedings, and draft agreements.

37 Whalley, *The Tithe Act* (see note 28), 291.

38 Whalley, *The Tithe Act* (see note 28), 295-6, 312.

[39] Evans, *Contentious tithe* (see note 3), 152.

[40] BPP (HC), 1837, VI, 'Report from the Select Committee on Survey of Parishes (Tithe Commutation Act); with the Minutes of evidence', 52.

[41] Andrews, 'Ordnance Survey in nineteenth-century Ireland' (see note 19), 36-7.

[42] See the 'correspondence' in H. Barty-King, *Scratch a surveyor …* (London, Heinemann, 1975), 109-11.

[43] Devon Record Office 2165A/PB59-102—Correspondence, 1838-41, from Snell, assistant overseer, Drewsteignton; Jole, surveyor, Plymouth; landowners of Drewsteignton; Tithe Commission and others. We are indebted to Dr. J.B. Harley for directing out attention to these papers.

[44] F.M.L. Thompson, *Chartered surveyors: the growth of a profession* (London, Routledge and Kegan Paul, 1968), 106. The process of valuation and its associated costs are described in great detail in R. Davies, *The tithe maps of Wales: a guide to the tithe maps and apportionments of Wales in the National Library of Wales* (Aberystwyth, National Library of Wales, 1999).

[45] J. Farncombe, 'On the farming of Sussex', *Journal of the Royal Agricultural Society of England*, 11 (1850), 75.

[46] BPP (HC), 1857, IV, 363.

[47] BPP (HC), 1837-8, XXXVIII, 'Return of Agreements for the Commutation of Tithes', 189.

[48] Hansard, 3rd series, 36, 585.

[49] 'Report on the Survey of Parishes' (see note 40), 25.

[50] BPP (HC), 1837, XLI, 'Copy of Papers Respecting the Proposed Survey of Lands Under the Tithe Act', 9.

[51] BPP (HC), 1839, XVI, 335.

[52] BPP (HC), 1844, XXI, 419; D.W. Howell, *Land and people in nineteenth-century Wales* (London, Routledge and Kegan Paul, 1978), 83-5.

[53] PRO IR 18/4420 Great Claybrook, Leicestershire.

[54] BPP (HC), 1839, XVI, 335.

[55] BPP (HC), 1840, XXVIII, 139.

[56] BPP (HC), 1843, XXIX, 391.

[57] BPP (HC), 1849, XXII, 549; Evans, *Contentious tithe* (see note 3), 143.

[58] BPP (HC), 1849, XXII, 549.

[59] See respectively, PRO IR18 5418, 5617, 4113 (though the documents which would probably explain the delay have been weeded from this tithe file), 5415, and 9567 (Barham), 9785 (Hemingstone), and 9786 (Hemingstone, lands titheable to Barham). Unfortunately the last-named file, which might once have contained an explanation of this delay, has been heavily weeded.

[60] BPP (HC), 1857 second session, XXI, 350.

[61] Act of 49 and 50 Vict., cap. 54 (1886).

[62] Act of 54 and 55 Vict., cap. 8 (1891).

[63] Act of 8 and 9 Geo. V., cap. 54 (1918).

[64] Act of 15 and 16 Geo. V, cap. 87 (1925).

[65] Act of 26 Geo. V and I Edw. VIII, cap. 43 (1936).

[66] C. Fox, *The countryside and the law* (Newton Abbot, David and Charles, 1971).

Chapter 3: Tithe Maps, Apportionments and Files, pp.31-71

[1] BPP (HC), 1837, XLI, 'Copy of papers respecting the proposed survey of lands under the Tithe Act'.

[2] 'Copy of papers' (see note 1), 10.

[3] 'Copy of papers' (see note 1), 9.

[4] 'Copy of papers' (see note 1), 11-16.

[5] 'Copy of papers' (see note 1), 11.

[6] 'Copy of papers' (see note 1), 12. In the event, 32 per cent of tithe maps were drawn at one inch to three chains, 14 per cent at one inch to four chains, and 33 per cent at one inch to six chains; see R.J.P. Kain and R.R. Oliver, *The tithe maps of England and Wales: a cartographic analysis and county-by-county catalogue* (Cambridge, Cambridge University Press, 1995), 726.

[7] Article 28 of Colby's 'Instructions for the Interior Survey of Ireland' reproduced by J.H. Andrews, 'The Ordnance Survey in nineteenth-century Ireland', unpublished Trinity College Dublin M. Litt. Thesis (1971), Appendix B, 521-37.

[8] 'Copy of papers' (see note 1).

[9] An Act for the Commutation of Tithes in England and Wales, 6 & 7 Will. IV, cap. 71.

[10] BPP (HC) 1837-8, XXXVIII, 'Return of Agreements for the commutation of tithes …'

[11] BPP (HC), 1837, VI 'Report from the select committee on survey of parishes (Tithe Commutation Act); with the minutes of evidence', 47-8.

[12] 'Copy of papers' (see note 1), 16.

[13] 'Copy of papers' (see note 1), 17.

[14] 'Copy of papers' (see note 1), 4.

[15] 'Report on survey of parishes' (see note 11), 66 pages of evidence and report.

[16] 'Report on survey of parishes' (see note 11), 15, 24, 27.

[17] 'Report on survey of parishes' (see note 11), 47.

[18] 'Report on survey of parishes' (see note 11), 13.

[19] *Journal of the House of Commons*, 92 (1837), 14 and 18 April.

[20] An Act to Amend an Act for the Commutation of Tithes in England and Wales, 1 Vict. cap. 69; 2 & 3 Vict. cap. 62 extended the amendments to maps accompanying compulsory awards.

[21] R.J.P Kain, 'R. K. Dawson's proposal in 1836 for a cadastral survey of England and Wales', *Cartographic Journal*, 12 (1975), 81-8.

[22] F.M.L. Thompson, *Chartered surveyors: the growth of a profession* (London, Routledge and Kegan Paul, 1968), 105.

[23] BPP (HC), 1852-3, LXXXV, Appendix pp.clvii-clxi.

[24] R. Oliver, *Ordnance survey maps: a concise guide for historians* (London, Charles Close Society, 1993).

[25] BPP (HC), 1844, XVII, 'Minutes of evidence taken before the commission inquiring into the state of large towns and populous districts', 371.

[26] Tithe Commission, 'Instructions as to forms of apportionment and maps', issued 31 July 1837; a transcript of these instructions is printed in G.H. Whalley, *The Tithe Act, and the Tithe Amendment Act* (London, Shaw and Sons, 1838), 194-8.

[27] Copies of the 'instructions' have occasionally found their way into parish tithe files; for example, PRO IR 18/4323. They may also be found among the papers of solicitors and land surveyors in county record offfices.

[28] 'Instructions as to forms of apportionment and maps' (see note 26).

[29] 'Instructions as to forms of apportionment and maps' (see note 26).

[30] W. Eagle, *The acts for the commutation of tithes in England and Wales*, 3rd edition (London, Saunders and Benning, 1840), 138.

[31] Leicestershire Record Office DE380/36 and DE380/25/8.

[32] Leicestershire Record Office DE380/30/1 and 2.

[33] Whalley, *The Tithe Act* (see note 26), 313.

[34] BPP (HC), 1852-3, LXXXV, clvii-cixi. Letter from Major Dawson, RE, to the Registrar General, 20 July 1852.

[35] Kain and Oliver, *The tithe maps of England and Wales* (see note 6), 708-14.

[36] BPP (HC), 1854, XLI, 'Correspondence respecting the scale for the Ordnance Survey ...' Letter dated 24 February 1854 from James Walker, FRS, to the Master General of Ordnance, 333.

[37] Kain and Oliver, *The tithe maps of England and Wales* (see note 6), 732-42.

[38] R.J.P. Kain, 'Interpreting tithe map evidence', *Rights of Way Law Review*, Section 9.3 (1998), 97-106.

[39] R.J.P. Kain and Sarah A.H. Wilmot, 'Tithe surveys in national and local archives', *Archives*, 20 (1992), 106-17.

[40] This section is based closely on Kain and Wilmot, 'Tithe surveys in national and local archives' (see note 39), pp.106-17.

[41] Clawton, Halwell (Black Torrington Hundred), Morchard Bishop and Sampford Spiney tithe maps in Devon CRO, Exeter and PRO IR30 9/115; 9/193; 9/293; 9/356. Kimpton and Little Munden tithe maps, Hertfordshire County Record Office, Hertford and PRO IR30 15/59 and 15/70.

[42] BPP (HC), 1837 second session, XXI. Letter dated 30 October 1854 from H. Pyne, Clerk to the Board of Copyhold and Tithe Commissioners to the Royal Commission on Registration of Title and Sale and Transfer of Land, 347.

[43] A.D.M. Phillips, 'A study of farming practices and soil types in Staffordshire around 1840', *North Staffordshire Journal of Field Studies*, 13 (1973), 30, 34 and Kain and Oliver, *The tithe maps of England and Wales* (see note 6), 8-11, 468-9.

[44] 'Royal Commission on Registration of Title', evidence of William Blamire, 259.

[45] Secretary of the Tithe Redemption Commission, 'The records of the Tithe Redemption Commission', *Journal of the Society of Archivists*, 1 (1957), 136; E.A. Cox and B.R. Dittmer, 'The tithe files of the mid-nineteenth century', *Agricultural History Review*, 13 (1965), 1-16.

[46] Cox and Dittmer, 'The tithe files' (see note 45), 3-9. The use of the files in the study of mid-19th-century farming is discussed in Chapter 5 below.

[47] PRO IR 18/454.

[48]   Harriet M.E. Holt, 'The tithe files of Norfolk', *Norfolk Research Committee Bulletin*, 23 (1980), 6-7.

[49]   PRO IR 18/14266.

[50]   The full index in machine-readable form is deposited in the Economic and Social Research Council's Archive at the University of Essex. Those parts relating to agriculture and the rural landscape are printed in R.J.P. Kain, *An atlas and index of the tithe files of mid-nineteenth-century England and Wales* (Cambridge, Cambridge University Press, 1986) and are available on a CD-ROM with searching software as Kain, *A socio-economic survey of land use and the agricultural economy: the 1836 national tithe files database on CD-ROM* (Marlborough, Adam Matthew, 1995).

[51]   G. Slater, *The English peasantry and the enclosure of common fields* (London, Constable, 1907), 189.

[52]   List and Index Society, *Inland Revenue tithe maps and apportionments* (London, Swift (P. and D.), 1971 and 1972), Vols. 68 and 83.

[53]   A project is being developed at the Public Record Office to electronically scan the entire holding of tithe maps and apportionments. It is conceived as a long-term venture and is conditional on funding.

[54]   Kain, *An atlas and index of the tithe files* (see note 50).

Chapter 4: The Accuracy of the Tithe Surveys, pp.72-84

[1]   Janet M. Hooke and R.J.P. Kain, *Historical change in the physical environment: a guide to sources and techniques* (London, Butterworth, 1982), 68-94; see also J.B. Harley's comments on the evaluation of the whole 'family' of privately produced estate, enclosure and tithe maps in *Maps for the local historian. A guide to the British sources* (London, National Council of Social Service, 1972), 36-9.

[2]   Reply of John Meadows White to a Treasury circular concerning the scale for future Ordnance Survey maps printed in BPP (HC), 1854, XLI 'Correspondence respecting the scale for the Ordnance Survey and upon contouring and hill delineation', 107-10.

[3]   BPP (HC), 1856, XIV, 'Report from the select committee on Ordnance Survey of Scotland together with the proceedings of the committee, minutes of evidence, appendix and index', evidence of Lieutenant-Colonel R.K. Dawson, 31.

[4]   P.W. Millard, *The law relating to tithes and payments in lieu thereof*, 3rd edition (London, Butterworth, 1938), 84-6.

[5]   Ordnance Survey, *Account of field surveying and the preparation of the manuscript plans of the Ordnance Survey* (Southampton, Ordnance Survey, 1873).

[6]   F.M.L. Thompson, *Chartered surveyors: the growth of a profession* (London, Routledge and Kegan Paul, 1968), 98.

[7]   BPP (HC), 1857, second session, XXI, 'Report of the commissioners appointed to consider the subject of the registration of title with reference to the sale and transfer of land', 256.

[8]   'Report ... registration of title ... sale and transfer of land' (see note 7), 256.

[9]   BPP (HC), 1844, XVII, 'Minutes of evidence taken before commissioners of inquiry into the state of large towns and populous districts', 371.

[10]   'Minutes of evidence ... state of large towns' (see note 9), 371.

[11]   BPP (HC), 1841, XII, 'Report of the tithe commissioners for England and Wales', dated 9 February 1841.

[12]   'Report of the tithe commissioners', 9 February 1841 (see note 11).

[13]   'Report of the tithe commissioners', 9 February 1841 (see note 11).

[14]   'Report ... on Ordnance Survey of Scotland' (see note 3), 31.

[15]   BPP (HC), 1844, V, 'Report of select committee on commons enclosure and minutes of evidence', 159.

[16]   'Report ... on commons enclosure' (see note 15), 159.

[17]   'Report ... registration of title ... sale and transfer of land' (see note 7), 261.

[18]   'Report ... on Ordnance Survey of Scotland' (see note 3), 32.

[19]   'Report ... on Ordnance Survey of Scotland' (see note 3), 32.

[20]   BPP (HC), 1861, XIV, 'Report from the select committee on the cadastral survey', 54.

[21]   'Report ... on the cadastral survey' (see note 20), 58.

[22]   'Correspondence respecting the scale for the Ordnance Survey' (see note 2), 205.

[23]   'Correspondence respecting the scale for the Ordnance Survey' (see note 2), 222.

[24]   Janet M. Hooke and R. A. Perry, 'The planimetric accuracy of tithe maps', *Cartographic Journal*, 13 (1976), 177-83.

[25]   Inconsistency and ambiguity are likely where landowners adopted units other than individual parcels of land as the basis for apportionment; A.R.H. Baker, in 'The field system of an east Kent parish (Deal)', *Archaeologia Cantiana*, 78 (1963), says on p.99, 'The tithe map here is an unreliable guide to the open or enclosed state of the fields, for all the boundaries are shown as continuous lines. These

boundaries are ownership rather than field boundaries'. In the Chilterns, dotted lines were also used
to demarcate one person's lands from another's where this division was not marked adequately on the
ground; see F.D. Hartley, 'The agricultural geography of the Chilterns *c.*1840', unpublished University
of London M.A. thesis (1953), 115.

[26] For example: J.E.G. Mosby, *Norfolk, Report of the Land Utilisation Survey of Britain*, part 70 (1938),
144; B.L. Davies and H. Miller, *Carmarthenshire, Report of the Land Utilisation Survey of Britain*, part 39
(1944), 549; Hartley, 'The agricultural geography of the Chilterns', 20-1; A. Harris, *The rural landscape
of the East Riding of Yorkshire, 1750-1850, a study in historical geography* (Oxford, Oxford University
Press, 1961), 112; M.R. Postgate, 'Historical geography of the Breckland, 1600-1850', unpublished
University of London M.A. thesis (1961), 272; E.A. Cox, 'An agricultural geography of Essex *c.*1840',
unpublished University of London M.A. thesis (1963), 39; J.M. Powell, 'Tithe surveys and schedules:
some Montgomeryshire examples', *Journal of the National Library of Wales*, 16 (1969), 87-96; J.
Chapman, 'Agriculture and the "waste" in Monmouthshire from 1750 to the present day',
unpublished University of London Ph.D. thesis (1973), 21-6; R.J.P. Kain,'The land of Kent in the
middle of the nineteenth century', unpublished University of London PhD thesis (1972), 93-102.

[27] PRO IR 18/3603, 3710.

[28] PRO IR 18/3560, 3407, 371 1.

[29] PRO IR 18/3506, 3699.

[30] Cox, 'An agricultural geography of Essex' (see note 26), 39.

[31] Cox, 'An agricultural geography of Essex' (see note 26), 41.

[32] Hartley, 'The agricultural geography of the Chilterns' (see note 25), 20-1.

[33] William Eagle, *The acts for the commutation of tithes in England and Wales*, 3rd edition (London, Saunders
and Benning, 1840), 83-4; the quotation is from G.H. Whalley's discussion of the Tithe Commission's
'Form of Instructions No. 6 "Form of agreement ... with form of schedule annexed" ', in *The Tithe
Act and the whole of the Tithe Amendment Acts, with explanatory notes*, 2nd edition (London, Shaw and
Sons, 1848), 245.

[34] R.J.P. Kain and Harriet M.E. Holt, 'Agriculture and land use in Cornwall circa 1840', *Southern History*,
3 (1981), 142-3.

[35] Hartley, 'The agricultural geography of the Chilterns' (see note 25), 12.

[36] PRO IR 18/3531.

[37] PRO IR 18/3501, 3792.

[38] PRO IR 18/9983.

[39] A.D.M. Phillips, 'A study of farming practices and soil types in Staffordshire around 1840', *North
Staffordshire Journal of Field Studies*, 13 (1973), 34-5.

[40] A.D.M. Phillips, 'Agricultural land use, soils and the Nottinghamshire tithe surveys circa 1840', *East
Midland Geographer*, 6 (1976), 288.

[41] PRO IR 18/454.

[42] PRO IR 18/1407.

[43] PRO IR 18/3074.

[44] BPP (HC), 1850, XXXII, 'Report from the registration and conveyancing commission', 5.

[45] 'Report ... registration of title ... sale and transfer of land' (see note 7), 257.

[46] R.E. Sandell (ed.), *Abstracts of Wiltshire tithe apportionments* (Devizes, Wiltshire Record Society, 1975),
10.

[47] 'Report ... registration of title ... sale and transfer of land' (see note 7), 260.

Chapter 5: Tithe Surveys as a Historical Source, pp.85-126

[1] H.L. Gray, *English field systems* (Cambridge, Mass., Harvard University Press, 1915), 15.

[2] Roger J.P. Kain and Richard R. Oliver, *The tithe maps of England and Wales: a cartographic analysis and
county-by-county catalogue* (Cambridge, Cambridge University Press, 1995), 827-30.

[3] BPP (HC) 1852-3 LXXXV, Census of 1851: Population Tables. I. vol.1 lxxix.

[4] J.B. Harley, 'England *circa* 1850', in H.C. Darby (ed), *A new historical geography of England* (Cambridge,
Cambridge University Press, 1973), 531-3.

[5] Kain and Oliver, *The tithe maps of England and Wales* (see note 2), 17-19.

[6] D. Fletcher, 'The Ordnance Survey's nineteenth century boundary survey: contexts, characteristics
and impact', *Imago Mundi*, 51 (1999), 131-46; F.G. Aldsworth, 'Parish boundaries on record', *Local
Historian*, 15 (1982), 34-40; Christopher Cox, 'Parish boundary markers and the decline of parish
authority', *Local Historian*, 18 (1988), 58-64. There are some 12,900 Boundary Remark Books in
PRO OS 1/26.

[7] J.D. Marshall, *The old poor law, 1795-1834* (London, Macmillan, Econ. Hist. Soc., 1968)

8 Richard R. Oliver and Roger J.P. Kain, 'Maps and the assessment of parish rates in nineteenth-century England and Wales', *Imago Mundi*, 50 (1998), 156-73.

9 S. and B. Webb, *The parish and county. English local government*, vol. 1 (London, Longmans Green, 1906); W.E. Tate, *The parish chest: a study of the records of parochial administration in England*, 3rd edn. (Cambridge, Cambridge University Press, 1969).

10 Roger J.P. Kain and Hugh C. Prince, *The tithe surveys of England and Wales* (Cambridge, Cambridge University Press, 1985), 148-71. For references to the work of Dorothy Sylvester see 155-6.

11 Alan R.H. Baker and Robin A. Butlin (eds.), *Studies of field systems in the British Isles* (Cambridge, Cambridge University Press, 1973); Robert A. Dodgshon, *The origins of British field systems: an interpretation* (London, Academic Press, 1980).

12 Ruth Downing, 'The field-names of some Suffolk parishes: a comparison', *Local Historian*, 17 (1987), 285-89.

13 Christopher Taylor, *Village and farmstead: a history of rural settlement in England* (London, George Philip, 1983); Brian K. Roberts, *The making of the English village* (Longman, 1987).

14 D.R. Mills, *Lord and peasant in nineteenth century Britain* (London, Croom Helm, 1980).

15 J.B. Harley, *Maps for the local historian. A guide to the British sources* (London, National Council of Social Service for the Standing Conference for Local History, 1972).

16 T.R. Slater, 'The analysis of burgage patterns in medieval towns', *Area*, 13 (1981), 211-16.

17 M.W. Beresford and J.K.S. St Joseph, *Medieval England: an aerial survey* (Cambridge, Cambridge University Press, 1958), 154.

18 D. Ward, 'The preurban cadaster and urban pattern of Leeds', *Annals Assoc. Amer. Geog.*, 52 (1962), 150-66.

19 H.J. Dyos, *Victorian suburb: a study of the growth of Camberwell* (Leicester, Leicester University Press, 1961); M.A. Jahn, 'Suburban development in outer west London 1850-1900', in F.M.L. Thompson (ed.), *The rise of suburbia* (Leicester, Leicester University Press, 1982), 94-156.

20 R.J.P. Kain, 'Interpreting tithe map evidence', *Rights of Way Law Review*, 9.3 (1998), 97-106.

21 John Field, 'Street names', *Local Historian*, 16 (1984), 195-203.

22 S. and B. Webb, *The story of the king's highway: English local government*, vol. 5 (London, Longmans Green, 1913).

23 L.D. Stamp, *The land of Britain, its use and misuse*, 3rd edn. (London, Longmans, 1962), 55 and 58.

24 Malcolm R. Postgate, 'Historical geography of the Breckland, 1600-1850', unpublished University of London M.A. thesis (1961).

25 David B. Grigg, *The agricultural revolution in south Lincolnshire* (Cambridge, Cambridge University Press, 1970).

26 S.R. Eyre, 'The upward limit of enclosure on the east moor of north Derbyshire', *Trans. Inst. Brit. Geog.*, 23 (1957), 61-74; Alan Digby, 'Regional variations in land use in Ribblesdale since late medieval times', unpublished University of Leeds M.A. thesis (1960).

27 John Chapman, 'Changing agriculture and the moorland edge in the North York Moors, 1750-1960', unpublished University of London M.A. thesis (1961); Chapman, 'Agriculture and the "waste" in Monmouthshire from 1750 to the present day', unpublished University of London Ph.D. thesis (1973).

28 E.C. Willatts, 'Changes in land utilisation in the south-west of the London basin, 1840-1932', *Geographical Journal*, 82 (1933), 515-28.

29 H.C.K. Henderson, 'Our changing agriculture: the distribution of arable land in the Adur basin, Sussex, from 1780 to 1931', *Journal of the Ministry of Agriculture*, 43 (1936), 625-33; Henderson, 'Changes in land utilisation in Derbyshire, 1837-1937', in A.H. Harris, *Derbyshire. Report of the Land Utilisation Survey of Great Britain*, Part 63 (1941), 71-4.

30 J.E.G. Mosby, *Norfolk. Report of the Land Utilisation Survey of Great Britain*, Part 70 (1938).

31 F.D. Hartley, 'The agricultural geography of the Chilterns, *c.*1840', unpublished University of London M.A. thesis (1953).

32 M.C. Naish, 'The agricultural landscape of the Hampshire chalklands, 1700-1840', unpublished University of London M.A. thesis (1961).

33 B.R. Dittmer, 'An agricultural geography of northwest Wiltshire, 1773-1840', unpublished University of London M.A. thesis (1963).

34 E.A. Cox, 'An agricultural geography of Essex, *c.*1840', unpublished University of London M.A. thesis (1963).

35 A. Harris, *The rural landscape of the East Riding of Yorkshire, 1750-1850: a study in historical geography* (Oxford, Oxford University Press, 1961); J.A. Yelling, 'Open field, enclosure and farm production in east Worcestershire, 1540-1870', unpublished University of Birmingham Ph.D. thesis (1966).

36 A.D.M. Phillips, 'A study of farming practices and soil types in Staffordshire around 1840', *Staffordshire*

Journal of Field Studies, 13 (1973) 27-52; Phillips, 'Agricultural land use, soils and the Nottinghamshire tithe surveys, *circa* 1840', *East Midland Geographer*, 6 (1976), 284-301; Phillips, 'Agricultural land use and the Herefordshire tithe surveys, *circa* 1840', *Transactions of the Woolhope Naturalists' Field Club*, 43 (1979), 54-61.

[37] R.J.P. Kain and Harriet M.E. Holt, 'Agriculture and land use in Cornwall, *circa* 1840', *Southern History*, 3 (1981), 139-81; Sarah Wilmot, 'Farming in the nineteenth century', in R.J.P. Kain and W.L.D. Ravenhill (eds.), *A historical atlas of south-west England* (Exeter, University of Exeter Press, 1999), 294-306.

[38] R.J.P. Kain, 'The land of Kent in the middle of the nineteenth century', unpublished University of London Ph.D. thesis (1973); Harriet M.E. Holt and R.J.P. Kain, 'Land use and farming in Suffolk, about 1840', *Proceedings of the Suffolk Institute of Archaeology and History*, 34 (1982), 123-39; R.J.P. Kain and Harriet M.E. Holt, 'Farming in Cheshire, *circa* 1840', *Transactions of the Lancashire and Cheshire Antiquarian Society*, 82 (1983), 22-57; A. Harris and R.J.P. Kain, 'Agricultural land use in the mid-nineteenth century', in Susan Neave and S. Ellis (eds.), *An historical atlas of East Yorkshire* (Hull, University of Hull Press, 1996), 70-1.

[39] D.W. Harvey, 'Fruit growing in Kent in the nineteenth century', *Archaeologia Cantiana*, 79 (1964), 95-108.

[40] Prize essays on the farming of various counties were published in the *Journal of the Royal Agricultural Society of England* between 1845 and 1869; J. Caird, *English agriculture in 1850-51* (London, Longmans, 1852).

[41] W. Cobbett, *Rural rides*, 1830, Everyman edition (London, Dent, 1912), Penguin edition (Harmondsworth, 1967).

[42] G.E. Mingay (ed.), *The agrarian history of England and Wales*, vol. VI 1750-1850 (Cambridge, Cambridge University Press, 1989); M. Overton, *Agricultural revolution in England: the transformation of the agrarian economy* (Cambridge, Cambridge University Press, 1996).

[43] Roger J.P. Kain, *An atlas and index of the tithe files of mid-nineteenth-century England and Wales* (Cambridge, Cambridge University Press, 1986), 23.

[44] BPP (HC) 1836 VIII. First report from the select committee to inquire into the state of agriculture: with minutes of evidence and appendix. Evidence of John Rolfe Q.1481; Second report ... Evidence of John Ellman Q.4739; George Webb Hall Q.4968.

[45] J.H. Clapham, 'Tithe surveys as a source of agrarian history', *Cambridge Historical Journal*, 1 (1924), 201-8; J.A. Venn, 'The economy of a Norfolk parish in 1783 and at the present time', *Economic History*, 1 (1926), 76-88.

[46] Kain and Oliver, *The tithe maps of England and Wales* (see note 2), 8, 11.

[47] G.R.J. Jones, 'The Llanynys quillets: a measure of landscape transformation in north Wales', *Transactions of the Denbighshire Hisorical Society*, 13 (1964), 133-58; Naish, 'Hampshire chalklands' (see note 32); E.D.R. Burrell, 'An historical geography of the Sandlings of Suffolk, 1600 to 1850', unpublished University of London M.Sc. thesis (1960); D.W. Gramolt, 'The coastal marshland of east Essex between the seventeenth and mid-nineteenth centuries', unpublished University of London M.A. thesis (1961); Postgate, 'Breckland' (see note 24); Chapman, 'North York Moors' (see note 27); A.R.H. Baker, 'The field systems of Kent', unpublished University of London Ph.D. thesis (1963); J.W. Edwards, 'Enclosure and agricultural improvement in the Vale of Clwyd, 1750-1875', unpublished University of London M.A. thesis (1963); Cox , 'Essex' (see note 34); Dittmer, 'Northwest Wiltshire', (see note 33).

[48] E.A. Cox and B.R. Dittmer, 'The tithe files of the mid-nineteenth century', *Agricultural History Review*, 13 (1965), 1-16, quote from 16.

[49] Phillips , 'Staffordshire', 'Nottinghamshire', 'Herefordshire' (see note 36).

[50] Phillips, 'Nottinghamshire' (see note 36), 297-300.

[51] Holt and Kain, 'Suffolk' (see note 38).

[52] Jennifer R. Baker, 'Tithe rent-charge and the measurement of agricultural production in mid-nineteenth-century England and Wales', *Agric. Hist. Rev.*, 41 (1993), 169-75.

[53] E.H. Hunt and S.J. Pam, 'Essex agriculture in its "Golden Age" ', *Agricultural History Review*, 43 (1995), 160-77.

[54] R.E. Porter, 'Agricultural change in Cheshire during the nineteenth century', unpublished University of Liverpool Ph.D. thesis (1974).

[55] Kain and Holt, 'Cheshire' (see note 38).

[56] Michael Sill, 'Using the tithe files: a county Durham study', *Local Historian*, 17 (1986), 205-11, quote on 210.

[57] Kain, *An atlas and index of the tithe files* (see note 43).

[58] ibid, 70.

[59] ibid, 461.

[60] Most relevant are those compiled by A.H. John in Mingay, *Agrarian history* (see note 42), 1038-68.

[61] R. Cobden, *Speeches on questions of public policy* (London, Macmillan, 1878), 144.

[62] F.M.L. Thompson, 'Landowners and the rural community', in G.E. Mingay (ed.), *The Victorian countryside* (London, Routledge and Kegan Paul, 1981), 459-62.

[63] B.A. Holderness, 'The Victorian farmer', in Mingay, *Victorian Countryside* (see note 61), 229.

[64] R. Howes, 'Joseph Pitt, landowner', in B.S. Smith (ed.), *Gloucestershire Historical Studies*, 7 (University of Bristol Department of Extra-Mural Studies, 1976), 20-4; J.D. Marshall, *Furness and the industrial revolution* (Barrow-in-Furness, Library and Museum Committee, 1958), 73-8; Sue P. Farrant, 'The management of four estates in the lower Ouse valley (Sussex) and agricultural change, 1840-1920', *Southern History*, 1 (1979), 155-70; Farrant, 'The changing structure of land ownership in the lower Ouse valley, 1780 to 1840', *Sussex Archaeological Collections*, 116 (1978), 261-8; W.K. Ford, 'Boltro Farm, Cuckfield', *Sussex Archaeological Collections*, 114 (1976), 81-96; L.W. Lloyd, 'Corsygedol, Ardudwys's principal estate', *Journal Merioneth Historical and Record Society*, 8 (1977-8), 27-60, 157-90; J. Weller (ed.), *Coleshill model farm Oxfordshire: past, present and future*, Architects in Agriculture Group Occasional Paper 1 (1981).

[65] Examples of such maps are found in W.S.G. Thomas, 'Changing land utilisation, occupation and ownership in south-west Carmarthenshire', unpublished University of London Ph.D. thesis (1965) and R.F.J. Chiplen, 'The rural landscape of the Blackmore vale *c.*1840', unpublished University of Exeter M.A. thesis (1969). Tithe surveys illustrating the persistence of boundaries of early manors and divisions between differing forms of customary tenure are referred to in F.A. Barnes, 'Land tenure, landscape and population in Cemlyn, Anglesey', *Transactions of the Anglesey Antiquarian Society and Field Club*, unnumbered series (1982) 15-90.

[66] A.M. Carpenter, 'The value of the tithe surveys to the study of landownership and occupancy in the mid-nineteenth century, with special reference to south Hertfordshire', *Hertfordshire Past and Present*, 7 (1967), 48-52.

[67] Postgate, 'Breckland' (see note 24).

[68] D.R. Mills, 'Landownership and rural population with special reference to Leicestershire in the mid-nineteenth century', unpublished University of Leicester Ph.D. thesis (1963), 131-51; Mills, *Lord and peasant* (see note 14), 64-97.

[69] J.A. Yelling, 'Open field, enclosure and farm production in east Worcestershire, 1540-1870', unpublished University of Birmingham Ph.D. thesis (1966).

[70] J.S. Ingleson, 'Settlement, agrarian systems, and field patterns in central Durham, 1600-1850: a study in historical geography', unpublished University of Durham M.A. thesis (1972); Heather A. Fuller, 'Landownership and the Lindsey landscape', *Annals of the Association of American Geographers*, 66 (1976), 14-24; Heather A. Clemenson, *English country houses and landed estates* (London, Croom Helm, 1982); Brian Short, *Land and Society in Edwardian Britain* (Cambridge, Cambridge University Press, 1997), 252-69.

[71] Alastair Pearson and Peter Collier, 'The integration and analysis of historical and environmental data using a geographical information system: landownership and agricultural productivity in Pembrokeshire *c.*1850', *Agricultural History Review*, 46 (1998), 162-76.

[72] F.M.L. Thompson, *English landed society in the nineteenth century* (London, Routledge and Kegan Paul, 1963), 122-7.

[73] D.B. Grigg, *The agricultural revolution in south Lincolnshire* (Cambridge, Cambridge University Press, 1966).

[74] W.M. Williams, *A west country village, Ashworthy: family, kinship and land* (London, Routledge and Kegan Paul, 1963).

[75] C. Thomas, 'Estate surveys as sources in historical geography', *Journal of the National Library of Wales*, 14 (1966), 451-68.

[76] Sarah J. Banks, 'Open and close parishes in nineteenth-century England', unpublished University of Reading Ph.D. thesis (1982).

[77] F.M.L. Thompson, *Hampstead: building a borough, 1650-1964* (London, Routledge and Kegan Paul, 1974).

[78] M.J. Daunton, *House and home in the Victorian city: working-class housing, 1850-1914* (London, Edward Arnold, 1983), 74.

[79] K.A. Cowlard, 'The urban development of Wakefield, 1801-1901', unpublished University of Leeds Ph.D. thesis (1974).

[80] J.R. Kellett, *The impact of railways on Victorian cities* (London, Routledge and Kegan Paul, 1969), 126.

[81] P.S. Richards, 'The growth of towns—a study in methodology', *Local Historian*, 9 (1970), 190-5.

[82] Audrey Perkins, 'Middle-class yeomanry in the Kentish parish of Rainham in the nineteenth century',

Local Historian, 26 (1996), 16-35.

83   R.E. Sandell (ed.), *Abstracts of Wiltshire tithe apportionments* (Devizes, Wiltshire Record Society, 1975).

84   V.H.T. Skipp (ed.), *Discovering Sheldon* (Birmingham, University Extra-Mural Department, 1960).

85   Mosby, *Norfolk* (see note 29), 128-37, 148.

86   Jean East, 'The form and function of settlements in relation to types of farming in England and Wales (with an analysis of specific examples from the west midlands and elsewhere)', unpublished University of London Ph.D. thesis 1947; J.T. Coppock, 'Changes in farm and field boundaries in the 19th century', *Amateur Historian*, 3 (1958), 292-8; D.H.C. Bennett, 'Settlement patterns and farm units in western Pembrokeshire: a study in historical geography', unpublished University of Wales M.A. thesis (1955); J.C. Grove, 'Land use changes in west Gower, 1840-1950', unpublished University of Wales M.A. thesis (1956); J.G. Thomas, 'Some enclosure patterns in central Wales, a study in landscape modification', *Geography*, 42 (1957), 25-36; J.M. Powell, 'An economic geography of Montgomeryshire in the nineteenth century', unpublished University of Liverpool M.A. thesis (1962); Colin Morgan, 'The effect of parliamentary enclosure on the landscape of Caernarvon and Merioneth', unpublished University of Wales M.Sc. thesis (1959).

87   R.J.P. Kain, 'Tithe surveys and the study of land occupation', *Local Historian*, 12 (1976), 88-92; Clare T. Lukehurst, 'The Stour marshes: a study of agricultural changes 1840-1966', unpublished University of London Ph.D. thesis (1977); B.M. Short, 'Agriculture in the High Weald of Kent and Sussex, 1850 to 1953 (a case study in the application of multivariate techniques in the field of historical geography)', unpublished University of London Ph.D. thesis (1973).

88   Anne and Jim Andrews, *Quarries and brickworks in Stafford and district* (Stafford, Staffordshire Industrial Archaeological Society, 1983).

89   Shane Beadle, 'Tracing coal mining in Somerset and south-west Lancashire', *Local Historian*, 18 (1988), 5-12.

90   G. Shaw, 'The content and reliability of nineteenth-century trade directories', *Local Historian*, 13 (1978), 205-09; M.J. Lewis and R. Lloyd-Jones, 'Rate books: a technique of reconstructing the local economy', *Local Historian*, 17 (1987), 277-80.

91   Gillian Cookson, 'Large scale problems: the neglect of building plans', *Local Historian*, 19 (1989), 3-7.

92   Spencer Thomas, 'Land occupation, ownership and utilization in the parish of Llansantffraid', *Ceredigion*, 3 (1957), 124-55; 'The enumerators' returns as a source for a period picture of the parish of Llansantffraid, 1841-51', *Ceredigion*, 4 (1963), 408-21; 'The agricultural labour force in some south-west Carmarthenshire parishes in the mid-nineeenth century', *Welsh History Review*, 3 (1966), 63-73.

93   Thomas, 'South-west Carmarthenshire', (see note 92), 65.

94   G.J. Lewis, 'The demographic structure of a Welsh rural village during the mid-nineteenth century', *Ceredigion*, 5 (1966), 290-304; C. Thomas, 'Rural society in nineteenth-century Wales: south Cardiganshire in 1851', *Ceredigion*, 6 (1971), 388-414.

95   June A. Sheppard, 'East Yorkshire's agricultural labour force in the mid-nineteenth century', *Agric. Hist. Rev.*, 9 (1961), 43-54.

96   A. Henstock, 'Group projects in local history—house repopulation in the mid-nineteenth century', *Bulletin of Local History, East Midlands Region*, 6 (1971), 11-20. This has been reprinted with a few amendments in *Local Population Studies*, 10 (1973), 27-52.

97   ibid, 17.

98   Gee Langdon, *The year of the map: portrait of a Wiltshire town in 1841* (Tisbury, Compton Russell, 1976).

99   D.R. Mills, 'A social and demographic study of Melbourn, Cambridgeshire, *c.*1840', *Archives*, 12 (1976), 115-20, the passage quoted is from 118.

100   D.R. Mills, 'The technique of house repopulation: experience from a Cambridgeshire village, 1841', *Local Historian*, 13 (1978), 86-97.

101   E.M. Yates, 'The evolution of the English village', *Geographical Journal*, 148 (1982), 182-206.

102   D.R. Mills, 'The residential propinquity of kin in a Cambridgeshire village, 1841', *Journal of Historical Geography*, 4 (1978), 265-76.

103   E. A. Wrigley (ed.), *Identifying people in the past* (London, Edward Arnold, 1973).

104   Edward Higgs, 'The definition of the "house" in the census of 1841', *Local Historian*, 19 (1989), 56-7.

105   Dennis and Joan Mills, 'Rural mobility in the Victorian censuses: experiences with a micro-computer program', *Local Historian*, 18 (1988), 69-75.

INDEX

Numbers in **bold** refer to page numbers of illustrations